Tate Modern
The Handbook

Edited by Frances Morris
With essays by Michael Craig-Martin,
Andrew Marr and Sheena Wagstaff and a
special foreword by Nicholas Serota

Tate Publishing

First published 2000 by order of the Tate Trustees
by Tate Publishing, a division of Tate Enterprises Ltd,
Millbank, London SW1P 4RG
www.tate.org.uk/publishing

First revised edition published 2006
Second revised edition published 2010, 2011

A catalogue record for this book is available
from the British Library

ISBN: 978-1-85437-967-2

Designed by Rose
Printed by Grafos, Barcelona

Mixed Sources
Product group from well-managed
forests and other controlled sources
www.fsc.org Cert no. SGS-COC-005160
© 1996 Forest Stewardship Council

Front cover, page 9 and pages 52–53 :
Tate Photography/ Andrew Dunkley/ Marcus Leith
Frontispiece: Shigeo Anzai
Pages 10–11: Tate Photography/ Dave Clarke

Contents

Director's Foreword

When Tate Modern opened its doors in 2000 no one could have anticipated the sheer volume of visitors and the extent of interest that have resulted from its spectacular building and its engaging programmes. One of the most exciting and gratifying aspects of this has been the extent to which Tate Modern's innovative and dynamic rotating collection display has energised visitors' experiences of twentieth and twenty-first century art, by providing fresh and often controversial displays of familiar iconic works as well as presenting new and unfamiliar works to a broad public for the first time.

Tate Modern's collection displays are drawn from Tate's important holdings of International Modern Art including British Art, and they span the period from 1900 to the present day. The collection includes many individual works of acknowledged significance and certain periods in art are especially well represented. The establishment of Tate Modern was driven by the need to find additional space to house Tate's ever increasing collection as well as the ambition to provide London and the UK with superb spaces for temporary exhibitions of exceptional quality.

The conventional way of organising a collection, either in book form, or in the form of a display, is to present it as a linear chronology. In 2000 Tate Modern's opening display of the collection dispensed with this tradition by presenting four suites of galleries grouped by theme, allowing different stories and histories to be presented at the same time. Six years on, in 2006, the first major rehang of the collection built on the opening display by exploring the complex ways in which artists respond to the art of their own times as well as to the innovations of earlier generations. The display reflects the way artists tend to work, looking backwards in order to go forwards, as well as the ways in which contemporary art encourages us to review and revise our understanding of history. Alongside masterpieces from Tate's collection and displays reviewing periods of recognised importance to art history visitors will encounter work by artists who fit less easily into a conventional reading of art history as well as major installations of very recent and contemporary art. Each of the new wings opens with a dialogue between two works of art from different generations, pairings that point to the incredible affinities as well as the differences between works of art separated by time, and suggest unexpected perspectives on the old as new ways of approaching the contemporary art.

Tate Modern's Display team, led by Matthew Gale and assisted by Ann Coxon, continues to develop the new displays. Many colleagues past and present across Tate have had an input and we are deeply grateful for their contributions. We would particularly like to thank those individuals in the current display team: Tanya Barson, Stuart Comer, Mark Godfrey, Jessica Morgan, Helen Sainsbury, Rachel Taylor, Sheena Wagstaff and Catherine Wood, as well as Frances Morris, who heads the International Collection, and Simon Bolitho and Gabriela Salgado from Tate Learning. We would very much like to acknowledge Stephen Mellor and Phil Monk for their careful management and technical planning, as well as the skill and dedication of Tate conservators, registrars and technicians and the many back and front of house teams who continue to make this major project possible.

Tate displays depend for their quality on the strength and vitality of the works of art in the collection. We work in continuous dialogue with artists in the collection and many of our displays are informed by their judgements and opinions. We are deeply grateful to them for their sustained interest in Tate Modern and their commitment to presenting the collection in the best possible way. The displays at Tate Modern have been enormously enriched by superb loans from individuals and institutions in Britain and abroad and we are indebted to them for their generosity in allowing works from their collections to amplify our displays. We would especially like to thank a number of lenders with whom we have developed longer term partnerships including the Davenport Collection, David King, the Wilson Centre for Photography, the Joan Mitchell Foundation, the National Gallery, and the Victoria and Albert Museum. Finally, the arrival of ARTIST ROOMS in 2008, acquired jointly with the National Galleries of Scotland through The d'Offay Donation with assistance from the National Heritage Memorial Fund and the Art Fund, has brought new dimensions to Tate Modern as it has done for institutions across the country.

This handbook has been written to accompany the new installation of the collection at Tate Modern. It is intended to complement and extend a visit to the museum by providing an overview of the first five years of programme and a critical introduction to the next five years of collection displays. An illustrated A to Z includes entries on over 100 artists in the collection who will be on display at Tate Modern over the next few years, as well as brief texts on important movements and artistic concepts of the twentieth century. Many individuals across and beyond Tate have contributed informed and accessible texts to this volume and we thank them for sharing their expertise. The Handbook presents four extended essays, and we are especially grateful to their authors: to writer and broadcaster Andrew Marr for his lively and thought provoking essay on the impact of Tate Modern, Frances Morris and Sheena Wagstaff of Tate Modern for their respective overviews of displays and exhibitions, and to the artist Michael Craig-Martin for granting us permission to reprint his essay from the first Handbook. We would also like to thank Simon Elliott and Terry Stephens of Rose for their creative vision, and Beth Thomas who has taken over from Mary Richards at Tate Publishing in overseeing this publication.

Alongside the reinstallation of the collection a number of important new 'tools' have been originated to assist in visitor orientation and interpretation. The very generous ongoing support from Bloomberg has enabled Tate Modern to create a fascinating and multi-layered Interactive Zone as well as to provide a collection Multimedia guide that will transform the experience of visiting the museum for many visitors. Ab Rogers Design has undertaken a major redesign of the concourses. We are grateful to them and to many others who have contributed to the project.

The rehang of the collection in 2006 and its continuing reconfiguration was enormously challenging to all those involved in the process, from inception to completion. It simply could not have taken place without a uniquely creative partner together with a significant level of financial support. We would like, therefore, to reserve our very warmest thanks to UBS for collaborating with Tate and above all sharing a vision to open up art to new audiences. This partnership has not only enabled us to rehang the collection, but also to introduce a number of exciting new elements including an annual cultural festival, a bi-monthly series of live-events and an enhancement of our family activities, all of which will vastly increase the scope and impact of Tate's programme. In addition we have also been able to draw on key works from UBS's unique art collection as a means of further enriching our own displays.

Vicente Todolí
Director, Tate Modern

TATE
MODERN

Authors
Andrew Marr
Frances Morris
Sheena Wagstaff
Michael Craig-Martin

In the decade since it opened, Tate Modern has been visited by over 45 million people and has become an established part of the experience of London. It is now difficult to remember the city and its culture without Herzog & de Meuron's powerhouse for art and Norman Foster's elegant Millennium Bridge. However, in the wake of this success it is also easy to overlook the fact that Tate Modern is only half built and that further benefits to the city and its culture will flow from the completion of the next phase of work that begins in the summer of 2010.

Any city is an economic, social and physical organism that is in a constant state of flux. For decades Bankside lay dormant. Sir Christopher Wren's house, occupied by the architect while he was designing St Paul's, sits as a reminder that this area was once at the centre of the city and surrounded by the bustle of the theatre district with The Globe and Rose nearby. In the nineteenth century the needs of the metropolis for heat and light brought coal and then oil-fired installations for the generation of power. Giles Gilbert Scott's magnificent post-war building was completed in the 1960s, only to be made redundant by the early 1980s. It had become a dark, brooding presence as it slowly decayed over the following fifteen years; notwithstanding its central location in the city, life was passing Bankside by.

However, an urban fabric needs constant new investment and the decision to redeploy the power station as a museum of modern art and to create a new footbridge across the Thames acted like pebbles thrown into a stagnant pond. Slowly, transformation has gathered pace with office and residential developments stimulating improvements to the public realm. The structure of Bankside nevertheless remains tight and small in scale, with the exception of Southwark Street, driven through the area in the late nineteenth century. The most promising development in the wake of Tate Modern has therefore been the initiative to create a new character for the public realm, the Bankside Urban Forest, led by a group of local companies and a team of architects, Witherford Watson Mann. Their proposal is designed to green and humanise the city through planting and change the balance between vehicles and pedestrians in favour of people in order to bring scale and humanity to a somewhat harsh, utilitarian realm dominated by the railway viaducts, through traffic and small-scale industrial activities that service the more prosperous parts of the city. Over the next decade the steady implementation of the Bankside Urban Forest will transform our experience of this triangle of London running south from the river between Blackfriars Road and Borough High Street, culminating at Elephant and Castle, the gateway to London from the South.

Tate Modern's success as a museum has grown from a powerful combination of the building, the collection and the imagination of its curators. It was the brilliance of Herzog & de Meuron to see the potential of the redundant Turbine Hall, transforming it into a covered street, almost a city square, within the museum. It is a space that changes its character according to the time of day, the quality of light and the number of visitors, but it is always welcoming and offers the community a place for congregation. The architects also created a series of rooms for learning and social engagement as well as galleries that can rival those in any of the new museums across the world. Yes, we all complain that the galleries are too full on a weekend afternoon, but at other times the side-light from the Thames or from above, through the clerestory lights of Level 5, encourages a moving and often surprisingly intimate encounter with art.

The collection itself has grown dramatically in the past ten years. The relative neglect of the visual arts in Britain in the twentieth century means that the collection has far fewer recognised masterpieces than the museums in Paris or New York, but Tate Modern has created new favourites such as Rebecca Horn's *Concert for Anarchy* 1990 and the group of Anselm Keifers that have recently been seen on display as a result of Anthony d'Offay's extraordinary gesture in giving his collection to the nation in the form of ARTIST ROOMS. Above all, it is the imagination of the team of Tate Modern curators that has defined the originality of the institution, showing collections in new configurations that have been adopted by others across Europe and North America. In working with artists in the Turbine Hall, or in devising the innovative displays of the collection, in one structure from 2000–06 and since then under a different frame, the curators have set out to make vivid the ideas, achievements and connections between different generations of artists. Contemporary art lies at the heart of the debate about ideas and values, not, as often elsewhere, relegated to the end of a long historical line where it suffers in comparison with the now-established masters of the early twentieth century: Picasso, Matisse, Mondrian, Beckmann and Duchamp. These initiatives are described in detail by Frances Morris and Sheena

Tate Modern is Ten
Nicholas Serota
Director, Tate

Left:
Detail of the overview of
Bankside Urban Forest
© Witherford Watson
Mann Architects

Right:
New Development of Tate Modern,
view from the south at dusk
© Hayes Davidson and
Herzog & de Meuron

Wagstaff later in this volume, but they have established Tate Modern as an institution that serves its audience by suggesting new ways of seeing.

The very success of Tate Modern in opening up our experience of contemporary and modern art and in changing our relation to the city compels us to seek ways of realising the further potential of the site and of the building itself. Herzog & de Meuron's new plans for Tate Modern will be realised over the next few years. Work has begun and will create new gallery and social spaces to relieve the overcrowded rooms in the present building and respond to the changing nature of art, with facilities for new media and spaces to reflect Tate's new commitment to photography and art from across the world, not just from North-West Europe and North America. There will be enhanced spaces for learning, with access to studios, seminar and study rooms that will be places for dialogue and exchange not simply instruction. Beneath these exciting new facilities lie the former oil tanks from the power station: rough, raw spaces where we shall present special installations by artists, and performance in the realm of dance, music, the spoken word and film. As it enters its second decade, Tate Modern is continuing to explore new ways to interpret the art that we already know and to present emerging trends. Artists oblige us to look again and to think again. Tate Modern gives us the opportunity to join them in that search.

The story of Tate Modern is a new story. It is a tale on a big scale, about huge risks, a river of millions of visitors alongside London's river; it's a story brimming with symbols, above all the obvious one of an old industrial power station scooped out and remade as a cultural powerhouse. And what of those of us passing time here – perhaps squatting down to stare at a completely unfamiliar sculpture, or standing and gawping upwards in the awesome Turbine Hall, or browsing through the shop, acutely aware of sore soles, watching other watchers, daydreaming? In a busy, grindingly urban world, we learn to value our time. What do we hope to get by spending it here: little spasms of pleasure, a slightly grander sense of ourselves, a time of contemplation, freed from the usual demands of earning, shopping and moving?

Church or holiday?

The contemporary art museum is often compared to a secular cathedral, where agnostics come to engage in a pale mimicry of worship. The artist Jake Chapman, a ferocious critic of Tate Modern, expressed the complaint that its architecture is 'concussive': 'You feel very small in the face of the magnitude of this cathedral. It sends messages for miles: this is important, this is a sacred place, everything here is sacred. Things that are sacred aren't questioned, and that's the problem.' Every honest visitor to a contemporary gallery knows what he means. You just have to look at the false-pious expressions, the dazed reverence, on some faces; or hear the hushed murmuring; or attempt to read some of the hectoring prose written about modern art. Yes, there is an attempt by some people, some of the time, to mimic religion and browbeat visitors. Whether it is fair to judge Tate Modern in that way is another question. Is there laughter here? Is there 'art impiety'? Are there arguments going on around the building? Do people gasp with actual pleasure or are they really solemn and intimidated? This is a difficult thing to analyse. My impression as a regular visitor is that the Tate is not concussive, despite its almost ludicrous size, and is rather a welcoming place. But yours may be different.

In other words, Tate Modern does not feel like a cathedral. For one thing, to make an obvious and mildly barbarian point, it is a great deal more popular than most cathedrals. It draws in around four million visitors a year, more than double the number originally planned for, and apparently holding steady. In raw pulling power, that makes it the most successful modern art gallery in the world, easily outstripping New York's Museum of Modern Art. It is the third most popular free attraction in London, this constantly distracting, 'watch me', 'do this' mayhem of an international city. Its audience is relatively young. Cathedrals, perhaps sadly, tend to attract older congregations, but six out of ten visitors to this place are under thirty-five. Walk around and you will find all ages, colours and styles of ambulant human. Tate Modern works hard to attract children, in groups and individually, and there are plenty of them, particularly on week days. All of which is not bad, you may think, for a building full of allegedly difficult art.

The days are long gone when we were taught a story of one genius or group of them following and eclipsing previous schools, so that a line of advance is discovered, and art moves ahead, as if artists were explorers or experimental scientists. A major contemporary gallery, like this one, exists to teach and to expose us to new art and new experience. That involves history, including the history of ideas. But modern art, with its complex, writhing pattern of movements, its glittering dead ends and its surprising passages, has become hard to categorise into hierarchies of good and bad. We lack the words. If you are dealing with oil paint on a flat surface, or an etching, then comparison between two works is relatively easy. Comparing a huge colour-field painting by an American abstract painter with a Fragonard may be hard, but it is not impossible. How, though, do you compare an arrangement of Brillo boxes by Andy Warhol, a Sam Taylor Wood DVD of fruit rotting, Joseph Beuys's basalt columns and a Dan Flavin light sculpture? We are lacking in a common language for this. Calling one of these works more or less successful than another pushes us back into our own individual responses, which are in turn shaped by the chances of our lives and personal experience. In earlier eras, people could fall back on using technical ability as their criterion, highlighting the work's craft and artifice. We have been taught that there is something barbarian about this, but for centuries it gave people a jumping-off point. But craft is almost irrelevant to an age when artists employ others to do the actual making, sub-contracting the welding, assembling and occasionally even the painting or mark-making.

Art has also consciously disconnected itself from external systems of values. There are overtly political works in Tate Modern, reflecting our unease about the environment and global warming. There is Tony Cragg's sideways map of Britain made out of junk, and an Irish dirty protest, an electric chair, as well as Germanic anti-heroes, throwing out thoughts on the darkest time of the twentieth century. But when we ask what contemporary art says about the world around it, the words continue to scrabble and slide. A medieval Londoner could read the

Andrew Marr
The Magic Box

symbolic iconography of saints, a lexicon of images that was instantly accessible, summoning stories heard orally and their moral conclusions. An art lover in Georgian times understood the classical fables, reading off the fauns and Dianas like notes on a score, and could bask in the memory of sunlit afternoons among Roman ruins. A mid-Victorian gallery goer had a whole internal dictionary of romantic responses to waterfalls, Shakespearean scenes and the like. As with the concept of skilfulness, this gave them ways into the art. They could come away feeling the truth of a Bible story more strongly, or preening themselves on appreciating subtle jokes about Bacchus, and thus on being part of the educated elite, or feeling soulful, and liking themselves the better for it. But a lot of what is in Tate Modern repels 'reading' in that way; the shiny metal, abstract canvas or curved wood has cut itself adrift from anything verbal. That makes things hard. It can mean our responses are more intensely personal; but it can also stop us describing, or discussing those responses with one another in anything other than the blandest way, in terms of how it makes us feel. Perhaps we suspect there are secret societies of adepts who know more, but if so, they speak to us rarely.

As compared to the agreed stories and hierarchies of Christianity or Islam, Tate Modern offers puzzles, questions and dilemmas. One critic, John Carey, argues that this demonstrates conclusively that such art is inferior to literature, which contains the eloquence to criticise itself. I would say, rather, that all our moving around rooms, the time we spend in front of artworks, and how they hold up in the memory once we depart, adds up to a kind of perpetual market of emotion and imagination. Works fail if they cannot attract an audience, a glow of enthusiasm. They succeed, or survive, if enough people enjoy them enough … which, after all, is much the same with books. Tate Modern is an ordered, or at least curated, quasi-chaos of creative and mental activity. The curators are provoking us, challenging us to decide what moves us. Some work survives; other work fails. And, as we know, one era's failures may be regarded, in time, as successes. Almost certainly, in the galleries you may have visited, there are examples of art that will in the future be seen as ultimately unsuccessful. Through the obscure working of art fashion, paintings and sculptures currently standing proudly in the light-washed, thronged rooms, will one day be packed away into Tate storage, to sit in silence and dark, relegated and forgotten. Then, perhaps, a few decades later they will be rediscovered. (Wouldn't it be wonderful if all the seen-too-often Monets and Bacons, for instance, could be hidden away for a generation and revealed in their radical glory to fresh eyes? Ha! Surprise!)

So this is a bogus cathedral whose worshippers disagree about basic tenets of the faith. It does contain common stories, from the tale, or fable, of Joseph Beuys's near-death wartime experience, to Richard Long's discovery of the walk as art. Stand behind other people, room by room, listen to them talking and you will hear the parables of contemporary art being retold again and again. Yet for most people, the experience of the work will be full-on, of the moment and unclouded by even these stories. This is not necessarily a good thing. It can make the work seem dull, off-putting or incomprehensible: as with other art forms, the audience has to work a bit, too. There is a sentimental assumption sometimes, that you can put anyone in front of a work of art and they will respond to it – that this is the ultimate democratic experience. It is a nice thought, but untrue. Put a twelve-year-old in front of a Donald Judd and what happens? First, the talking has to start, the gabble of explanation.

But if the galleries can be thought of as side-chapels to the cathedral, each with a different clutch of images and questions, then the Turbine Hall is where the communal acts take place. With the help of generous sponsors and an awesome space, a string of artists have produced public art on a blow-your-mind scale. Louise Bourgeois's disconcerting huge spider and Olafur Eliasson's *Weather Project*, with its great, hazy, apricot sun disc, were among the works – or events – that were surrounded by crowds of awed observers hour after hour. We have had moments at Tate Modern when contemporary art folded into mass experience, if not an act of collective worship then perhaps a silent, optical rave.

In the end, though, we should be nervous of the simile between art and religion. Religion is supposed to give people answers to questions about life and death, fundamental meanings and a code by which to live. Art may 'ask questions', console and delight, but it rarely presumes to offer new ways to live. Tate Modern contains some works of obvious profundity, which have the power to shake and provoke serious reflection – I am thinking in particular of the extraordinary Rothko room, which is for me among the most sobering places on the planet. Other works instantly delight and somehow reassure – think of Matisse's *Snail*, or the work of Anish Kapoor. Others genuinely provoke questioning. But the heterodox, jumbled, multiform nature of contemporary art, ranging from satire to

Previous page:
Olafur Eliasson (born 1967)
The Weather Project
16 October 2003 – 21 March 2004

Above:
Visitors to Tate Modern during
the Edward Hopper exhibition
27 May – 5 September 2004

Right:
Aerial view of the partially built
Bankside Power Station, 1951

solemnity, wax and hair to oil paint and DVD, Pop to abstract cerebration, beauty to extreme ugliness, means that to talk of any single typical or ideal experience in a building such as Tate Modern, is hooey – marsh-gas and night-soil, as denizens of London's South Bank might have put it centuries ago.

Dirt and money

The place matters too. London is moving home again – back east, where the original city hugged the slimy riverbank, after the best part of three centuries of spreading west. The area around Tate Modern was originally a zone of pleasure and luxury, then squalor and wildness. Southwark was outside the limit of the city, which was on the northern bank of the Thames. From the southern entrance to London Bridge, the laws and enforcement of London's civic rulers lapsed. Rich merchants' houses, squatting across the road south, gave way over time to bear-baiting and cock-fighting, prostitution, crime of all kinds, and eventually, famously, to the great theatres of Elizabethan times. In the rebuilt Globe, crouching beside Tate Modern, there is a modern remembering of that. But Tate Modern's building, the old power station, recalls the later fate of Southwark as a grimy industrial area. London was once a manufacturing city, a centre of the industrial revolution, and nowhere was as ruthlessly disfigured by factories and crammed slum housing as Southwark. It must have stank with the smells of iron-making and brewing, distilling and glass-making. Along the river, where you can now saunter so easily, there were crammed wharves, jostling masts and barges, the constant clamour and shriek of dockers, cranes, cables and steam engines. The air was thick with smoke and the streets slimy with filth. Just across the sewer-like river were the finer buildings and opulent offices of the City, already a world hub of banking. Its wealthy citizens looked and lived to the West, where parks and terraces, new villages and crescents, were springing up. But back in Southwark there was danger and discomfort. No-one would have dreamed of building something as necessary as a power-station on the other bank.

By the time the great British architect Giles Gilbert Scott was asked to design Bankside power station, Southwark was already in steep decline, well on the way to the neglected and decaying era it is now beginning to escape. Scott, who had in fact designed a cathedral too, in Liverpool, produced a massive and instant landmark, almost as dramatic as his other London power-station, Battersea, further along the river. The thick, blunt chimney at its centre, somewhere between a cubist Doric column and a proletarian spire, rises from what is essentially a big brick shed, interestingly detailed but simple in form. Readers intrigued by the story of how this industrial-era building became Tate Modern are directed to Michael Craig-Martin's gripping essay later in this handbook.

In modern times, the area around Bankside had become a classic example of what happens to post-industrial land without enough money and imagination. Large, gloomy blocks of social housing, bomb-sites, railways – some still operating – and spectacularly ugly office-blocks hemmed it in to the south. Schools, scraps of green urban park and fairly dismal shopping struggled to compete with choked, busy roads. It was a place people moved out of when they could. The good life was elsewhere. It was in the London villages, Blackheath, Highgate, Chiswick, even Clapham; or in the more spacious suburbs, or in the wealthier housing of Westminster, Chelsea and beyond. The working-class population remaining after deindustrialisation was, here, mostly white. But across East London, the ethnic mix was changing fast. Poorer immigrants moved in. The old white working classes began to move out, to Essex and Kent. More recently still, the story began to change again. Somehow, after nearly three centuries when London was moving west, and the centre of gravity swinging away from the old city, that mysterious pendulum is swinging back. London is coming east. London is coming home. Whether it is the migration of artists and restaurants to Hoxton, or the somewhat crass commercial development of the old docklands, or the revival of the Thames riverside, there is a return migration of money and energy. It has certainly affected the area around Tate Modern, though when the decision to create the gallery was taken, there were few signs of what was about to happen.

One of the best food markets in London now operates nearby, filled at the weekend with delicious smells, exotic and homely supplies from across England, and visitors cramming bags and mouths with all manner of good things. Specialist shops, restaurants and cafés have opened all over the area. Warehouses have been converted into expensive riverfront lofts; the Thames has been straddled by the Millennium Footbridge – which infamously, but rather enjoyably, wobbled as you crossed it, until it was de-wobbled at some expense. On the other side, Tate Modern has encouraged the development of pedestrian space, sunnier and more open lines of sight and regeneration at street level. Some of the duller old buildings have been pulled down. Students have colonised other areas.

I don't want to overplay the changes, because this part of London is still home to some of the ugliest buildings in the Western world, notably on the Thames's north bank. But there is an air of hope, a genial buzz, at Bankside these days. It has become part of a linear sweep, a riverbank boulevard, which connects it to the concrete galleries, theatres and concert halls of the South Bank, home of the post-war Festival of Britain, and ultimately to Westminster. There has been dramatic change too: the former Greater London Council buildings became empty after Margaret Thatcher's Conservative government abolished the leftist GLC and now house, among other things, a hotel and an aquarium. The pleasant walk under trees extends east from the huge O of the London Eye, past Tate Modern and the rebuilt Globe theatre. It is briefly obliterated by buildings, and then picks up again towards Tower Bridge, a berthed Second World War cruiser and the new London Assembly building, variously compared to a fencer's mask and a testicle. In its childlike geometric variety – circle, block, stick, globe, bobble – this is the frontage of contemporary London. Tate Modern has its place firmly in the middle of a new family photo.

Who comes, and why?

So what are we looking for, when we stop here and come inside? Is Tate Modern simply a convenient, decorated space to amble through, a destination in itself, the ultimate excuse for slowing down? Among its many functions, it is a refuge. We need refuges. We are carried through our lives in a constant gurgle of activity and anxiety, defined by what we are doing – as workers, consumers, travellers, followers, leaders. Every few hundred metres of the modern city calls on us to buy, to change our lifestyle, to do better, earn more, look smarter. We live in a cacophony; not only the obvious one of electronic bleeps, traffic and plane noise, half-conversations through mobiles, recorded voice messages and sirens, but also in a visual cacophony of image and colour designed to make us buy. If we travel between cities, on business or holiday, we touch down and re-enter the cacophony. We have become urban creatures and we rarely escape it. Behind this noise are the deeper pressures we live with – to survive an illness or thrive in a place of work; to pass exams; to retain contact with friends, children, parents; to mourn; to achieve a difficult change of life. Then, like a distant grinding, are the wider anxieties, the worries about global warming, pollution, poverty and ultimate meanings.

In many ways we may have been living through a golden age in the West, a time of cheap travel and huge material affluence. The warning rumbles about rising sea-levels or mass migrations are just that, not imminent. Most of us are not oppressed in any direct way. We do not fear the state, as so many millions feared it during the middle of the last century. There are no near-at-hand tyrannies. Ugly prejudice, aimed at skin colour, sexuality or religion, is comparatively rarely expressed, particularly given the mixed societies of most large European cities. Yet we are harried people too. We are busier than ever, living faster than ever, surrounded by buzz, questioning and the jabbing finger of choice. In such a life, there are surprisingly few places that let you alone, that stand back and do not demand that you buy, or state your business, or explain yourself. The modern public gallery is one such place. It is constantly available to be probed and thought about, but it doesn't press itself on you. It waits. It lets you be yourself, at your own pace, following your own track and thinking your own thoughts. Drenched in light, surrounded by the work of tense, alert minds, you can feel yourself washed and strengthened before the cacophony begins again.

Or so it is for me. I revel in being able to enter a free gallery for half an hour and spend it with one or two works, as I could not do in a paid-for exhibition. Around me will be knowledgeable students, unknown artists, academics, excitable tourists, local idlers, all with their own agendas. Tate Modern wasn't here a few years ago. It is only here because of the high-rolling gamble taken by some administrators and politicians, and then frantically hard work by the teams who redesigned, converted and opened this extraordinary place. Yet already, a few years on, it feels as much a part of this city as Tower Bridge or St James's Park. Its beautiful wooden floors are changing colour. Its gallery spaces are being reorganised and will soon expand to the south. The flow of people never stops, but there is a rhythm to the arrivals and departures, as the sun moves round the windows, a tide of walking and talking. It belongs to the world of contemporary art but it belongs to London too, a place we are already proud of. It shows that among the botched public works, overruns and administrative failures, things can be made on time, to cost, and can be popular without being crass. It knits an older English aesthetic with the neat decorations and burned-biscuit bricks of Gilbert Scott's power station, and the newer, cooler aesthetic of Herzog & de Meuron, and makes that pairing feel natural. It has brought jobs, helped revive local businesses, and will do more in the years to come. It has excited hundreds of thousands of people with its paying shows, from *Matisse Picasso* to *Frida Kahlo*, and has educated even more through clear labelling, talks, public education programmes, computer links and film.

It was a power station and is, of course, a powerhouse, pumping out energy of a different kind. It is not a cathedral or the site of a new mock religion. But it is both a refuge and a box of magic tricks. In the end, perhaps the simplest description is the best. Tate Modern is the most interesting box on these old and busy islands.

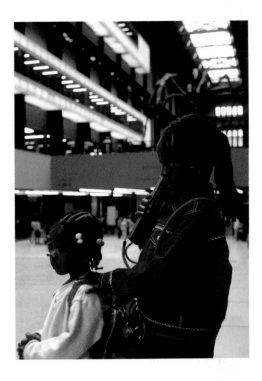

Above and right:
Visitors to Tate Modern during
the Louise Bourgeois exhibition
12 May – 17 December 2000

Above:
'The Tate Gallery and its Site at
Millbank', press cutting from
The Times, 1892
Tate Archive

Left:
Rachel Whiteread (born 1963)
EMBANKMENT
11 October 2005 – 1 May 2006

Frances Morris
From Then to Now
and Back Again:
Tate Modern
Collection Displays

Rachel Whiteread's *EMBANKMENT*, the major installation in Tate Modern's Turbine Hall in 2005, was rich in metaphor, from art history to personal memory. Its many translucent white casts of boxes forged a direct link, in their evocation of sugar cubes, to the sugar magnate and philanthropist Henry Tate, who lent his name and gave his wealth to the establishment of the Tate Gallery. The development, within the compass of just over a century, from his founding ambition – to celebrate and encourage national art – to the extraordinary institutional engagement with the production and display of contemporary art represented by *EMBANKMENT*, constitutes an enormous leap.

The first Tate Gallery was built in 1897 at Millbank, on the north side of the Thames, upstream from Westminster, on the sprawling, waterlogged site of the old Millbank penitentiary, once Europe's largest prison. As institutions, prisons and museums have a surprising amount in common. Within them, both inmates and works of art, removed from their original habitats, their private spheres, are gathered together, regulated and controlled. Once inside, they rub along with new companions from different backgrounds; changing governors choose the company they keep, determine their status, distribute privileges and control public access.

Not surprisingly, artists have always resisted such terms of confinement. To the painter Maurice Denis, writing in 1907, museums were 'cemeteries abandoned to decay, where the silence and the musty smell denote the lapse of time'. Two years later, F.T. Marinetti, poet and spokesman for the Futurist movement, dismissed them as 'musty graveyards' dedicated to the 'futile worship of the past'. More recent artists, such as Marcel Broodthaers and Susan Hiller, have made the museum itself a subject for their critical gaze, no longer calling for its destruction, but laying bare in their work the conventions and values that underpin its practices. Others, like Hans Haacke, have exposed the ideological frameworks that lie behind the museum, or, like Mark Dion, have excavated rich seams of poetry latent within museum systems of classification and display. Battered but unbowed, art museums – Tate among them – have shown themselves to be both remarkably resilient and responsive to such onslaughts, riding the storm waves but also responding to the ebb and flow of the tide.

While the prison and the museum may share a common root in the emphasis they place on the value of instruction, art museums, from the outset, were intended as stages for revelation, prisons as sites of containment. Jeremy Bentham, architect of Millbank prison, invented the instantly recognisable panopticon plan, based on a notion of an all-seeing eye, that determined the shape and ethos of so many early nineteenth-century prisons as well as influencing the development of other institutional building types. Bentham's vision has no counterpart in the evolution of the museum, which has developed in a remarkably free way. Throughout its history, the art museum has offered architects and curators a wonderfully open challenge – witness the countless different types of museum – and the last few decades have seen the development of a dazzling range of innovative new museum buildings across the world, as well as the dramatic expansion of museum programmes responding to a broadening public interest in contemporary art.

Since it first opened in May 2000, Tate Modern has been inundated with visitors, young and old, from near and far. It has become a people's palace, a national treasure, cresting the wave of cultural effervescence as well as spurring the economic regeneration of its neighbourhood. It is a phenomenal visitor attraction – its bars, restaurants and bookshops packed, its public spaces animated with late-night entertainments, its galleries heaving with human traffic, embedded in the chaos and momentum of contemporary life.

But to enter the museum through the exhilarating space of the Turbine Hall is also to escape, momentarily, from the onslaught of everyday life and work. Fabulous for people-watching as well as London's coolest party venue, the Turbine Hall is first and foremost a vast and hugely challenging project space for contemporary artists. Beginning with Louise Bourgeois in 2000 and running to the more recent contributions of Dominique Gonzalez-Foerster in 2008 and Miroslaw Balka in 2009, artists have responded to it in utterly different ways, and in the process significantly extended the range of their own practice. Throughout its varied spaces, Tate Modern has found opportunities to inspire and support myriad new artistic initiatives, from commissioned interventions in the galleries themselves and live events staged in the Turbine Hall to smaller-scale projects and group presentations, and commissions for its restaurant, members' room and outside landscape. Like art galleries and museums everywhere, Tate Modern is intent on encouraging and promoting new artistic initiatives, on participating in debate, on responding to and promoting emerging art.

If Tate's emphasis on the contemporary increasingly occupies centre-stage, what has become of its original aim, and its task of defining and safeguarding heritage? What should museums such as Tate Modern do with their permanent collections? And how should they balance the needs and priorities of the contemporary and the modern, the temporary and the permanent? Curators nowadays are faced with a dual challenge: to engage in and make sense of new art and to re-present the old; to approach and communicate history, and display works of art in such a way that meaning can be communicated and experience can be felt by audiences of every kind.

The expectation that permanent-collection displays must somehow address both the history of the works they contain and the wider history from which those works are born is a forceful legacy of the first generation of nineteenth-century art museums, rooted as they were in Enlightenment thinking. Of course, museums have always had to grapple with the restrictions imposed on their historical narratives by the partial nature of their holdings: the 'history' that any collection can address is guided by its particular strengths and weaknesses. Nineteenth-century curators displayed plaster-casts of originals to stand in for the 'missing links', while today, the need to 'fill gaps' often drives a museum's acquisitions policy. Until the advent of photography, students of art history seeking to view art were necessarily confined to those museums they could conveniently visit and to what they could see there. Photography, as André Malraux's famous *Imaginary Museum* of 1947 demonstrated, opened up limitless possibilities for the historian: any work from any era could be reproduced in combination with any other, on the printed page. Far from denuding museums of their function, however, this in fact prompted a reassessment of their role. It was Walter Benjamin, exploring the impact of photographic reproduction on the work of art a decade earlier, in 1936, who had identified the notion of 'aura' as the unique power of the work of art, which can only be appreciated in the presence of the original and is lost in the business of reproduction. Museums, rather than art books, are where you can see the real thing, engage with the original work of art and its 'aura'. That is why people visit and revisit museums, why they care, sometimes passionately, about curator's choices, and why they love or loathe interpretative texts, or other means by which the museum might mediate their experience of the work of art.

Tate has developed two complementary collections: one following the history of British art – the purpose for which it was originally founded – and, since 1917, one of modern international art. The collections have their own characters: the British collection is more broadly based and the international more selective and idiosyncratic. Tate's collection reflects both the visions of different directors and curators and the realities of taste, economics and opportunity. Until recent years, its geographical focus was principally on Europe and North America, and its strengths and weaknesses were easily categorised according to recognisable historical/stylistic focal points. Surrealism, Abstract Expressionism and Pop were well represented; Dada, interwar realism and Expressionism were notably lacking. Highlights include celebrated individual works – August Rodin's *The Kiss* 1901–4 (p.209), Edgar Degas's *Little Dancer Aged Fourteen* 1880–1 (p.100), Henri Matisse's *The Snail* 1953 (p.169) – as well as significant groups of works by key artists including Pierre Bonnard, Mark Rothko, Alberto Giacometti, Germaine Richier, Donald Judd and Joseph Beuys.

Beyond these triumphs of acquisition, Tate's history is punctuated by moments when it failed, or passed up the opportunity, to secure important and now highly regarded masterpieces. Other areas of omission emerge over time. As women or black and ethnic-minority artists play an increasing role in shaping the field of contemporary art, it has become apparent that these constituencies are largely absent from the earlier part of the modern collection. For many years, Tate focused its collecting exclusively on painting, sculpture and works on paper. The amazing vitality of new art in video, film and photography, which Tate has actively pursued since, highlights the absence of these media from its holdings of earlier contemporary art. Changing role models and shifting agendas as well as the impact of new research in art history cause a continuous rethinking of collecting priorities.

Tate's collection, rich in texture and depth, and yet uneven, is available to us in its entirety only as a virtual experience on its website, through a database that allows users to access artists by name, date, medium and other categories. The collection is physically spread over multiple sites – at Tate Britain on Millbank, Tate St Ives in Cornwall, Tate Liverpool as well at Tate Modern on Bankside. A fifth site, a warehouse in Southwark,

Above:
Press cuttings from the launch
of Tate Modern, May 2000

Right:
André Malraux's *Imaginary
Museum*, 1947

houses works currently not on view and manages the daily transaction of objects as they are shifted between Tate sites as well as travelling as loans to temporary exhibitions in the UK and abroad. Each of the four gallery sites calls for a different means of organisation for its permanent collection displays, reflecting its principal focus and inflected by the different physical qualities of its spaces.

Tate Modern is in effect a new building, created within the imposing brick skin of an older one. Bankside power station was designed by Sir Giles Gilbert Scott during the middle years of the twentieth century, and is an emphatic design statement of its own era. It was transformed at the end of the century by the Swiss architectural team of Herzog & de Meuron into an equally powerful statement of contemporary cultural life. A solitary visitor to the Turbine Hall, listening carefully, will still hear the quiet but insistent throb of the transformers, still functioning and housed behind the southern wall. Other echoes of the past abound. Some, such as the gantry crane in the Turbine Hall or the vertiginous windows, are original. Others, like the compact metal floor grilles or the untreated oak floors, are new but represent a conscious response on the part of the architects to the character of the original building. Galleries for the permanent collection were provided within the seven-storey refurbishment of the building's river-facing side. Instead of a series of uniform spaces, the architects designed a range of different rooms – some exhilarating expanses lit from high clerestories, others smaller and more domestic in scale – to provide for the display of huge contemporary works as well as for more intimately scaled paintings and photographs. Views onto St Paul's Cathedral interrupt the walls on the (north) river facade, while high balconies project into the Turbine Hall on the galleries' south side, generating a continuous interplay between outside and in, city and museum, life and art. The architectural solution answers both the ambitions of the 'white cube' as an isolated, neutral space, and the tradition of the 'enfilade', of galleries unfolding in sequence. The floor plan allows for four

26

Below and right:
'Head to Head'
Display at Tate Modern,
30 May – 30 August 2004

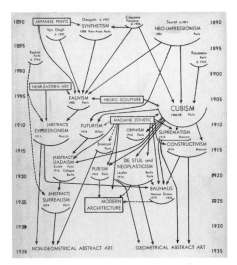

separate wings of permanent collection galleries, on two storeys. Each wing offers the possibility of multiple entry points and a number of alternative routes, allowing visitors to determine their own journey through the displays.

Alongside the constraints and opportunities afforded by its collections and buildings, every museum display is also guided by a set of assumptions determining the layout of works of art. Until recently, most collections of modern and contemporary art have tended to follow a structure of display originated by the famous founding director of the Museum of Modern Art in New York, Alfred Barr. His brilliant and influential flow-chart of artists and movements, compiled in 1936, reflected and reinforced a particular and subsequently widely shared view of modern art's lineage and development. Centring on Europe and North America, it traced a succession of moments of innovation, 'isms', all leading towards pure abstraction. Barr's model not only informed the way in which he displayed his museum's collection; it also guided the growth of the collection itself, and its acquisitions policy and priorities, especially during the period of his own tenure as director. His template suited the classic decades of twentieth-century avant-garde movements but it has proved less adequate as a means to interpret more recent international developments in art. The weight of its influence continues to be felt in the new MOMA, which, when it reopened after a massive expansion in 2005, opted for a clear historical divide in its displays between old (modern) and new (contemporary). This stance reflects the consensus view of its curators that contemporary art is 'too recent to present in the form of a synthetic overview'.

The manner in which MOMA's extraordinary collection addresses and narrates the history of modern art has been under question since the 1960s, as artists have sought new alliances with mass culture and innovative technologies, and reflected on their own practice and its history in fresh and revealing ways. As many younger artists are unwilling to accept modernism as the defining force in their cultural heritage, old hierarchies of art, gender and geography are constantly assailed and dismantled. Art history, developing within a wider theoretical context informed by semiology, Marxism, feminism, psychoanalysis, analytical philosophy and the politics of identity, has explored the powerful yet complex impulses of politics, society and geography on art. It no longer seems possible to account for the diversity and dexterity of artistic innovation through a single, all-embracing historical narrative, nor to see art as a continual and inexorable progression, of reaction and innovation, towards a commonly agreed end. This open and fluid situation was what the new Tate Modern, inaugurated in 2000, felt called upon to confront and address.

Tate Modern's first five-year display, unveiled in 2000, challenged the idea of a synthetic overview of history by adopting four broad themes – Landscape, Still Life, The Nude and History – through which it explored connections between artists and works of art over the whole field of twentieth-century art. A mix of single artists, small groupings and more complex thematic displays across the century, often juxtaposing works and artists of different periods, allowed for a continuously shifting viewpoint, in which famous works could be seen in new contexts, and new works could be brought into play with more familiar ones. It deliberately avoided a general chronological disposition of displays, proposing alternative ways of looking at the history of art. 'Head to Head', an installation assembled in 2004 of portrait busts in the collection, from Auguste Rodin's bronze *Balzac* 1892, to Bruce Nauman's video work *Good Boy Bad Boy* 1985, ranked over eighty pieces in strict date order, disregarding conventions of hierarchy and style and allowing new connections to be made. In 'The Shape of a Year: 1951', in 2001, a wide range of works all made in the course of a single year were brought together to reveal the diversity of artistic practice at any given moment in time. A series of 'In Focus' displays took single 'iconic' works from the collection – such as Pablo Picasso's *Weeping Woman* 1937 (p.194) – and explored, through accompanying documentation, the artist's intention and the work's context and early reception, to highlight the ways in which its meaning and importance evolve over time and through the vagaries of public opinion, the judgement of critics and fellow artists, and the market place. Finally, a series of displays brought together two artists 'in dialogue'. Some of those who were paired, such as Alberto Giacometti and Barnett Newman, belonged to the same era. Others, like Claude Monet and Richard Long, worked at opposite ends of the twentieth century. These displays, met variously with delight or derision, hinted at unexpectedly poetic as well as engaging and provocative ways by which the art museum can animate relationships over time.

The current displays, opened in 2006, is the collective endeavour of many curators, the result of wide-ranging consultations and lengthy, heated debate. Building on what was learnt over the opening five years, an entirely new scheme for display restates Tate Modern's

Above:
Diagram of artistic movements devised by Alfred H. Barr, from the cover of *Cubism and Abstract Art*, The Museum of Modern Art, New York 1936

ambition, declared in the opening hang, to pursue a discussion of art and its meanings; not to replace orthodox art history with an alternative narrative, but to suggest the possibility of multiple readings, conflicting stories and different agendas. In place of the single, institutionally authored history, the current display embraces different viewpoints and different framing devices, both in the works and in their disposition and presentation; it aims, crucially, at fresh reflection on history from the perspective of the present day.

A fluid dialogue between past and present animates the current display. It goes with the grain of the collection, acknowledging the particular character, and relative strengths of Tate's holdings, as well as the reading of modern art history that has shaped the collection's development over the last century. It also works against the grain of a sequential narrative, allowing for the interplay of different timeframes. It acknowledges that history is not static: hierarchies and interpretations of which we once felt certain can be upset and reconsidered in the wake of subsequent developments. In the 1960s, for example, abstraction seemed to be the pre-eminent achievement of twentieth-century art. From today's perspective, however, the invention of collage appears to be more vividly connected to the way in which artists work now in an ever more multi-dimensional, virtual world dominated by digital technologies and visual spectacle. Connections – stylistic, conceptual and poetic – between movements and artists are neither simple nor sequential. What links Marcel Duchamp to Richard Hamilton, Monet to Pollock, or experiments with construction of the 1910s and 1920s to Arte Povera in the 1960s cannot be explored solely through chronology. Works of art belong to their moment but they have varying genealogies and in different eras become part of new histories. Over time, they accrue meanings, are interpreted and reinterpreted. Experience of artworks and readings of their meanings evolve in dialogue with the company they keep, guided by the perspectives of those who encounter, respond to and interpret them, and as collections grow and are redeployed and revalued, each generation discovers the old in new ways.

The current display is divided into four sections in each of the wings on levels 3 and 5: 'States of Flux', 'Poetry and Dream', 'Material Gestures', and 'Energy and Process'. Each of these revolves around a central 'hub', which presents a key period of particularly heady experimentation in twentieth-century art history – 'crucible' moments that radically altered the artistic landscape of the times, and whose shock waves continue to be felt. The central space in 'States of Flux' is occupied by 'Cubism, Futurism and Vorticism'. At the core of 'Poetry and Dream' is a display focusing on 'Surrealism and Beyond', which includes painting, objects and film from the movement's inception to the mid-1940s. The hub of 'Material Gestures' combines American Abstract Expressionism and European Informel art, while 'Energy and Process' revolves around post-Minimalist practices associated with Arte Povera artists and their contemporaries internationally.

Thus the basis of the four sections is formed by familiar 'movements' – whether defined immediately by the artists themselves with manifesto zeal, coined soon after by critics identifying a new stance, or confirmed later by art historians seeking to clarify and categorise, in retrospect, the history of art. But these terms are treated as relatively elastic. They remain open to fresh interpretation. The display has been configured to offer a mind-map of their possibilities. In each wing, a series of satellite displays – some of which change on an annual basis, allowing for a continuous re-mapping as fresh connections are made between present and past – unfold around the hub, creating a network of connections. These tributaries, parallel streams and contra-flows allow other stories to unfold: alternative forms of Realism are seen adjacent to Surrealism, the continuation of post-Impressionism is presented alongside Cubism, the aesthetics of assemblage are seen in relation to Arte Povera, German Expressionism is reviewed in the light of the later Abstract Expressionism. Contemporary artists, working in different media, and returning to different moments of history and modern art at will, enter the displays as solo voices, pairings or groups. These interjections are deliberately staged to suggest the ways in which meaning can emerge and alter over time; artists most steadfastly set on breaking with the immediate past rarely do so without reflection on and response to historical precedents. Even if they do, interpretation and understanding of their work by others is often mediated by the search for antecedents and influences.

Left (top):
International Surrealist Exhibition,
New Burlington Galleries, London
1936
Scottish National Gallery
of Modern Art Archive

Left (below) and right:
Installation views of 'Poetry and
Dream', Tate Modern, March 2006

States of Flux

'States of Flux' centres on Cubism, Futurism and Vorticism. Pioneered by Pablo Picasso and Georges Braque between 1907 and 1914, Cubism marked a radical rethink of notions of representation; it rejected the idea of the painting as a static illusion of reality that had held sway since the Renaissance, in favour of a fragmented, multi-dimensional form of representation that reflected the complex realities of modern sensibility. Together with initiatives in other parts of Europe at the time, Cubism was in tune with new philosophies of perception in reflecting the dynamism of the machine age. Despite this, the pioneering innovations of Braque and Picasso were most commonly played out in the conventional genres of still-life and portrait painting. Co-opting their vocabulary but fusing it with a heady obsession with new technology, the Italian Futurists celebrated, as their 1909 manifesto declared, the beauty of 'a roaring car', and the 'sleek flight of planes'. In Britain too, the Vorticists extolled action, speed, movement and modernity.

The central display of these interrelated 'isms' – expanded to embrace other artists of the period caught up in and extending the field of experimentation – is surrounded in the series of satellite spaces by a changing sequence of individual contemporary voices. Collage, appropriation and montage are all parts of Cubism's legacy and are explored in the spaces that follow and make a bridge to similar concerns in Pop art. Other displays focus on moments when groups of artists have pursued equally passionate struggles to reconnect art and life: a sense of chaos, experimentation and indeterminacy underpins the radical excesses of the international Fluxus group of the 1960s, while the Pop art generation is seen to revisit and vitally transform the language of collage, combining high and low culture, art and commerce into new and compelling visions of their era. The innate radicalism of Cubist innovations and its vivid connection with modernity also encouraged the appropriation and extension of its formal innovations by artists driven by more radical political agendas.

Not all artists, of course, were caught up in the sway of Cubism in these years; there were many who ignored or rejected its attractions. In the art of Pierre Bonnard and Henri Matisse, among many others, a vision of tranquillity and domestic stability countered the pull of the modern world. This wing of galleries not only embraces the dynamism of the Cubist revolution, but also explores its ramifications and subsequent lineage, and reflects on its counterpoint: stasis and continuity. It opens with the pairing of Marcel Duchamp's *Large Glass* and the work of Richard Hamilton who set about reconstructing Duchamp's work in the 1960s. They shared concerns with an erotically charged reinvention of the body, but each work speaks of its time.

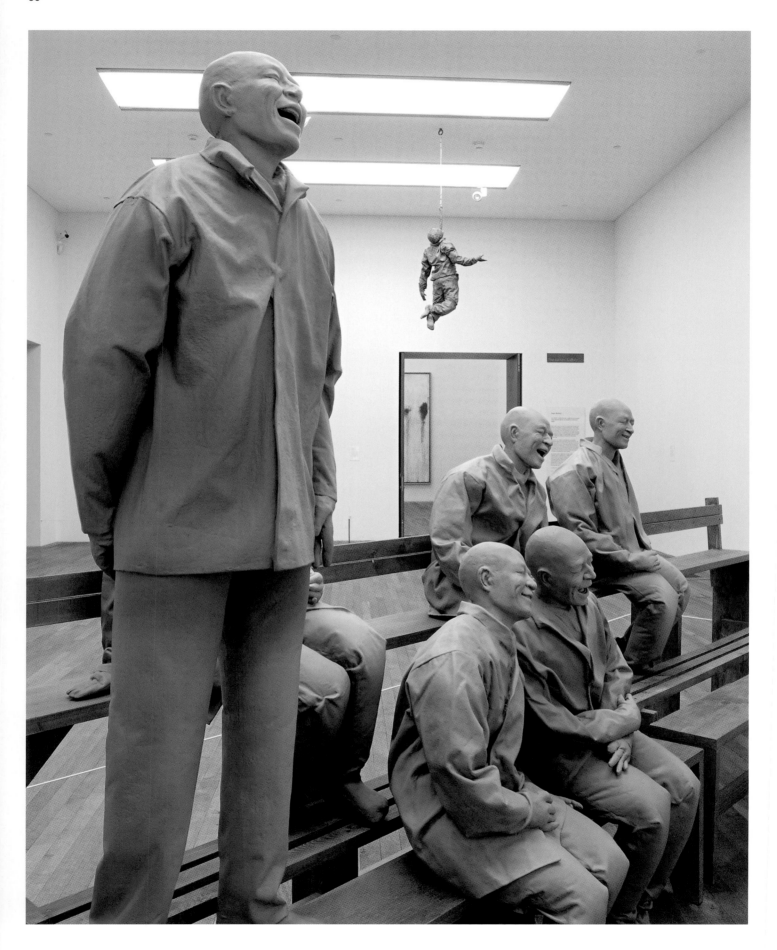

Juan Muñoz (1953–2001)
Towards the Corner 1998
Installation view, 'Poetry and Dream',
Tate Modern, March 2006

Poetry and Dream

'Poetry and Dream' spans Surrealism and its legacies, from 1920 to the 1940s. Surrealism was launched in 1924 in a manifesto published by the poet André Breton, and has been hugely influential in shaping the course of subsequent art. It drew on Sigmund Freud's work on dreams and the unconscious as well as Marxist political theory, making a direct connection between the liberation of the creative potential of the irrational mind and social revolution. For some artists the unconscious could be unleashed through techniques of automatism, involving free-association and the effects of chance. Others evolved highly realistic styles through which to present bizarre, dream-like narratives. The dense, multilayered installation of works at the heart of this wing combines painting, sculpture, objects, photography, prints and film, and reflects the intense, immersive experience that the Surrealists themselves sought from their art. Adopting an extended timeframe, this hub also explores how artists from Pablo Picasso to Jackson Pollock transformed key Surrealist strategies in responding to the horrific realities of the middle years of the century.

Surrounding galleries allow a range of artists to be seen in relation to Surrealism. Francis Bacon and Pablo Picasso, for example, followed distinct and separate paths, while conceiving a, sometime violent, reinvention of the figure. Other artists resisted the urge towards inner expression, and more conventional aspects of realism are also on display in this wing. Surrealism's widespread, complex and often troubled legacies extend into much of the most interesting recent art, and this allows for frequent changes of displays that embody these contemporary responses.

While some displays look forward in time from the hub, others also look back. The opening dialogue between Giorgio de Chirico (1888–1978) and Jannis Kounellis (born 1936) adopts a broad time span, with the work of the Italian metaphysical painter who exercised a profound influence on Surrealism, shown alongside a wall drawing and installation of 1979 by the Greek-born sculptor, who was associated with the radical Italian Arte Povera group in the 1960s. Affinities between the highly charged, dream-like atmospheres and strongly metaphorical content of these two works suggest interesting ways of reconsidering the history of Arte Povera, a movement explored in greater depth in 'Energy and Process'. The display also demonstrates how powerful figures such as de Chirico can exercise influence over artists at different moments in time.

Material Gestures

New and seemingly unprecedented forms of abstraction and realism emerged on both sides of the Atlantic as artists responded to the traumatic experiences of the Second World War and its aftermath. In 'Material Gestures', the central focus on post-war experimental art brings together artists from Jackson Pollock and Mark Rothko to Alberto Giacometti and Jean Dubuffet, who shared a fundamental belief in the ability of materials and gestures to evoke and communicate internal states of consciousness and strong human emotions. Spanning both American Abstract Expressionism and European Informel art, it includes works that, at the time, seemed to bring painting and sculpture to the brink of its own destruction, such as Jackson Pollock's drip paintings or Jean Fautrier's sculptures.

Another display looks at post-war painting by a number of more senior artists, including Henri Matisse and Joan Miró, who continued to pursue their own concerns but responded, in their work, to the scale and ambition of the new art. Other stories also unfold around the hub. The presence of Claude Monet, as well as of German Expressionist painting, suggest ways in which the seemingly unprecedented innovations of the post-war era were anticipated in strategies evolved by previous generations. Dialogues between past and present are prompted by the opening display of the wing, which brings together the tense physical presence of Francis Bacon's work with the more elegiac experience of Anish Kapoor's *Ishi's Light* 2003.

Energy and Process

The conceptual and political radicalism that boiled up towards the end of the 1960s found an outlet in the radical revision of art associated with a rejection of Pop and Minimalism and a return to simpler materials and actions. The Italian artists associated with Arte Povera (poor art) and those internationally who worked in parallel ways are the focus of the hub of 'Energy and Process'. All turned to materials more generally associated with craft or everyday life, reinforcing the connection to natural forces and activities. The resulting works, sometimes residues of performances at other times redolent of natural processes, embrace new and richly poetic visions of the world. This openness to new materials and their indeterminate form is seen as much in the work of Giovanni Anselmo and Guiseppe Penone working in Europe as Lynda Benglis and Robert Morris in the USA. Around this central gallery radiate, as elsewhere, spaces in which echoing displays explore works that enlarge upon this aesthetic. The tone is set by the confrontation of Kasimir Malevich and Richard Serra in the opening space, which captures a sense of the different ways in which notions of energy can be fixed at different moments in the century. Other precedents for 'anti-form' art are found in 'Beyond Painting' where the transition from the canvas through collage and assemblage in Picasso and Schwitters acquires a startling energy in the slashed and shot canvases of Fontana and Saint-Phalle. Further displays radiate around these to show some of the many ways in which related practices have developed.

Tate Modern's displays are temporary and experimental. Like the inaugural hang, on which it builds, this new configuration will evolve over time. The framework, artists and themes will be replaced by different ones as future curators seek to accommodate Tate's ever-evolving international collection and review and respond to new thinking about the nature of history and aesthetic experience. This open-minded commitment to speculation, experimentation and change is crucial. No single museum collection or gallery display can begin to enunciate all the multiple histories alive within a work of art, or the full range of connections between artists in and beyond their time. But art museums can reclaim and reanimate history for a contemporary audience, as well as providing a sense of context for the apprehension of contemporary work. Just as the search for antecedents and historical roots guides our understanding of the present, so contemporary practice opens up unforeseen perspectives on history. Artists go backwards to go forwards. The past only exists for us in the present. To suggest a fixed and permanent disposition would be to dare to impose a gagging order on a wonderfully rich and open-ended narrative that will continue to be contested for as long as artists make art, galleries are built to house collections, and audiences visit them.

Below:
Anish Kapoor (born 1954)
Ishi's Light 2003
Installation view, 'Material Gestures',
Tate Modern, March 2006

Right (above):
Tacita Dean (born 1965)
The Roaring Forties: Seven Boards in Seven Days 1997 (detail)
Installation view, 'Material Gestures',
Tate Modern, March 2006

Right (below):
Installation view, 'Material Gestures',
Tate Modern, March 2006

Raw Materials, the provocative new work created by Bruce Nauman for the fifth Unilever Series commission (2004), filled Tate Modern's vast, imposing Turbine Hall not with conventional sculptural forms but with intangible acoustic material. Loudspeakers slotted into the vertical I-beams lining the space emitted twenty-two voices, from the sombre tones of an older man, to the shrill careful pronunciation of a little girl, to the tirade of an exasperated male, each enunciating simple texts or single words in an explosive or insistent way that tested language to its very limits. Led by curiosity, moving intently from one sound zone to the next, visitors became aware that the disturbing, cacophonous or humorous effect of the repetition of words or phrases made what they were hearing hover at the edge of unknowingness. 'Language is a very powerful tool', Nauman has said. 'I think the point where language starts to break down as a useful tool for communication is the same edge where poetry or art occurs.' Through this project, the artist wanted to expose the way in which words shape our perceptions of the world, making us realise that we can see – and see through – language. 'The tension is very interesting … I think art forms in general are most interesting when they function in the same way.'

It is this tension in art – a dynamic oscillation between what we see, what we think we know, and the revelation that there are other ways of responding to and thinking about our world – that Tate Modern's programme is devised to reflect. This potent quality is at the very core of the best of modern and contemporary art – inherent in the entire spectrum of visual culture, whether film, photography, installation, sculpture, performance, painting, video, live art or the hybrid interdisciplinary branches that grow up between these forms.

Each of the museum's exhibition projects, commissions and events is debated and often disputed by the curators and directors, who are ever-conscious of the responsibility of making decisions about what is shown to audiences. This process challenges the curators' choices and the viability of their concepts, tests how artistic ideas can be unfolded in the museum's spaces, debates the placing and timing of the show within the overall programme, and struggles with how the art can be presented so that the diversity of its possible meanings comes across to a large and varied audience, which can then make up its own mind about what it sees.

To take on the daunting challenge of making a new work within the enormous space of the Turbine Hall is a courageous and risky task, which can be undertaken successfully by only a handful of artists, each of them conscious of the spectres of the preceding projects and the prospect of creating a distinctly different one. The Turbine Hall, so enormous that it is officially designated as 'a covered street', is at the very heart of Tate Modern thus each experimental and dynamic commission for this space resonates beyond the significance of the work itself. In 2001, when he was developing the second commission in the Unilever series, the sculptor Juan Muñoz said he came 'to look at the Turbine Hall as part of a city rather than part of a museum. It's a fragment of the urban experience … It is a space of our time … These kinds of architectural spaces are very recent. They are a condition of our modernity.'

Tate Modern has come to epitomise that urban sensation. Standing by the edge of the Thames, linked to the civic and economic centre of the city by the Millennium Footbridge, the museum offers startlingly different views north and south from its galleries and restaurants. On the one side, the grandeur of St Paul's is the iconic focal point of a meticulously planned civic environment. On the other is the vast sprawl of south London, an intricate grey tapestry combining pockets of intriguing new construction with neglected city planning projects. At the interstice of this complex, chaotic and exhilarating social space, Tate Modern sits in a position to blend the energy and history of the surrounding city with the social function of the museum, via the stimulus of its programme of exhibitions and collection displays.

One of the first exhibitions at Tate Modern, *Century City: Art and Culture in the Modern Metropolis* (2001), addressed the modern urban condition. It presented, through diverse curatorial points of view and via the different global contexts of ten cities at significant periods of their cultural flourishing in the twentieth century, the ways in which the visual arts have addressed the vigour of the metropolis. Using the constant flux, contradictions and changes inherent in city life at a given moment in time, both as subject matter and as an active metaphor for the public function of art, was an enterprising and risky proposition. The ambition of this project set the tone for Tate Modern's programme, prefiguring the increasing international reach of the artists it presents and whose work it collects. It also heralded Tate Modern's subsequent recognition as a museum that has radically shifted the public attitude to modern and contemporary art within both the city and the nation as a whole, with an impact unrivalled by any other international museum.

As one of the most important secular spaces in London, a social destination and gathering place for a huge number of people, the generous volume of the Turbine Hall is the first space a visitor to the museum encounters. It invites us to enjoy a democratic, communal experience within a massive space, although this does not mean that the work sited here must forgo a

Sheena Wagstaff
Raw Materials:
Tate Modern Programme

human scale or a more individual experience. The first Unilever Series installation for the Turbine Hall was by Louise Bourgeois (2000). Her idea was to create a sculptural theatre for the masses, tempered by the opportunity for intimate human encounters within that spectacle. Three gigantic steel towers, as well as a colossal sculpture of a spider named *Maman*, which has since assumed iconic status, created a monumental dialogue with the architectural scale of the Turbine Hall. In quieter significance, they also laid out a personal iconography, analogous to a four-part 'journey of life'.

Two intensely erotic sculptures made forty years earlier by Bourgeois were included in the exhibition *Surrealism: Desire Unbound* (2001), illustrating a link to her Surrealist predecessors. Part of an exhibition strand devoted to surveys of a movement, or a period in which artists have dealt with similar issues or have formal or stylistic affinities, *Surrealism*'s central theme focussed on desire, seen as the 'authentic voice of the inner self', flickering lustfully in art, literature, poetry and film. This topic provided a distinct perspective on one of the most important artistic and intellectual movements of the twentieth century whose resonance is still pertinent to art made today. As familiar and extensively documented as this period has been, research for the show uncovered previously unseen material, creating new scholarship on Surrealism.

Deserving more recognition of its historical significance for post-war art was Arte Povera, a clustering of work by a loosely affiliated group of artists who emerged in Italy during the 1960s. *Zero to Infinity: Arte Povera 1962–1972* (2001) was the first comprehensive examination in the UK to explore those artists' understanding of how 'poor' materials could convey a vital energy and bodily experience through painting, sculpture, installation and performance – in contrast to the media-oriented, consumerist work of American Pop artists whose fame had historically eclipsed the achievements of their European peers. In response to a more conventional interpretation of Pop art, *Pop Life: Art in a Material World* (2009) proposed a vigorous rereading of a major legacy of Pop art. Taking a cue from the its chief protagonist Andy Warhol, whose notorious provocation that 'good business is the best art', the show looked at the various ways that some artists since the 1980s have deliberately infiltrated the world of commerce and publicity, cultivating celebrity personas and creating their own signature 'brands'. Both these exhibitions, as well as *Open Systems: Rethinking Art c.1970* (2005), were barometers of an historic moment identified and seized by curators as timely opportunities to re-think or define a theme or shared artistic sensibilities. They demonstrated the need to challenge orthodox historical wisdom about past cultural periods by posing questions informed by the perspective of the present.

Another way to create stimulating exhibitions that present the sheer diversity of artistic innovation in the past is to chart the artistic friendships between some of the great figures of early twentieth-century art, such as the exhibition *Matisse Picasso* (2002), which revealed how these twin giants of modern art inspired – and provoked – one another to create a fascinating and complex artistic narrative. Through an exploration of the striking affinities and parallels between three of the following generation of artists, the exhibition *Duchamp, Man Ray, Picabia* (2008) demonstrated that while each artist pursued a separate career, it was their personal interaction that amplified the resonance of each other's works through a complex web of echoes and allusions that together had a significant impact on their contemporaries. In the same vein, the pairing of the two pioneers of Russian Constructivism, Aleksandr Rodchenko and Liubov Popova, concentrated on work made from 1917, the year of the October Revolution, to 1925. Coincident with the radical political notion of a new society conditioned by social justice, these constructivist artists – who regarded themselves as engineers of this utopian vision – engaged modern technology to create abstract painting and utilitarian work manifested in myriad cultural forms, including film, theatre design, photography, graphic design and fashion. The creative dialogue between *Rodchenko & Popova: Defining Constructivism* (2009) testified to their utter conviction in the potential of art to transform the individual and society at large. By contrast, in its mapping of the journey from Weimar Germany to post-war America of the two visionary artists, *Albers and Moholy-Nagy: From the Bauhaus to the New World* (2006) posed probing questions regarding the transitioning of utopian belief in a new social order to the profound dystopia of Nazi Germany and World War II, alongside the migration of Modernist ideas from 1930s Europe to post-war America. While Albers and Moholy-Nagy's careers overlapped only intermittently, their artistic practice was informed by similar concerns, made manifold in highly individual responses to an emphasis on experimentation and formal innovation, a refusal to be confined by conventional media and, most notably, an ongoing understanding of artistic production as an ethical activity.

Previous page:
Louise Bourgeois (1911–2010)
I Do, I Undo, I Redo
12 May – 17 December 2000

Below:
Katharina Fritsch (born 1956)
Man and Mouse 1991–2 and
The Dealer 2001
Installation view, *Katharina Fritsch*, 7 September –
9 December 2001

Right:
Albers and Moholy-Nagy: From the Bauhaus to the New World
Installation view, 9 March –
4 June 2006

Spanning 110 years, from those whose work is historically well established to younger artists whose practice at a 'mid-career' point is notably consistent and inventive, large-scale Tate Modern exhibitions devoted to the work of single artists are conceived either as concisely selected retrospectives or focus on specific aspects of an artist's oeuvre. As the architecture of the museum enables two exhibitions to be staged simultaneously, the opportunity occasionally arises to devise an informal 'pairing' between these two ages of artists, where the link between the shows is implied but not over-determined. One such example of complementary exhibitions occurred with *Surrealism: Desire Unbound* and the mid-career profile of Katharina Fritsch (2001), in which the latter's enigmatic subjects have certain parallels with the sensuality, dark humour and obsessive sensibility of the Surrealists. A more deliberate correspondence occurred through a profile of the painter Luc Tuymans alongside a retrospective of the works of Edward Hopper (2004). Tuymans was intrigued by the prospect of this correlation, since one of his early interests had been Hopper's smaller paintings, which he regards as toy-like 'fetishes'. He described the filmic aspect of Hopper's work as deriving from an 'elusive space, slipping away into the diagonals', a quality that has infused his own series of 'toy-world' paintings. Tuymans decided to acknowledge his affinity with the older artist's work by including in his own exhibition three Hopper-inspired pieces, which he regards as crucial to the development of his art.

The enduring mystery of Hopper's melancholy narratives and his achievement in literally and metaphorically casting light on the modern human condition continues to excite enormous public interest, and attracted large numbers of visitors to the exhibition. Tate Modern does not undertake such exhibitions simply because they attract a broader public, privileging mass appeal over educational value. Rather, the decision to include these and other shows within the programme is taken because the subject deserves re-examination, or because a new angle on old work suggests itself. Comparably popular was the first solo exhibition at Tate Modern dedicated to a Latin American artist, Frida Kahlo (2005). Due to the diffusion of many of her searingly intense, visceral self-portraits into forms of popular culture – from biopics to bumper stickers – and the fact that her personal mythology has been used to debate wider issues central to post-revolutionary Mexican cultural politics, Kahlo's work has often been regarded as exemplifying the idea of an 'authentic' Mexico. Likewise, Hopper's paintings are often presumed to represent a genuine American experience. Both exhibitions were devised to retrieve the creative expressions of these artists from the symbolic ciphers and carriers of other mythologies they had come to assume. A more recent analogy can be found in prevailing assumptions about the painterly vision of Mark Rothko, whose progressively sombre darkening of his late canvases has provoked simplistic projections about their being an 'authentic' corroborative expression of the artist's melancholic state of mind before his eventual suicide. Ever since its inauguration in 1970 when the artist himself selected the works for Tate, the 'Rothko room', as it has become popularly known, has been one of the iconic highlights of the Tate Collection. Concentrating on the less-explored sequence of Rothko's late series, the exhibition (2008) presented the nine Seagram murals from the 'Rothko room' in a completely new context, uniting them with a selection of key related paintings. In so doing, the show also made visible one of the museum's core functions, namely, the ongoing questioning, enquiry and research into works in its care by curators and conservators.

Retrospectives of two of the most influential international sculptors of the post-war period, Eva Hesse (2003) and Donald Judd (2004), gently de-bunked previous critical appraisals of their work. While the latter explored Judd's engagement with philosophy, architecture and design, it also revealed the striking contrast between the formal austerity of his work and its sensual richness of material and colour. Hesse's exhibition focused on her work as a synthesis of contemporaneous European and American artistic sensibilities, where the febrile and visceral tactility of her work is held in balance by an internal rhythm or formal seriality. It owed as much to the artistic ferment of 1960s New York, which included Judd, as it did to the evocatively inchoate and organic sculpture of Joseph Beuys, encountered by Hesse when she was living near Düsseldorf.

The exhibition *Joseph Beuys: Actions, Vitrines, Environments* (2005) included the eccentric objects that Beuys (1921–86) deployed in his installation works, which were imbued by his unique fusion of political activism and utopian vision. By contrast, although never associated directly with a political ideology, Hélio Oiticica (1937–80), a major artist of the Brazilian avant-garde in the 1960s and 1970s, considered art to be an anarchic form of revolt against all forms of oppression, whether intellectual, institutional or social. Yet the emphasis on the artist as rebel has tended to obscure other aspects of his artistic project, in which colour was central to his investigations. *Hélio Oiticica: The Body of Colour* (2007) took as its starting point his assertion that 'Colour is the first revelation of the world'. From the vivid hues of early environmental installations, Oiticica

Left (top):
Mark Rothko (1903–1970)
Black and Gray series 1969
Installation view, *Rothko*,
26 September 2008 –
1 February 2009

Left (below):
Hélio Oiticica (1937–1980)
Grand Nucleus 1960–66
Installation view, *Hélio Oiticica:
The Body of Colour*, 6 June –
23 September 2007

Above:
*Cy Twombly: Cycles and
Seasons*
Installation view, 19 June –
14 September 2008

gradually de-coupled colour from its traditional role to propose it as pure sensory stimuli. His work reached its climax through seducing viewers to become participants in his late performative works, indulging in the visual and tactile sensations of richly coloured textile costumes combined with rhythm, dance and music, in which his radical conceptual insights were finally integrated and reconciled with his experience of life. The belief in art as an all-embracing social system was shared by Martin Kippenberger (1953–1997), whose saying 'one of you, among you, with you' proposed communication as the very basis of human existence. Focusing on the various forms of expression manifest in a richly prolific body of work, the comprehensive survey of the work of Martin Kippenberger (2005) charted an oeuvre that drew from popular culture, music, architecture, art, politics and history. Anticipating its later reception, he once declared that he was the ultimate embodiment of the art of the 1980s: many of his works deal caustically with political issues from the last decade of the Cold War, dipping into Punk, New Wave and Neo-Expressionism, while his notoriously razor-sharp wit and loudly communicative personality impressed and influenced countless subsequent generations of artists.

To create exhibitions of artists whose work and life were as inextricably linked as that of Beuys, Oiticica or Kippenberger – and who are no longer alive to inform and shape an exhibition to reflect and invigorate that union – presents a significant challenge to the curator. How to site installations or perfomances regarded by the artists themselves as flexible propositions, so that they continue to create a dynamic relationship between visitor, object and the space? The crucial issue here is how empathetically close the curator can come to the vision of an artist in order to represent the work with the utmost integrity. When working with living artists who have achieved substantial bodies of work such as Louise Bourgeois (2007), Robert Frank (2004), Sigmar Polke (2003), Per Kirkeby (2009), Jeff Wall (2005), Peter Fischli & David Weiss (2006), Roni Horn (2009) and Pierre Huyghe (2006), the curatorial role is necessarily different and varies considerably from one project to another. A hallmark of success is the degree of receptivity that the curator has for an artist's ideas, engendering the close working relationship necessary to fulfil the artist's ambitions whilst also providing the optimal viewing conditions, both environmental and informational, for visitors.

The most effective artist-and-curator teams are conscious that every aspect of developing a show is a form of interpretation, which therefore presents the work to the public from a particular viewpoint. The selection of the works, their groupings or the way in which they are installed, the architectural arrangement and route through the spaces, the colour of the walls, the quality of the lighting: all these choices contribute to the spatial dynamics and visual phrasing of an exhibition, and are as crucial to people's experience and appreciation of art as the wall texts and brochures. Rather than attempt a comprehensive overview of a career spanning almost sixty years, the curator of *Cy Twombly: Cycles and Seasons* (2008) chose instead to present cycles of work within the artist's oeuvre to evoke an experience similar to being in the studio at the moment when a work evolves. In his assembling of graphic signs, vivid accumulations of rich colour and allusions to classical civilisations and mythology that are part metaphorical, part suggestive, Twombly often scrolls fragments of poetry, scraps of narratives or names into the pictorial tapestries of his drawings and paintings. *John Baldessari: Pure Beauty* (2009) demonstrates a similar fascination with the connection between working with words and the visual field (although approaching the making of art from the conceptual end of the critical spectrum), combining painting, photography and film into elaborate formal structures that play deftly and humorously with language and meaning. A fellow key instigator of international Conceptual art, Cildo Meireles (2009) combines abstract thought and direct physical experience in his extraordinarily diverse body of works, often originating from a life experience or memory connected to a wider concern with Brazilian history and its political and human rights predicament. Varying dramatically in scale and appearance, each of Meireles's unique large scenarios within the exhibition 'defined its own space', determined the way the visitor encountered and experienced each installation, and allowed them to gradually discover the artist's perceptual or ethical proposition through the work.

Invited in 2007 not least for her exceptional ability to engage with architectural space in the public sphere, Doris Salcedo chose to inscribe negative space into the Turbine Hall floor rather than fill its cavernous volume. The title, *Shibboleth*, refers to a story from the Old Testament in which the already-defeated Ephraimites are then horrifyingly slaughtered trying to gain access to their homeland simply due to the fact that their pronunciation of the word 'shibboleth' was not the same as that of their conquerors. Known for creating works and critical spaces informed by her political sensibility living and working in Colombia, Salcedo's complex response to the Turbine Hall referred to the language and legacy of violence by forcibly drilling open a long multi-branched crack that extended the length of the hall, laying bare and potentially de-stablising the

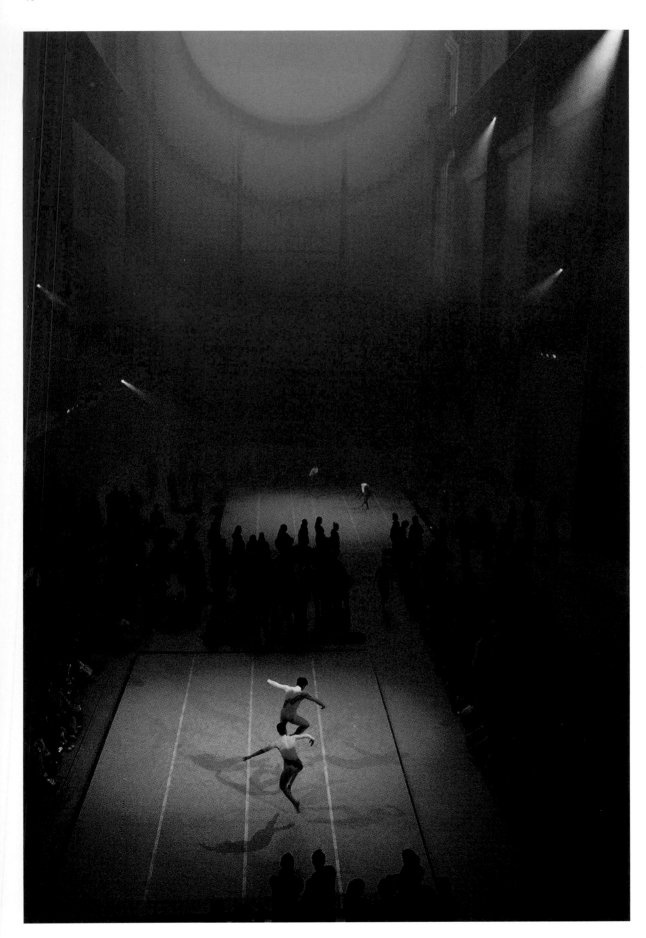

Left:
Anniversary Events
Merce Cunningham / Dance
Umbrella performance in the
Turbine Hall, November 2003
Photo: Gigi Giannella

Right (top):
Paul McCarthy (born 1945)
Blockhead
19 May – 26 October 2003

Right (below):
Cildo Meireles (born 1948)
Red Shift I: Impregnation 1967–84
Installation view, *Cildo Meireles*,
14 October 2008 – 11 January
2009

solid underpinnings of the vast building. Its edifice long recognised as a beacon of cultural power, Tate Modern stands at a juncture of history, its Collection still umbilically connected to the ideology of nationhood and the obverse colonialist aspect of the Enlightenment, at the same time as its acquisition and programme strategy is geared to making a far broader international account of artistic practice in a world in which the political plight, social inequity and exploitation of the so-called 'third world' nonetheless remains an urgent often unacknowledged and unresolved crisis. The result of painstaking labour by Salcedo's Colombian studio crafting hand-made concrete slabs with meticulously-finished surfaces, *Shibboleth* cracks opens a critical space that runs literally and metaphorically right through the heart of Tate Modern. Unique in the strength of its confrontation with and physical breaking of the building, *Shibboleth* permanently marked Tate Modern, transforming it through a remarkable artwork whose critical resonance continues to be felt. Where visitors once felt compelled to walk along its length from the delicate hairline incision to the gaping jagged depths, there now remains a scar.

As *Shibboleth* refused to be visually consumed from a single position, so Anish Kapoor also opted to create a form in the Turbine Hall whose massive volume prevented a complete view. His work *Marsyas* (2005) comprised three massive, circular, steel rings: two angled vertically and attached to each end of the Hall, and one suspended horizontally above the bridge. Between them stretched a continuous tubular span of dark red PVC fabric seamed in long strips like bleeding slices of peeled skin spliced together, their blood-red colour viscerally suggestive of the flayed muscle and sinew of the satyr Marsyas, who was brutally skinned alive at the hands of the Greek god Apollo. A heroic amalgam of art and engineering, this membranous form was powerfully torqued, its twisted seams describing a tensile strength, holding its colossal architectonic form in trembling tension: its relationship with the architecture evoked a sense that if one of the rings were to slip, the building itself might inwardly collapse. To address his intial misgiving that the work's massive scale would give it an unwanted theatricality, Kapoor's solution was to ensure that in his artistic collaboration with the engineer Cecil Balmond, the materials and engineering techniques used to create *Marsyas* were as much a part of the content as the form itself.

Another project created in collaboration with an engineering and technical team was the scaling-up in 2003 of Paul McCarthy's small maquettes into two giant inflatable sculptures. *Daddies Bighead* and *Blockhead* were vaguely figural shapes standing six storeys high, ebulliently dazzling in bubblegum-pink and pitch black. A collaboration with the Henry Moore Foundation, the works were installed on the north landscape, their monumental scale and visual spectacle vying with that of the building itself. *Blockhead*'s black nose, evoking a Pinocchio-like duplicity, and *Daddies Bighead*'s pink proboscis, a priapic balloon, both pointed across the river towards the City of London, literally cocking a snook at the establishment.

It is impossible to understand the forces behind today's visual production without representing other fields of visual culture through the museum's programme. To be able to achieve this, creative partnerships with organisations such as Dance Umbrella, the Live Art Development Agency or Sadler's Wells, are vital for sharing different areas of expertise, for introducing fresh ideas into artistic and curatorial practice, and for generating new audiences. Over the past ten years, Tate Modern has pioneered a programme of live performance, to create a different context through which to explore an increasingly interdisciplinary and ever-expanding international arena of contemporary art. Amongst presentations by over 200 artists, seminal historical works staged in collaboration with Dance Umbrella include: Merce Cunningham's 50th 'golden' anniversary performance (2003), staged under the glow of Olafur Eliasson's commission in the Turbine Hall; a re-staging of Joan Jonas's *Lines in the Sand: Helen in Egypt*; Trisha Brown's *Man Walking Down the Side of a Building* (2006); and Robert Morris's *Bodyspacemotionthings* (2009), a reconstruction of his 1971 Tate exhibition, the museum's first participatory show. The Live programme also proffers cutting-edge work by both emerging and established artists, amongst whom are Tania Bruguera, Tony Conrad, Ulla von Brandenburg, Pablo Bronstein, Keren Cytter, Matt Mullican, Cyprien Gaillard and Sturtevant. As is often the case, many performances are multi-disciplinary, involving aspects of theatre, music and film; particularly memorable was Alvin Curran's *Maritime Rites* (2007) when the London Symphony Orchestra led volunteer musicians in a sculptured sound piece staged on a barge on the Thames. The musicians joined the bells of St Paul's Cathedral to create a collage of harbour sounds, bell-peals, foghorns and music inspired by the river.

Launched in 2006 as an annual arts festival for the late May Bank Holiday, The Long Weekend has provided the opportunity to present a series of dramatic live events and music, often in thematic connection with Tate Modern's Collection displays. One such programme in 2008 resuscitated the idea of a Flux-Olympiad, conceived by founding Fluxus artist George Maciunas but never realised. Fluxus artist Larry Miller programmed a number of events, in which

Flux-athletes and visitors participated in a range of Flux-sports including soccer played on stilts, obstacle shoe races, slow speed bicycle races and balloon shotput. The evening was distinguished by Nan Goldin's seminal slide shows *The Ballad of Sexual Dependency* and *The Other Side*, with new soundtracks performed live by musicians Patrick Wolf and John Kelly. Afrobeat DJ Rita Ray set the scene for African filmmaker Djibril Diop Manbety's powerful, rarely seen films, and a screening of early experiments in computer animation featured among others Ed Emshwiller, Pierre Hebert, Malcolm Le Grice, Lillian Schwartz and Stan VanDerBeek.

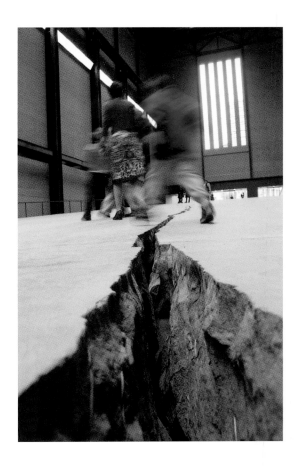

Since 2003, Tate Modern has developed Tate's first dedicated film and video screening programme, now considered London's premiere platform and forum for artists working with the moving image. In addition to numerous film series related to Tate's exhibitions, an acclaimed series devoted to international histories of experimental film and video has included extensive programmes devoted to work from Brazil, Eastern Europe, France, Germany, India, the Middle East and USA. Moving image works by hundreds of influential artists have been screened at Tate Modern, often for the first time in London. Highlights have included surveys of films and videos by artists ranging from Bas Jan Ader, Pedro Costa, Robert Frank and Harun Farocki to David Lamelas, Daria Martin, Marie Menken, Deimantas Narkevicius, Ulrike Ottinger, Trinh T. Minh-ha, Margaret Tait, Lawrence Weiner and Akram Zaatari amongst many others. Ambitious film performances and installations by Tony Conrad, Steve Farrer, Luke Fowler, Tamara Krikorian, Malcolm Le Grice, Daria Martin, Anthony McCall, Rabih Mroué and Lis Rhodes also have been presented in spaces ranging from the Starr Auditorium to the Turbine Hall and the Level 2 Gallery. Several major conferences and screening programmes have investigated related subjects such as animation, archival and found footage film-making, the relationship between still and moving images, and the Expanded Cinema movement.

Another strand of the programme 'takes the temperature' of the current social, political, economic and environmental climate across our many continents, capturing in large group shows the momentum of a new artistic idea amongst mostly younger artists. Ideas about chance, play, process and the possibility of the unexpected occurring as a result of audience interaction with the work characterise the approach of the artists whose works were included in the exhibition *Common Wealth* (2003). Acknowledging the rich historical relationship between visual art and theatre, *The World as a Stage* (2007) challenged the often-negative connotation of 'the spectacle' within the realm of visual art by making obvious the extent to which a sense of theatre is often prevalent in the gallery space. The idea of theatre was treated by artists as a fertile terrain to be experimented with or plundered.

The propensity of some of the artists to make art with political intent without considering themselves 'political artists' is shared by a number of the international panoply of artists, usually at the first stage of their vocation, represented in the Level 2 Series, launched in 2004. This has included individual projects by Elmgreen & Dragset, Julia Loktev, Julika Rudelius, Cui Xiuwen, Mohamed Camara, Simparch, Damian Ortega, Meshac Gaba, Jan de Cock, Catherine Sullivan, Simryn Gill, Brian Jungen, Roman Ondak, Latifa Echakhch, Nicholas Hlobo, Jill Magid and Michael Rakowitz. Interspersed with a series of eleven mini exhibitions of artists grouped by shared concerns identified by the younger curators at Tate Modern, this strand responds to and, crucially, promulgates the ongoing exchange of ideas on the international artistic network.

While most artists embrace the opportunity for a one-person show or project to present and reflect on their artistic endeavour to date, some are nevertheless ambivalent about the ideological basis on which large institutions like Tate Modern operate. When Olafur Eliasson was commissioned to make work for the Turbine Hall in 2003, *The Weather Project* began with the idea of revealing the 'construction behind the construction' through his work. He wanted to create an installation that would 'hold up a mirror to the institution', reflecting upon the ways in which it influences or 'mediates' the experience of art for its audience; at the same time he was aware that simply by undertaking the commission, he was already complicit with the museum's public agenda. Using three simple elements – a huge half-sun made of low-sodium yellow bulbs, vaporised water and a mirrored ceiling – he created an installation whose visual impact and perceived sublimity had an immediate and unprecedented popular effect. Reflected as a dazzling orb in the grand silvered ceiling, the monumental golden sun captured the imagination of a global public and has since become an iconic image, inextricably enmeshed in the public memory with the experience of Tate Modern's building.

Juan Muñoz was just as aware as Eliasson of the potential power of the Turbine Hall commission to create a tension between the illusory and the real, the act of looking and

Left:
Doris Salcedo (born 1958)
Shibboleth
9 October 2007 – 6 April 2008

Right:
Juan Muñoz (1953–2001)
Double Bind
12 June 2001 – 10 March 2002

perceiving, and the poignant isolation of detecting and acknowledging the individual amidst a mass of people. This resulted in an architectonic allegory called *Double Bind* (2001), a vast hollow structure whose lower and upper planes extended horizontally from those of the hall's bridge to touch all three walls of the west end of the Turbine Hall, its upper face a trompe l'oeil floor visible to people standing on the bridge. Enclosed within the cavity between the planes, discernible by people below who could look up through partial openings, was a sequence of disquieting sculptural figure-tableaux, partially obscured in grey light. Muñoz speculated 'that 10,000 people are going to be there some days, and I'm trying to build a work to which they can pay attention as if they were the only one there.' Like the great architects of the Baroque period, he wanted 'to make the world larger than it is … You have to make this person trust for a second that what he wishes to believe is true. And maybe you can spin that into another reality and make him wonder.'

Artists are indeed agents of transformation. They change the way we think and how we look at our world, its past and its present. They are also crucial in defining the identity of the museum and conveying the spirit of the place. Those who have made work in the Turbine Hall over the past ten years have demonstrated that it is not only an awe-inspiring architectural space and the pulsating public heart of Tate Modern, but that it also functions as an imaginative, intellectual and ethical framework for both the programme and the museum itself.

I had the good fortune to be appointed as an Artist Trustee of the Tate Gallery in 1989. The ten-year period of my Trusteeship proved to be one of the most proactive and expansive in Tate history. As a Trustee I had the opportunity to participate in the sequence of discussions and decisions that led to the creation of Tate Modern at Bankside.

Soon after his appointment as Director in 1988, Nicholas Serota initiated a number of key changes. He decided to restore the original architectural integrity of the Millbank building by the removal of all the temporary walls and false ceilings that had been constructed over the years. Most significantly, he decided to entirely reorganise the display of the collection. These changes brought into sharp focus the limited and inadequate exhibition space, and the urgent need for new buildings.

In the early 1980s an architectural master plan for the Millbank site had been created by James Stirling, shortly after his design of the Clore Gallery in 1981. On reconsideration of this plan, the Trustees decided that it did not provide for sufficient new exhibition space for the present and anticipated needs of the gallery. Although significant development possibilities at Millbank were identified, it was clear that these alone would not be adequate for the Tate properly to fulfil its responsibilities while maintaining and enhancing its international status.

The Trustees concluded that a second site in London would have to be found. This decision raised the critical curatorial and administrative problem of determining the basis on which work would be shown at each site. Should the collection be divided, and if so along what lines? Extensive discussions were held with a wide range of participants from both inside and outside the institution.

The Trustees decided to maintain and continue to develop the collection as a single holding, but to divide what might be shown at each London site on the basis of its two principal areas of responsibility: British art at Millbank, international modern art at Bankside. This would mean, in effect, that Bankside would become the extension of the National Gallery, showing work from 1900 onwards. It would also mean the work of any modern British artist held in the collection could be shown at Bankside as well as Millbank.

A search was begun to locate a new site. The basic requirements were not extensive and more or less obvious, but had the effect of severely limiting the options: a large-scale central location, ready accessibility by public transport (particularly the tube), within reasonably easy reach of Millbank, and available for development in the near future.

A number of sites were considered, but most fell through or were rejected as inadequate: the car park area on the river between Hungerford Bridge and Jubilee Gardens (very limited for building because of height restrictions); at the centre of a new park to be created as part of a proposed redevelopment of the wasteland area behind King's Cross (project eventually shelved); a docklands site east of Canary Wharf (too isolated and inaccessible).

Francis Carnwath, Deputy Director at the time, came across the decommissioned Bankside Power Station in Southwark and recommended that Nicholas Serota and the Trustees consider it. Despite its immense size and its key location on the south side of the river opposite St Paul's Cathedral, this building, more or less inaccessible from the riverwalk and hidden by seedy office buildings on the south side, was largely unknown. Abandoned as a power station for more than ten years but still housing an electricity switch station, the building had become a brooding presence and a blight on the redevelopment of the surrounding area.

Bankside Power Station was designed and built after the Second World War by the distinguished British architect Giles Gilbert Scott, to provide electricity for the City. Scott is best known as the designer of London's other great power station at Battersea, now sadly derelict, and Liverpool Anglican Cathedral, as well as the once ubiquitous red telephone box.

The Bankside building was notable for its plain red brick exterior and the powerful symmetry of its horizontal mass, bisected at the centre by a single tall, square chimney. The building was articulated on three sides by a series of immense, well detailed windows. The only decoration came from the brickwork crenellation along the building's edging, cleverly mitigating its great bulk.

Inside, the building proved to be just as striking and unusual. Built to house the immense turbines, boilers and ancillary equipment of a power station, the building itself was architecturally simply a shell, a box. Its vast interior was divided along its entire length by a series of great steel columns, creating two interlocking spaces, the boiler house and the turbine hall. There were no normal floors, no staircases, no interior walls: everything inside had been built as part of the machinery, not part of the building. Removing the machinery would mean revealing a vast empty space within which virtually any construction might be possible.

The power station was far larger than anything we as Trustees had imagined building from scratch. From the beginning of the project, it had always been our assumption that we would

Michael Craig-Martin
Towards
Tate Modern

be commissioning an entirely new building. The discovery of Bankside dramatically altered our perception of the possible appearance, scale and function of the new gallery.

The Trustees decided to acquire Bankside and develop it as the site for the new gallery of modern art. The site answered all the criteria governing the search: an unparalleled large-scale central London location, excellent transport facilities (including the new tube station at Southwark), the possibility of a riverboat connection with the gallery at Millbank, and immediate availability for development. The local council, Southwark, recognising the potential impact of the Tate project on development and employment in this largely run-down area, enthusiastically supported it from the start.

The vast size of the building meant that the Tate would be able to more than double its capacity for showing its collection as well as housing major large-scale temporary exhibitions. Bankside also provided a remarkable bonus for an institution with the remit to increase its holdings constantly: even after realising our most ambitious development plans, more than a third of the space in the existing building (the present switch station on the south side and the cavernous underground area below) would remain untouched, waiting for development in due course.

Anyone who has had experience of working on a major architectural project will tell you that for it to be truly successful there has to be a single-minded project leader, someone who has a clear idea of what is needed and a vision of what the best might be, who oversees the project from conception to completion. In this case such leadership was provided by the Director, Nicholas Serota. Early in the planning stages of the project, he asked the sculptor Bill Woodrow and myself to tour a number of recently built museums of modern and contemporary art on the Continent, to consider them critically from our point of view as artists, and report to the Trustees. We went to a variety of institutions including those at Bonn, Frankfurt, Münchengladbach and Maastricht, and came to several conclusions. In general these modern museums seemed to serve the interests of architecture and architects more clearly than those of art and artists. Many architects clearly considered designing a museum to be a prime opportunity for high-profile signature work. On the other hand few architects seemed truly to understand or be interested in the needs of art.

In comparison with the entrance halls, staircases, restaurants and other facilities, the galleries for showing art were often, in our view, the least successful spaces in the building. Few architects appeared to have established properly considered criteria for the design of good modern galleries. They tended either to create sequences of more or less identical and characterless neutral spaces or to make self-consciously over-designed spaces where art was barely necessary.

By contrast we found that the most sympathetic and stimulating places in which to see modern and contemporary art were in older buildings converted from an earlier industrial or other purpose, such as the private Dupont Foundation in Tilburg (similar in character to the Saatchi Gallery in London) and the Hallen für Neue Kunst at Schaffhausen near Zurich. None of the purpose-built museums could match the stimulating quality and variety of these exhibition spaces, nor the opportunity for interaction between the art and the space.

We reported these views to the Director and to the other Trustees, and they were later confirmed by the majority of artists responding to a questionnaire on the subject initiated by the Tate. As a consequence, a decision was taken that *the* central concern of the design of the new building would be to address the needs of art through the quality of the galleries and the range of opportunities, both sympathetic and challenging, for showing art. While seeking the best possible architectural solution, we determined that the project would be art led not architecture led.

Many architects were bitterly disappointed by the Trustees' decision to make use of the existing Bankside building rather than to create something entirely new. Some, seeing this as the betrayal of a unique architectural opportunity for London, interpreted it as the result of a loss of institutional nerve. I believe that the Tate showed exceptional courage and ambition in its decision to go to Bankside, which in turn demanded a radical architectural solution.

Under the guidance of Richard Burdett, Director of the Architecture Foundation, an open international architectural competition was initiated with the stated aim of finding the right architect for the Tate to work with, rather than a highly resolved design proposal. A jury of ten members was appointed, with Janet de Botton and myself representing the Trustees. The jury sought to consider the proposal of each architect in the light of three principal questions: their approach to the architectural problem, particularly how to deal with the existing building and its position in the urban context, their ideas for the display and presentation of modern and contemporary art, and their interest in and understanding of art itself.

Nearly 150 architects entered the competition, including many of the world's most distinguished, but it was clear from the start that few were comfortable with the problem of working with the shell of the Giles Gilbert Scott building. Some essentially ignored the structure and designed within it the building they would have made had it not existed, while others attempted to neutralise it by completely altering or removing significant parts. Some sought to dramatise the architectural confrontation of old and new by having parts of their proposed new internal museum structure pierce through the older power station shell.

The six finalists in the competition could be seen to represent two generations of architects: the established masters Tadao Ando, Raphael Moneo and Renzo Piano, and the rising generation of David Chipperfield, Jacques Herzog and Pierre de Meuron, and Rem Koolhaas. It would be difficult to exaggerate how stimulating and challenging it was to be part of a jury charged with interviewing architects of this calibre and evaluating their proposals, and how daunting was the sense of responsibility in making a final selection for a building of such lasting national importance. In the end the jury came to a unanimous decision to recommend to the Trustees that they appoint the Swiss architects Herzog & de Meuron.

Why did Herzog & de Meuron win against such formidable competition? There are of course many reasons, but one seems to me to be absolutely central. All the other proposals treated the existing building as a shell within which their new structure would stand. Herzog & de Meuron's was the only proposal that completely accepted the existing building – its form, its materials and its industrial characteristics – and saw the solution to be the transformation of the building itself into an art gallery. They proposed a true union of their design with that of Giles Gilbert Scott, turning the box into a new building. Open, flexible and pragmatic, Herzog & de Meuron's approach to the project was concept rather than design based, reflecting the similarity of their practice with that of many contemporary artists.

Their proposals acknowledged the symmetry of the exterior by creating within the boiler house a new five-storey structure, with three floors given entirely to six suites of galleries, two to a floor, built around a central service core containing the main staircase, escalators, lifts and toilets. The intention was to divide the displays into manageable units for visitors and create a building in which, despite its great size, one would always have a sense of where one was. The galleries would all have high ceilings and whenever possible be lit by the large existing windows.

The most dramatic alteration to the appearance of the existing building would be a new two-storey-high frosted-glass beam running its whole length, acting architecturally as a translucent horizontal counterfoil to the dark vertical mass of the chimney. This light beam would clearly signal the change of function of the building from power station to art gallery, its welcoming beacon a striking addition to the London skyline. The beam would, of course,

Left:
Bankside Power Station
in 1994

Above:
Working on a double
height gallery

This page:
Transforming the Turbine Hall
and restoring the brickwork

Opposite:
Views of Tate Modern's light
beam from the roof

provide exceptionally beautiful skylighting for the top floor galleries, but also house all the building's service equipment and make possible a restaurant with views across the river to St Paul's. At ground level the architects proposed removing most of the building's smaller wings and outcrops to create a simpler perimeter. The building would rise dramatically from the newly created open piazza stretching to the river.

During the intensive design period following their appointment, the architects, led on site by Harry Gugger, proposed that the existing turbine hall should retain its character more or less unaltered and function as the entrance to the new gallery as well as providing a vast new exhibition space. However, instead of the ground floor being at ground level, they decided it should be established at basement level, opening up the existing space even more. This interior ground floor would be reached by the public from outside down a long concrete ramp the width of the turbine hall. The new building in the boiler house would thus effectively gain a complete floor in height rather than a windowless basement. The turbine hall would become even higher and be crossed at actual ground level by a wide bridge.

Regular and intensive discussions took place between the design team, led by the architects Jacques Herzog and Harry Gugger, with the engineers Ove Arup & Partners and quantity surveyors Davies Langdon & Everest, and representatives of the Tate, both Trustees and staff (notably Peter Wilson who led the Tate team). The final character of the building and especially that of the gallery spaces, emerged from those meetings. It is important to remember that despite constructing the new gallery within an old building, this is not, in a conventional sense, a conversion: everything one sees is new, except the windows – and even these have new internal fittings. It was decided, however, that the basic aesthetic of the old building, its strong simple industrial character, should be continued into the new.

The exhibition galleries were designed to have the feel of real rooms, with substantial walls, plain ceilings, and oak doors, rather than the temporary quality of partitioned spaces. The overhead light fittings are hidden in deep boxes and show only as translucent glass rectangles flush with the ceiling. To emulate the quality of natural light on every floor, they offer a wide and flexible range of light from warm to cool. Though fitted with tracks for supplementary spotlighting where necessary, they have eliminated the need for the banks of light fittings that clutter the ceilings of most galleries. The floors are either rough-cut unpolished oak, which will develop a natural patina over time from the footsteps of millions of visitors, or polished concrete. Set into these floors are the forthright cast iron grids of the air vents.

There is a great variety of gallery spaces, rooms large and small of true individual character. The pride of the new gallery are the grandest of these rooms, the double height gallery on the third floor, with its full-size window, and the four central galleries on the fifth floor. These beautifully proportioned galleries do not have the usual ceiling skylights but receive natural light through massive clear-storey bands of frosted glass above and flush with their side walls. In my view they are the most beautiful exhibition spaces to be found in any modern museum of art in the world.

I have had the pleasure of watching this project grow from dreams and ideas through drawings and more drawings, from models and mock-ups through raw construction to finished rooms. I believe that Herzog & de Meuron have given the Tate precisely what it sought from the beginning: a great building where concern for the needs of art are given the highest priority.

Above:
Detail of the Turbine Hall
and the concourse, level 5

Right:
View from the
Turbine Hall bridge

A–Z

American abstract artists, The Irascibles, including William Baziotes, James C. Brooks, Jimmy Ernst, Adolph Gottlieb, Hedda Sterne, Clyfford Still, Willem De Kooning, Bradley Walter Tomlin, Barnett Newman, Jackson Pollock, Theodoros Stamos, Richard Pousette-Dart, Robert Motherwell, Ad Reinhardt and Mark Rothko.
Photo: Nina Leen/Time Life Pictures/Getty Images

Abstract Expressionism

Abstract Expressionism developed as a movement in America during the later 1940s and throughout the 1950s. The artists associated with it, including Jackson Pollock, Mark Rothko, Clyfford Still, Franz Kline, Lee Krasner, Willem De Kooning, Robert Motherwell and Barnett Newman, were mostly based in New York City, and are sometimes known as the 'New York School'. They are linked not so much by a similar style as by a common aim to make new forms of abstract art that would be expressive or emotional in their effect.

Several of the Abstract Expressionists, including Arshile Gorky and Adolph Gottlieb, had spent time in Europe before the war and been inspired by the Surrealists' belief that art should come from the unconscious mind. As a result they strove to work as intuitively as possible. They rejected the external world as a source of subject matter, and instead explored how material gestures could be used to express internal states of consciousness. Several of the artists were interested in religion and myth, and drew inspiration from sources as diverse as the writings of the Swiss psychologist Carl Gustav Jung, the Jewish Kabbalah, and the Christian Stations of the Cross.

Two broadly distinct approaches emerged among the group. The so-called 'Action Painters', led by Pollock and De Kooning, emphasised energetic physical acts of painting: Pollock famously placed his canvas on the ground and danced around it, pouring paint direct from the can or trailing it from the brush or a stick. The 'Colour-Field' painters, including Rothko, Newman and Still, created simple compositions with large areas of a single colour intended to produce a contemplative or meditative response in the viewer. Both the Action and the Colour-Field painters shared common practices, ideals and an overall philosophy. The works are almost always made on large canvases, and brushstrokes and colour are applied across the whole space with equal importance.

With its emphasis on improvisation and the importance of process, Abstract Expressionism transformed the fundamentals of painting and sculpture in ways that were widely influential. It became the first American art movement to attain truly international status, putting New York City at the centre of the art world for the first time. Many factors contributed to the extent of this influence, including the championing of the movement by the influential American art critics Harold Rosenberg and Clement Greenberg, and its promotion as a symbol of American free thinking by the CIA during the Cold War.

The influence of the movement was strongly felt in Britain, where artists had the opportunity to see work by many of its key proponents in important exhibitions at the Tate Gallery in 1956 and 1959. The legacy for British artists continues to this day and is explored in a display at Tate Modern in which Barnett Newman's paintings *Adam* 1951–2 (p.186) and *Eve* 1950 are exhibited alongside Anish Kapoor's sculpture *Ishi's Light* 2003 (p.145), inviting comparison between the artists' concern with the spiritual and symbolic potential of light and colour. **(SH)**

Left:
Willem De Kooning (1904–1997)
The Visit
1966–7
Oil on canvas
152.4 x 121.9 cm
Purchased 1969

Above:
Clyfford Still (1904–1980)
1953
1953
Oil on canvas
235.9 x 174 cm
Purchased 1971

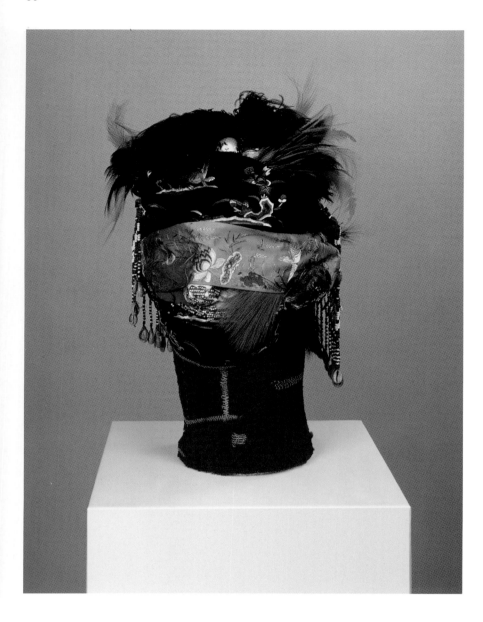

Angel of Anarchy
1936–40
Textiles over plaster
and mixed media
52 x 31.7 x 33.6 cm
Presented by the Friends
of the Tate Gallery 1983

Eileen Agar's imaginative imagery combined elements of humour and the uncanny with her fascination for the geometry of the natural world. Having studied at the Slade School of Art in London, a stay in Paris in the late 1920s brought her into contact with some of the most influential avant-garde art of the day. She drew on abstraction and Cubism, combining geometric forms with strange and quirky subjects through a range of techniques. As well as painting, she used found objects to create collages and assemblages. These highly innovative works brought her to the attention of Surrealist artists and her work was included in the International Surrealist Exhibition held in London in 1936, where she was the only professional British female artist whose work was shown.

Surrealism offered Agar an abundance of new possibilities in her quest to take art beyond the everyday. Turning to photography, she took shots of natural rock formations in a way that suggested new and extraordinary images. In the late 1930s she produced a number of plaster-cast heads, from which she created two versions of *Angel of Anarchy*, Tate's being the second; the first was lost and is now only known through photographs. Tate's version is at once colourful and playful, bizarre and macabre. Covered in exotic feathers and fabrics, the angel is blinded, suggesting a certain malign energy. The integration of African beads and bark cloth recall the important influence of non-European objects to artists working in the early part of the twentieth century. **(LA)**

Eileen Agar
1899–1991

Homage to the Square:
Study for Nocturne
1951
Oil on Masonite
53.3 x 53.3 cm
Presented by The Josef and
Anni Albers Foundation 2006

When Josef Albers arrived at the newly founded Black Mountain College, North Carolina, in autumn 1933, he described his educational mission as 'To open eyes'. He had arrived fresh from the Bauhaus in Berlin, which only months before had closed due to pressures by the Nazis. Having enrolled as a student in 1920 and risen through the ranks to the position of Assistant Director, his affiliation with the famous art and design school was longer than that of any other artist.

While at the Bauhaus he had made a series of highly innovative abstract glass pieces, which combined the semi-industrial technique of sandblasting sheets of coloured glass with the traditional format of easel painting. At Black Mountain, and later at Yale University, Albers continued the tradition of Bauhaus teaching, with its focus on liberating the creative potential he believed was universal to all mankind. Counting among his students the likes of Robert Rauschenberg and Eva Hesse, he became a critical link for the migration of modernist ideas from 1930s Europe to post-war America.

However, it was not until the age of sixty-two that he embarked on what would become his signature body of work, the *Homage to the Square*, a series of more than 1,000 variations on a formula of three or four different-coloured squares set inside each other and gravitating towards the bottom edge. Made by applying oil paint straight from the tube with a palette knife, the *Homages* subverted the then dominant notion of painting as a form of self-expression. Instead, their primary concern was with the psychology of visual perception and the *Interaction of Color*, the title of Albers's seminal book of 1963. **(ABH)**

Josef Albers
1888–1976

The Last Clown
1995–2000
Mixed media
Purchased with funds
provided by the American Fund
for the Tate Gallery 2002

Inspired by his experience of living and working in Mexico City, Belgian-born artist Francis Alÿs presents a decidedly urban view of everyday encounters, using a wide range of media including video, performance, drawing and painting. Alÿs is perhaps best known for his city walks, in which he uses props or enacts rituals in order to disrupt the everyday situations that he meets along the way. In one walk, he wore magnetic shoes, which gradually accumulated debris from the street as he proceeded. In another he sought out 'doppelgängers' – passers-by who resembled him – and walked alongside them until his footsteps fell into line with theirs. In all his walks, he relies on chance encounters in order to 'complete' the work.

Another theme explored by Alÿs is the role of the artist in contemporary society. The artist is seemingly expected to be a performer or entertainer but in doing so risks exposure to criticism and ridicule. The installation *The Last Clown* 1995–2000 may allude to this role by documenting a man who walks through the park and is tripped up by a passing dog. A painterly animation of the incident is repeated on a continuous loop and the installation is amplified by a series of paintings and drawings of the event. A soundtrack of circus music and canned laughter further emphasises the comedic quality and absurdity of the slapstick episode. **(HS)**

Francis Alÿs
born 1959

Controversy
Carl Andre's *Equivalent VIII* is one of the best known and arguably one of the most controversial works in Tate's Collection. Soon after it was acquired in 1972 the work caused a stir in the British press. Some commentators lambasted the 'Tate bricks' as a waste of public money. Others praised the work as an elegant example of Minimalism and a sign of Tate's engagement with important contemporary art movements.

Artists courted controversy throughout the twentieth century and continue to do so today. Marcel Duchamp's infamous *Fountain* 1917 (p.104), an up-ended urinal presented as a work of art, shocked the art world when it was submitted to the Society of Independent Artists exhibition in 1917. In more recent times the Young British Artists, who came to prominence in the 1990s, notoriously flaunted taboos surrounding the representation of sex and death. The work of Damien Hirst, Sarah Lucas, Jake and Dinos Chapman, and Tracey Emin has been deemed controversial and sensationalist. Controversy continues to surround Tate's presentations of contemporary art, notably during the annual media frenzy surrounding the Turner Prize. **(RT)**

Carl Andre is a seminal figure of American Minimalism. Since the 1960s he has made work that emphasises the inherent qualities of his materials. After a period carving wooden sculptures he began working with everyday industrial materials, arranging them in simple geometric shapes. These aestheticise the arrangements of industrial objects on the factory floor or in the forge. Andre has described his method of working as scavenging for 'physical realities' and he often seeks inspiration in the city streets.

In their elegant simplicity Andre's objects highlight the unique physical and sensual qualities of their materials. *Venus Forge* 1980 (p.172) is composed of steel and copper plates placed directly on the floor. The audience is invited to walk on the surface of the metal, experiencing the differences in density between the sculpture and the floor. The warmth and shine of the copper contrast with the dark, coarser surface of the steel. By placing his work directly on the floor rather than on the wall or plinth, Andre encourages the audience to interact with the objects in a much less hierarchical way.

Equivalent VIII 1966, otherwise known as the 'Tate bricks', is one of a series of eight works, each of which consists of 120 fire bricks in a different geometric configuration. When the *Equivalents* were first shown, the juxtaposition of the sculptures highlighted their similar volume and weight and the different configuration of their constituent parts. The artist intends the experience of walking around the two-brick height of *Equivalent VIII* to feel to the audience like wading through a shallow body of water. **(RT)**

Equivalent VIII
1966
Firebricks
12.7 x 68.6 x 229.2 cm
Purchased 1972

Carl Andre
born 1935

Jean (Hans) Arp
1886–1966

Jean (Hans) Arp was one of the leading figures of the Dada and Surrealist movements, and is perhaps best known for his distinctive sculptural reliefs and collages.

Born in France in 1886, Arp made his first abstract works in the early 1910s. In 1912 he met Wassily Kandinsky in Munich and took part in an exhibition of the Blaue Reiter (Blue Rider) group. However, it was not until 1916 that he came to prominence, as co-founder of Dada, a radical, international art movement that sprung from a Zurich night-club, the Cabaret Voltaire. Based in neutral Switzerland during the First World War, the artists aimed to question and even destroy traditional values in life and in art. As Arp himself stated, 'Revolted by the butchery of the 1914 World War we in Zurich devoted ourselves to the arts. While the guns rumbled in the distance, we sang, painted, made collages and wrote poems with all our might.'

Arp started to develop his personal style during the Dada period, when he made a number of wooden reliefs. Flat pieces of wood were cut into irregular, rounded shapes by a carpenter according to his instructions. They were then assembled and sometimes painted by the artist himself. These early reliefs expressed a number of themes that were continued in the free-standing sculptures he made from the mid-1920s until his later years. In particular, Arp was interested in the forms and processes of nature. In the mid-1930s he began to view his sculptures as a kind of 'concrete' art, their forms relating to those of the natural world, yet without deliberate imitation. **(AC)**

Left:
Constellation According to the Laws of Chance
c.1930
Painted wood
54.9 x 69.8 cm
Bequeathed by E.C. Gregory 1959

Right:
Pagoda Fruit
1949
Bronze
88.9 x 67.9 x 76.2 cm
Purchased 1951

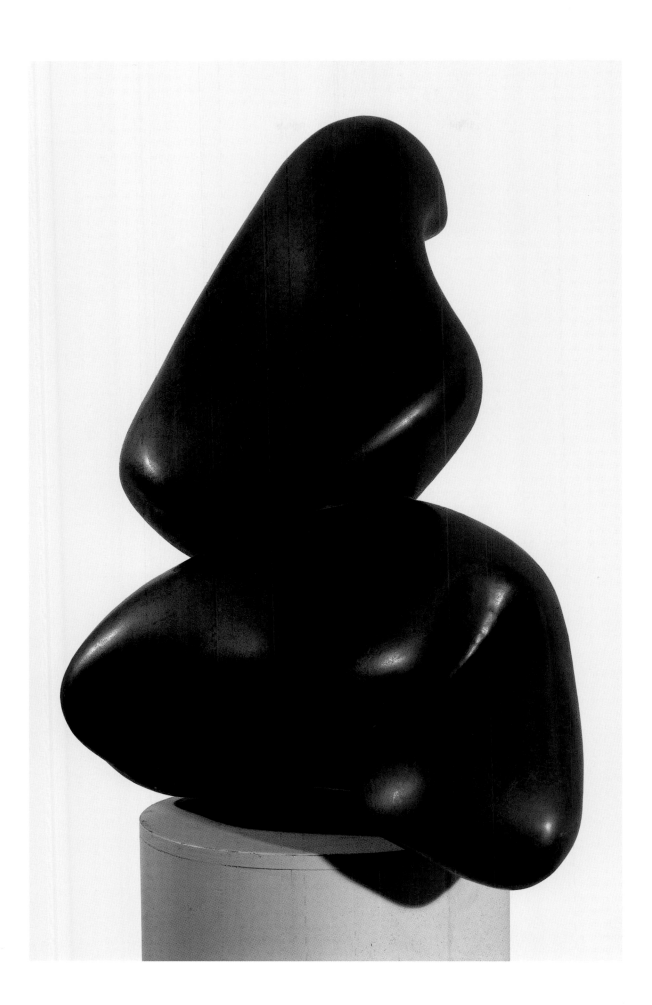

Chance

For the Surrealists, chance was a vital concept; accidental encounters, 'found' objects and automatic processes of drawing or writing were all valued as means to free the mind from the restrictions of logic and take it into the realm of the unconscious. Being open to chance, through play, creativity or other spontaneous actions was a quality celebrated by the Surrealists as the essence of radical or revolutionary living and the antithesis of rationalist, materialist norms.

Arp first introduced chance into his artistic practice in the Dada years, when he made collages of torn paper, which were arranged by dropping the pieces randomly onto a surface. In the 1930s he discovered that some of his earlier works had deteriorated whilst in storage. He chose to incorporate the wrinkled or cracked surfaces of these pieces into new works, tearing up the originals and pasting the pieces together in new configurations. These serendipitous abstract compositions can be seen as precursors to the works of a number of artists who came to prominence in the mid-twentieth century, such as Jackson Pollock. **(AC)**

Art Informel

During the years immediately after the Second World War, a number of artists were searching for a style of art that could convey their sense of irrationality and fear. To many, realist practices seemed to have been tainted by political use in propaganda, and geometrical abstraction seemed too cold and measured for the heated emotional climate. The broad constituency of artists whose work was dubbed *Informel* (literally 'without form') forged an impassioned form of abstraction characterised by a peculiarly physical handling of artistic materials. They included Karel Appel, Alberto Burri, Jean Dubuffet, Hans Hartung, Jean Fautrier, Georges Matthieu, Henri Michaux, Pierre Soulages, Antoni Tàpies and Wols. Many showed in the exhibition *Un Art Autre* (Art of Another Kind) organised in 1952 by the French writer and sculptor Michel Tapié, who saw the artists as trying to make a radical break with traditional notions of order and composition. In spite of this, their work can be seen as having pre-war roots in Surrealism and Expressionism, as well as the paintings of Wassily Kandinsky and Paul Klee.

Art informel is characterised by highly improvisatory styles of painting that emphasise spontaneity and gesture. Like the Abstract Expressionists in America, to which the movement is sometimes considered a European counterpart, many of the artists were influenced by the Surrealist idea of automatism, and often executed their works at speed, aiming for a direct expression of the subconscious. 'Speed, intuition, excitement – that's my method of creation', Matthieu explained. Hartung was typical of the movement in believing that painting should record and evoke his immediate inner experiences, tensions and energies. He rejected observation and memory as starting points and relied instead on spontaneous feeling and direct physical action. His painting *T1963-R6* 1963, with its repetitive calligraphic marks scratched into the top layer of a vinyl coating, is characteristic. Tàpies's *Grey and Green Painting* 1957 also shows a concern with texture: incised and scribbled lines, various lacerations and graffiti-like marks overlay a thick, highly textured base in which clay and marble dust have been mixed with the paint. Tàpies later wrote: 'My pictures became the truly experimental fields of battle.'

In the early 1960s, the introspection and bleakness of much of Art Informel was challenged by movements such as Nouveau Réalisme (New Realism) and Pop art, which sought a more direct engagement with everyday life and rejected the idea of art as the subjective expression of personality. However, the continued desire to express deep-seated creative impulses through gestural mark-making can be seen in the work of Lucio Fontana or Cy Twombly as well as younger painters including Fiona Rae and Luc Tuymans. **(SH)**

Above:
Cover of *Un Art Autre*
by Michel Tapié, 1952

Left:
Antoni Tàpies (born 1923)
Grey and Green Painting
1957
Oil, epoxy resin and
marble dust on canvas
114 x 161.3 cm
Presented by the Friends
of the Tate Gallery 1962

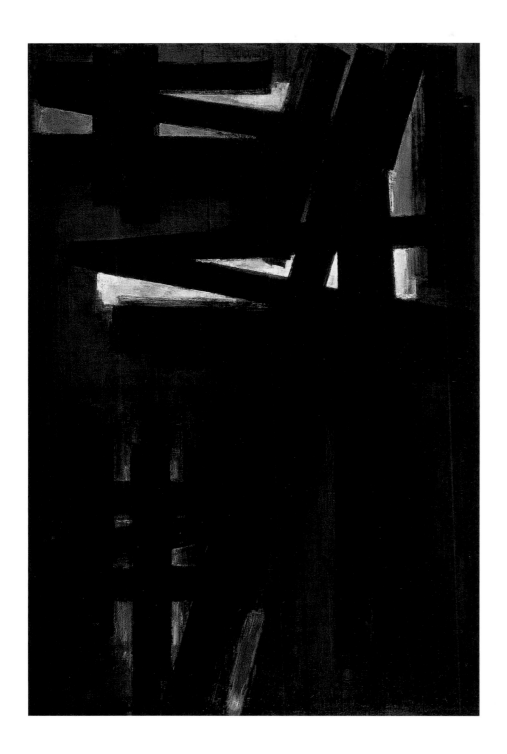

Left:
Pierre Soulages (born 1919)
Painting, 23 May 1953
1953
194.9 x 130.2 cm
Purchased 1953

Below:
Jean Dubuffet (1901–1985)
*Monsieur Plume with
Creases in his Trousers
(Portrait of Henri Michaux)*
1947
Oil and grit on canvas
130.2 x 96.5 cm
Purchased 1980

Arte Povera

The term Arte Povera (literally, 'poor art') was used for a loose and short-lived association of artists who first exhibited together in Italy in 1967. At a time of social and political unrest (which would climax in the student protests of the following year), this generation dismantled the role and function of art. In 'Arte Povera: Notes for a Guerrilla War' (published in November 1967) the critic Germano Celant described what he identified as an 'outlook' rather than a style. He wrote that it was concerned with 'contingency, events, ahistoricism, the present … and anthropological outlook, "real" man (Marx), and the hope (now a certainty) of discarding all visually univocal and coherent discourse'. As the subtitle of his essay indicates, Celant saw his friends as outside established practices, and characterised their interventions, installations and performances (using such diverse materials as earth, neon, water, plastic and trees) as assembling elements of reality rather than seeking to add gratuitously to the material world.

For this new phenomenological spirit Celant borrowed the term Arte Povera from the 'poor theatre' of the Polish director Jerzy Gorotowsky. Several of the artists, including Michelangelo Pistoletto, Luciano Fabro and Jannis Kounellis, were already established and responding to the conceptual and material experiments of the previous generation of Alberto Burri, Lucio Fontana and Piero Manzoni. The specifically Italian cultural context is evident in the maintenance of craft skills (despite the rejection of artistic traditions), and in the sophisticated relationship between past and present, history and the contemporary. That Arte Povera quickly became a national and international phenomenon was a testament to its timeliness. It had parallels with the growth in Conceptual, 'anti-form' and Land art of Joseph Beuys, Robert Morris and others, which was memorably dubbed the 'dematerialisation of the art object' by the American critic Lucy Lippard.

The first exhibitions in 1967 (in Genoa and Turin) included Giovanni Anselmo, Fabro, Kounellis, Giovanni Paolini, Pistoletto, Mario Merz, Marisa Merz and Gilberto Zorio, among others, building to a core group of around fourteen artists over the next few years. Many – especially those based in Turin – were bound together through collaboration. This fluidity was typified by the artworks (including Merz's wicker *Cone c*.1967), performances and interventions made for *Arte Povera – Azioni Povere* at Amalfi in 1968. Much of their work centred on an investigation of the relationship between nature and culture. The artist's position within nature is explicit in Giuseppe Penone's interventions in the landscape, while Mario Merz's exploration of the Fibonacci series (a mathematical formula describing incremental growth) identified a unifying structure to the world. At the same time, the phenomenological actuality of 'being in the world' underpinned works by Fabro and Pistoletto, who each used reflective surfaces to confront the viewer. Pistoletto also explored the legacy of classical culture through confrontation with contemporary reality, notably in the earliest versions of his iconic *Venus of the Rags* 1967.

A sequence of group exhibitions, such as *Live in Your Head: When Attitudes Become Form* held in Bern in 1969, confirmed Arte Povera's prominence and international connections. However, by 1971, Celant and many of the artists sought to abandon the term. They went on to extend their work in quite distinct ways, forming multiple legacies from Arte Povera's innovations. **(MG)**

Giuseppe Penone (born 1947)
Tree of 12 Metres
1980–2
Wood (American larch)
Each 600 x 50 x 50 cm
Purchased 1989

Above:
Jannis Kounellis (born 1936)
Untitled
1968
Wood and wool
250 x 281 x 45 cm
Purchased 1996

Right:
Marisa Merz (1925–2003)
Cone
c.1967
Wood (willow)
221 x 129.5 x 129.5 cm
Purchased 1983

Left:
Figure in a Landscape
1945
Oil on canvas
144.8 x 128.3 cm
Purchased 1950

Below and right (detail):
Second Version of Triptych 1944
1988
Oil and acrylic on canvas
Three panels, each 198 x 147.5 cm
Presented by the artist 1991

Though he had already been working as an artist for some years, Bacon became established in 1945 when he exhibited *Figure in a Landscape* 1945 alongside the original version of *Three Studies for Figures at the Base of a Crucifixion c.*1944. The coincidence of their display in London with the liberation of the concentration camps in Europe helped secure his reputation as a painter of the violence and horrors of modern times. Throughout the 1950s his work was seen in relation to Existentialist philosophy as the representation of humankind's inherent bestiality and inevitable isolation in a godless world. As such, though he has frequently been seen as a solitary figure in the history of art, his paintings perhaps relate to post-war European art more than to British work.

Bacon can also be positioned within a modernist tradition of appropriating photographs as sources for art that runs from Degas to the present. Even in these early pieces he drew upon photographs for their imagery. *Figure in a Landscape* 1945, for instance, was based on a snapshot of Bacon's lover sitting on a chair in a park. Bacon particularly explored the ambiguity of images and what they represent, an aspect that became especially marked in his use of Eadweard Muybridge's nineteenth-century photographs of the human body and animals in motion. Frequently, as here, Bacon's figures can appear both threatening and threatened, victims perhaps of their own inherent violence. The primary focus of his art was on such paradoxes, as well as the visual similarities between, for example, humans and animals, sex and violence, threat and vulnerability. **(CS)**

Francis Bacon
1909–1992

Whether he is depicting the banality of everyday life or appropriating film stills from Hollywood B-movies, the imagery of Southern California has always been central to John Baldessari's work. In the late-1960s, he was part of the group of West Coast Conceptual artists, including Ed Ruscha, whose work was characterised by deadpan wit in distinction to the analytical rigour of Conceptual artists based in New York.

Baldessari has consistently explored the tension between photography and painting. Early works deployed photo-emulsion paint to develop photographs of mundane urban scenes on canvas, accompanied by large captions. These make obvious or arbitrary statements about the images that foreclose the narrative possibilities usually associated with photographs in newspapers and magazines. Subsequently, his work has been strongly associated with cinema, due to his use of film stills as well as his application of Sergei Eisenstein's theory of montage, in which meaning is generated by the collision of two contrasting images. In a work like *Hope (Blue) Supported by a Bed of Oranges (Life): Amid a Context of Allusions* 1991, meaning is displaced across a rhythmic chain of thirteen collaged elements. The focal points of the images, such as faces or silhouettes, have been cut out and the resulting holes are filled in with different coloured paints. Consequently, the face ceases to be the starting point from which a narrative emanates, instead becoming an abstract painted form that sucks the rest of the picture into its vacuum. The constellation of elements echoes the shape of the figure that has fallen on the oranges, framed by and cut out against a blank wall that adopts the shape and scale of a cinema screen. **(BB)**

Hope (Blue) Supported by a Bed of Oranges (Life): Amid a Context of Allusions
1991
Colour and black-and-white photographs on paper, oil tint, vinyl paint, acrylic on board and sintra panels
381 x 701.5 cm
Purchased with assistance from the American Fund for the Tate Gallery and Tate Members 2004

John Baldessari
born 1931

Polish sculptor Miroslaw Balka came to prominence during the mid-1980s with a series of deeply autobiographical figurative sculptures and performances, which reflected his memories of a Catholic childhood in Poland under Martial Law. Towards the end of the 1980s he began to move away from complex narrative pieces. *Oasis (C.D.F.)* 1989 dates from this period. Despite the simple and austere appearance of the work, allusions to personal history continue to be strongly expressed. While the physical parameters refer to his own bodily dimensions, the formal components allude to the language of the home: the gable of a house, a drain pipe and door sill. In addition, Balka suggests the body through objects, such as the shallow bed, which evoke a human presence. He constructed the work from discarded domestic and industrial materials, some of them recycled from a previous work. Some parts, such as the weathered wooden planks, came from the family home in Otwock, near Warsaw. Balka has explained that such materials 'carry a history which I connect with when I touch them. It is like kissing the hand of history'. In combining these elements he makes connections between personal experience and the wider histories of family, community and country.

Since the 1980s Balka has continued to refine his sculptural language, but his materials, such as ash, soap and salt, as well as the forms and scales he employs, ensure that his works remain powerfully charged with a symbolism associated with life and death. **(FM)**

Oasis (C.D.F.)
1989
Mixed media
373 x 376.3 x 451 cm
Purchased 1999

Miroslaw Balka
born 1958

As a child, Lothar Baumgarten was taught by his anthropologist father an attentive way of looking at things in the world, profoundly influencing his later practice as an artist. Inspired by the accounts of the English explorer Sir Walter Raleigh and the writings of diverse ethnographers and anthropologists, he made imaginary maps of the New World (South America) many years before he visited it. Some of his earliest work was created in the swampy industrial wasteland on the banks of the Rhine, between Düsseldorf and Cologne, where he photographed incidental details of marshy vegetation, amphibious life and human rubbish. Between 1977 and 1983 he visited the Yanomámi people in the Orinoco basin in Venezuela, living with them for several months at a time. The installation *El Dorado – Gran Sabana* 1977–85 stems from this experience. It comprises a series of photographs taken by the artist in 1977 of the 'Gran Sabana' – the site of the legendary El Dorado sought by generations of European adventurers, an area spanning Venezuela, Brazil and Columbia. Between the photographs, paired words are painted on the wall, naming one of the heavy metals or minerals being mined in the region and an animal exterminated in the process. The creatures' names are upside down to signify death and mourning as well as the mining process of turning over the earth.

The plight of the indigenous people of this region became the subject of much of Baumgarten's work in the 1980s. Naming, as a means by which a culture may appropriate and inscribe itself on a landscape, is a central concept, used to draw attention to the erasure of one culture by another. **(EM)**

El Dorado – Gran Sabana
1977–85
Photographs and paint
195.5 x 1989 cm
Purchased with assistance from the American Fund for the Tate Gallery, courtesy of Edwin C. Cohen and Echoing Green 1990

Lothar Baumgarten
born 1944

Carnival
1920
Oil on canvas
186.4 x 91.8 cm
Purchased with assistance
from the National Art
Collections Fund and Friends
of the Tate Gallery and
Mercedes-Benz (UK) Ltd 1981

Max Beckmann was the most important German painter of the early twentieth century. In debates around contemporary art at the beginning of the century his early paintings, portraits, landscapes, mythological scenes and history paintings about modern catastrophes, aligned him with a more conservative trend. This viewed art as renewal and extension of a continuous tradition, while vanguard artists who seceded from established artists' societies to form their own groupings believed that modern art represented a break with the past.

However, Beckmann's experiences as a medical orderly in the First World War significantly changed his outlook and his art. Combining the legacies of Gothic art and, more recently, Cubism, he evolved densely packed compositions in shallow, stage-like spaces in his paintings of the early 1920s. Images of people he knew, sometimes in the guise of characters from the circus, cabaret or *commedia dell'arte*, as in *Carnival* 1920, displayed a sense of melancholy or world-weariness about the condition of humanity. Beckmann's mature style and increasing commercial success in the late 1920s can be traced through his lifelong sequence of self-portraits, the most important of which, *Self Portrait in a Tuxedo* 1927, depicts a confident, elegantly clad Beckmann confronting the viewer face on. Under the National Socialists his art was criticised then banned, and he went into exile in Holland, where he lived between 1937 and 1947. During this period he painted many of the complex allegorical triptychs upon which his reputation rests. He spent his final years in the United States and died days after completing his final triptych, *The Argonauts* 1950. **(SR)**

Max Beckmann
1884–1950

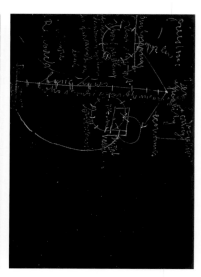

Joseph Beuys was one of the most influential German artists of the twentieth century. Following his wartime service as a radio operator in the Luftwaffe, he decided to become an artist rather than a natural scientist, another area of great interest to him. He evolved his ideas in the late 1940s to early 1960s, principally in the form of small sculptures and hundreds of drawings. In the 1960s, by now appointed professor at the Düsseldorf Art Academy, he became associated with the Fluxus movement. The nature of Fluxus, which collapsed boundaries between different disciplines, was markedly democratic and collaborative in character. This mirrored and influenced Beuys's own artistic approach. During the 1960s he came to international attention through his actions, which usually took place in galleries and extended over hours, and sometimes days. In the early 1970s he became increasingly active in the political spheres of educational reform and grass-roots democracy. His actions evolved to include public discussions and lectures, some of which were preserved in the form of blackboard drawings made while he talked.

Language was always vital to Beuys as an instrument for the formation and articulation of thoughts, and analogous to the manipulation of physical materials to make sculpture. As his fame, and sometimes notoriety, spread, he received invitations to make ever-more ambitious projects. Some of them, notably *7000 Oaks* 1982–7, for which he planted 7,000 oak trees in the city of Kassel, were only realisable outside the boundaries of museums and institutions. In parallel, he produced large numbers of editioned works, which took many forms, from sculptural objects to printed postcards. Through the production of multiples Beuys attempted to disseminate his ideas widely and make art objects that were widely available at affordable prices. **(SR)**

Above:
Four Blackboards
1972
Chalk on blackboard
121.6 x 91.4 x 1.8 cm
Transferred from
the Archive 1983

Right:
Felt Suit
1970
Felt
170 x 60 cm
Purchased 1998

Joseph Beuys
1921–1986

Materials
In the late 1960s, artists developed many new ways of working beyond the traditional media of painting and sculpture. Process art, Arte Povera, installation and site-specific art all expressed new attitudes towards the creation of art, often placing greater emphasis on the ideas behind or process of creating an artwork rather than the finished object. Artists such as Joseph Beuys, Robert Morris, Bruce Nauman, Jannis Kounellis or Barry Flanagan adopted a wide variety of materials with which to experiment. Although they were not part of a coherent movement, their works were brought together in several important exhibitions such as *When Attitudes Become Form* at the Kunsthalle, Bern, in 1969. Beuys's contribution to this exhibition included the smearing of fat along the bottom of a wall, and a bed of felt placed in a nearby room. Both of these materials held particular significance for Beuys and became part of his personal symbolism through their repeated use and surrounding mythology. **(AC)**

Umberto Boccioni was one of the most energetic members of the Italian Futurist group, which was founded in 1909 by the poet Filippo Tommaso Marinetti. The Futurists embraced industrialisation and celebrated speed, technology and power, advocating a complete break with the art of the past. The group's blend of avant-garde exploits and noisy publicity stunts set the stage for later movements such as Dada and Fluxus, and challenged the conventions of bourgeois good taste.

Boccioni's early painting style sought to express movement through the application of separate strokes of pure colour. However, his style evolved under the influence of the philosophy of Henri Bergson and Friedrich Nietzsche and the art of the French Cubists. Through several manifestoes, he promoted the representation of numerous viewpoints and moments in time in a single image, and the depiction of figures interpenetrating with their environments. He integrated Cubist decomposition of form, Impressionist light effects and his own emphatic brushwork to create distinctively animated paintings, but he was most innovative in the field of sculpture.

Boccioni considered *Unique Forms of Continuity in Space* 1913, purchased by Tate in 1972, to be his finest artistic achievement. The figure strides powerfully forward like a Nietzschian superman. Its flame-like curves and angular forms at once resemble a man and a machine, with muscles pulled backwards to reveal its trajectory. The extraordinarily dynamic treatment of volume makes this the perfect realisation of Boccioni's demand to 'split open our figures and place the environment inside them'. **(CM)**

Umberto Boccioni
1882–1916

The Bowl of Milk
c.1919
Oil on canvas
116.2 x 121 cm
Bequeathed by
Edward Le Bas 1967

Pierre Bonnard is best known for his paintings of domestic scenes rendered in luminous colours whose treatment is derived from late Impressionism. At the beginning of his career, around 1890, he became associated with the Nabis, a group of painters inspired by Paul Gauguin's use of flat areas of pure colour. The decorative aesthetic of Japanese prints, of which Bonnard made a study at this time, would prove to be another important influence. The 1890s saw Bonnard paired with another of the Nabis, Eduoard Vuillard, under the banner of Intimism, a term used to describe their small, decoratively designed and delicately coloured depictions of domestic settings.

His mature works, such as *Coffee* 1915, retain this interest in intimate household scenes but are infused with bold, complex, glowing colours that draw on Impressionist Claude Monet's later paintings. *Coffee*, with its idiosyncratic composition in which the objects of pictorial interest are arranged around the edges of the picture, continues to show the influence of Japanese prints. *The Bowl of Milk* c.1919, used similar means to create a quality that transcends decoration. The painting shows a girl bringing a cat a bowl of milk in the environs of a comfortably furnished apartment. Through dramatic lighting, a darker palette and an austere design dominated by verticals, Bonnard's trademark evocation of sensuous domesticity becomes psychologically charged. While the figure in *The Bowl of Milk* was probably based on an ancient Greek statue, Bonnard's favourite model was his wife, Berthe. She appears sipping from a cup in *Coffee*, her pet dog beside her, and she is thought to appear again in *The Table* 1925, apparently preparing a meal for the dog waiting by her side. **(MB)**

Pierre Bonnard
1867–1947

Trauma
Trauma derives from the ancient Greek word for 'wound'). In non-medical terms it is defined as emotional shock, often leading to neurosis, or an event that causes great distress or disruption. Typical causes for trauma are abuse or violence, especially during childhood, natural events, such as earthquakes, or man-made events such as war.

Expressions of trauma frequently feature in modern and contemporary art. Many artists have responded to collective or personal trauma through their art, either instinctively or deliberately, and in more or less explicit ways. Trauma has been the subject of numerous psychoanalytic and philosophical theories. These in turn have been critiqued or expanded by art theorists. Hal Foster's take on Jacques Lacan's theory of trauma is one such case. He states: 'Lacan defines the traumatic as a missed encounter with the real. As missed, the real cannot be represented; it can only be repeated … Repetition serves to *screen* the real understood as traumatic. But this very need also points to the *real*, and at this point the real *ruptures* the screen of repetition.'

The various facets of trauma are central to many artists' work, such as Louise Bourgeois, Cindy Sherman, Yayoi Kusama, Eva Hesse and Tracey Emin. **(EB)**

Highly individual, Louise Bourgeois's work spans the best part of the twentieth century, and has touched on many movements, from Surrealism to Abstract Expressionism, Minimalism and feminism. Her themes sprung from personal trauma and experience, exploring human relationships and psychological states. A constantly renewed interest in isolated human body parts and their symbolic potential dates back to the early 1960s, when she started making biomorphic sculptures using materials such as bronze, plaster, resin and latex.

Amoeba 1963–5 is seemingly an inchoate mass with a bulging surface and single opening. It suggests the evolution of a living organism, but also alludes to neonatal forms and pregnancy. *Avenza* 1968–9, named after a town in Italy where Bourgeois worked, is made of latex; clusters of phallic bulges allude to both sexual and landscape themes. Bourgeois often focused on relationships between men and women, most significantly those of lovers and that of daughter and father. Thirty years on from *Avenza* a frieze-like panel of pink breasts titled *Mamelles* (breasts) 1991, showed her continuing interest in exploring gender roles and psycho-sexual meaning through body parts.

Bourgeois was the first artist to exhibit in Tate Modern's Turbine Hall, with her installation *I Do, I Undo, I Redo* 2000 (p.35) and one of her signature spider sculptures, *Maman* 2000 (p.21). **(EB)**

Mamelles
1991
Rubber, fibreglass and wood
53 x 292 x 48 cm
Presented by the artist
(Building the Tate Collection) 2005

Louise Bourgeois
1911–2010

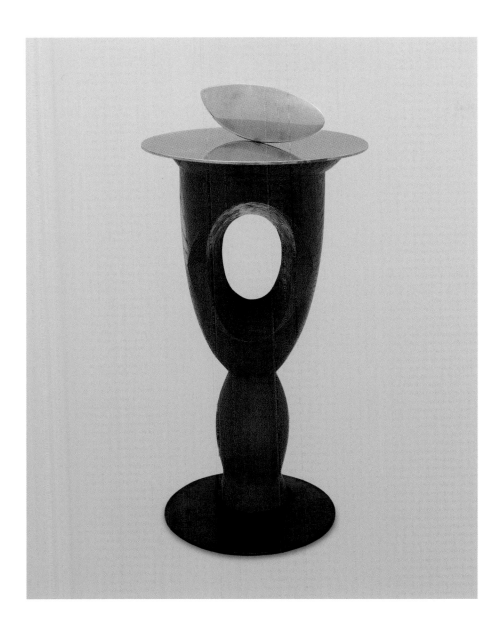

Primitivism
The term 'Primitivism' has been used to describe the adoption of artistic forms from outside the orthodox European canon, usually as a way of enriching or subverting that tradition. In the early twentieth century, artists inspired by Paul Gauguin's withdrawal to Tahiti in the 1890s sought out new objects in archaeological and ethnographic museums. The sources were extremely diverse, from the arts of Mexico, to Assyria, Alaska and Africa, especially the interpretation of the body found in West African carvings – notably of the Fang and Dogon peoples (see Karl Schmidt-Rottluff *Male Head* 1917 (p.110), or Pablo Picasso *Bust of a Woman* 1909). Although many artists questioned the colonialism that made these objects available, the new aesthetic did not preclude stereotypical notions about the childlike, the mysterious or the exotic nature of the 'primitive'. Many artists, including Picasso and Jacob Epstein, amassed significant collections of carvings, but few looked beyond their formal inspiration to consider the societies from which they came. **(MG)**

Developing forms of great purity on the verge of abstraction, the Romanian artist Constantin Brancusi epitomised what it meant to be a modernist sculptor in the first half of the twentieth century. He honed his extraordinary skills first in his native Romania, before moving to Paris in 1904. However, in 1907–9, he rejected modelling, as practiced by Auguste Rodin, and turned instead to carving. He chose rough indigenous stones and responded to 'primitive' examples outside the classical tradition, blending African sources with Romanian wood-carving. Superfluous form was radically reduced. His contemplative, gradual approach led him to generate extended series from essential forms. The *Fish* series (1922–1930), avoids zoological accuracy in order to capture the idea of streamlined motion. This is also evident in *Maiastra* 1911, an early sculpture in the series of *Birds* that Brancusi made in marble and bronze over a thirty-year period. The title refers to a Romanian folk-tale whose earthiness resonates in the roughly carved base, while the form of the up-rising, crowing, bird is almost ballistic in its simplicity.

It was this reduction and refinement that resulted in the famous New York trial associated with Brancusi's *Bird* in 1927–8. Custom's officials deemed it eligible for tax, like any machine-made object, since they did not recognise it as an artwork. The debate hinged around the legitimacy of abstraction and the verdict in Brancusi's favour became a milestone in the expanding definition of art. **(MG)**

Fish
1926
Bronze, metal and wood
93.4 x 50.2 x 50.2 cm
Accepted by H.M. Government in lieu of tax and allocated to the Tate Gallery 1996

Constantin Brancusi
1876–1957

Georges Braque's early training as an artisan decorator instilled in him a sense of craftsmanship that he retained throughout his career as an artist. His skill with and concern for paint made him a master of the medium. Rarely executing preparatory studies, he preferred to explore his subjects spontaneously on the canvas.

Braque's early artistic career was dominated by his crucial involvement in the development of Cubism. *Mandora* 1909–10 shows him at the height of his explorations with

Pablo Picasso in expressing volumes in space. Braque frequently integrated images of musical instruments into his Cubist still lifes, later commenting that 'a musical instrument as an object had the peculiarity that one could animate it by touching it'. The numerous fragmented planes seem to shift and shimmer across the canvas, suggesting the vibration of the strings of the lute-like mandora.

Even after Cubism had dissolved as a movement, Braque continued to distort conventional ways of representing objects on a two-dimensional surface, focusing on interiors and still lifes. *The Billiard Table* 1945 is from one of his most important and monumental late series. Devoid of any sense of traditional perspective, the composition is dominated by the strangely angled billiard table, which forms a barrier across the canvas and prevents an easy reading of the interior. The space is further flattened by an arrangement of horizontal and vertical lines that seem to imitate the frame of the painting. This visual rhyme, coupled with the theme of the billiard table, may be a playful reference to painting as a 'game'. **(LA)**

The Billiard Table
1945
Oil and sand on canvas
89.1 x 116.3 cm
Purchased from the Galerie
Louise Leiris, Paris, with
assistance from the gift of
Gustav and Elly Kahnweiler,
the National Art Collections Fund,
Tate Members and the Dr V.J.
Daniel Bequest 2003

Mandora
1909–10
Oil on canvas
71.1 x 55.9 cm
Purchased 1966

Georges Braque
1882–1963

Belgian artist Marcel Broodthaers began his creative life as a poet, a photographer and occasional avant-garde film-maker. Around 1945 he met the Surrealist artist René Magritte, who gave him a poem by Stéphane Mallarmé (1842–98). This inspired a life-long fascination with the French Symbolist poet and his brand of abstraction, in which condensed imagery and cryptic allusions are intended to allow space for the viewer's imaginative interpretation. The art that Broodthaers created during his short twelve-year artistic career (1964–76) emulates Mallarmé's enigmatic style. Using a wide range of media, Broodthaers imitated and subverted the artistic movements of his time – Nouveau

Réalisme, Pop, Minimalism and Conceptualism – while remaining rooted in traditional culture. He famously saw art as a way to create saleable commodities, which his poetry did not; his first artwork comprises volumes of his self-published poems embedded in plaster.

A central concern, inherited from Magritte, is the relationship between representation and reality. For Broodthaers this was expressed in the interplay between word and image or object. In 1973, the year he moved to London, Broodthaers created *Paintings*, one of a series of nine-canvas works comprising printed text. The words appear in varying configurations on the canvases, repeated at intervals in changing relationships to one another, forcing viewers to interpret meanings for themselves. Sixteen different words in red, yellow, blue and black refer to such elements of traditional painting as 'composition', 'perspective' and 'colour'. The elegant, old-fashioned cursive script evokes the high tradition of art, while the use of text and the spare, repetitive structure epitomise contemporary Conceptual and Minimal styles. **(EM)**

Paintings
1973
Oil on canvas
80 × 100 cm
Purchased 1983

Marcel Broodthaers
1924–1976

Sacking and Red
1954
Acrylic and hessian collage on canvas
86.4 x 100.3 cm
Purchased 1965

Alberto Burri was one of the pioneers of a new sensibility after the Second World War. Around 1948, while working in Rome, his highly wrought surfaces transformed the means and the impact of abstract art. He used discarded sacking and wood in place of canvas, mixing pumice, tar and other materials into his paint to lend it weight and texture. The sacks had been used for essential foods (floor, rice, sugar) imported under the US Marshall Plan aid scheme for European recovery and Burri often retained their stencilled lettering as part of his compositions. In this he anticipated the use of commercial signs found in the work of Robert Rauschenberg and others. During the mid-1950s, Burri also turned to destruction itself. Using a blowtorch, he licked the surface of wooden reliefs with fire, managing to contain the action of destruction with great immediacy. He took this further with the burning of plastic works in the early 1960s.

Burri's ruptured surfaces were readily understood as comments on the violence and isolation of the nuclear era. Early commentators drew attention to his wartime experience as a doctor serving with the Italian army. The association with the wounded body was powerful, and added to the controversy that surrounded his work. Exhibiting and working as much in America as in Europe, Burri was a dominant figure from the 1960s. There was no let-up in his activity, since his concern with materiality initiated a number of series with subtly pitted and cratered surfaces as well as monumental steel sculptures. Many of these explorations anticipated and inspired the Arte Povera generation. **(MG)**

Alberto Burri
1915–1995

Janet Cardiff is best known for a number of works in which visitors are given headphones and a Walkman and invited to follow her directions on tours through the city, walking in time with her footsteps. Perceptions of experience and memory are questioned by the coincidences and discontinuities between the world described on the headphones and the reality of walking through the space.

40 Part Motet 2001 is a sound installation based on *Spem in Alium* by Thomas Tallis (*c*.1505–85), a plain-song composition for a choir of forty voices. Unlike a conventional recording, which fuses the separate elements into a unified whole, the individual voice of each member of the choir is played back through a separate speaker. A significant section of the piece records the mundane chatter of the choir before the recital begins, and moving from speaker to speaker is like being in the stalls with the choir, eavesdropping on banal conversations that blend with the ambient sounds of visitors in the gallery. The presentation is minimal, simply a circle of forty speakers on stands. Even though this sparseness resists any visual interpretation, it still has a strong resonance with the codes of cinema. Each speaker functions like a close-up through which we discover the role played by individual members of the choir, revealing the alternating circuit of song and silence through which the full composition gains its texture. But when standing in the middle of the room, the voices blend and the recital functions like a panning shot, where viewers are given an immersive overview of the overall harmonies and composition. **(BB)**

40 Part Motet
2001
Mixed media
Lent by Pamela and Richard Kramlich and the American Fund for the Tate Gallery, fractional and promised gift 2003

Janet Cardiff
born 1957

Maurizio Cattelan (born 1960) has been well known since the early 1990s for the highly provocative nature of his practice. Once described as 'a bastard child of Duchamp and Boetti', he makes art that is as much about creating challenging situations as it is about producing objects. Cattelan's self-imposed persona as a kind of clown or court jester has enabled him to poke fun at the art world and can be seen as an attempt to side-step the pressures of being an artist. Early in his career his contributions to exhibitions included the act of knotting together sheets to escape from a museum window; bricking over the door to a gallery so that visitors had no access; and stealing the contents of another gallery in order to avoid having to make his own work.

Ironically, these subversive strategies and his deliberate admissions of failure, along with the creation of a number of powerful installations involving stuffed animals, mannequins and other diverse objects, have led him to become one of the most significant artists to have emerged onto the international arena of contemporary art in recent years.

Since 2002 Cattelan – along with curators Massimiliano Gioni and Ali Subotnick – has been running The Wrong Gallery. Until 2005 The Wrong Gallery took the form of a tiny exhibition space sandwiched between two doors on 20th St, Chelsea, New York. Since its eviction from this site, however, the gallery has found new life as an intervention into the Collection Displays at Tate Modern. Like a Trojan horse smuggling its own agenda into the larger institution, The Wrong Gallery provides an opportunity to show artists and works not normally displayed at Tate Modern. It therefore operates in a parasitic way, as its curators have stated, 'like a flea on the elephant's back, all the while growing and gathering energy from its surroundings'. **(AC)**

Maurizio Cattelan/ The Wrong Gallery

The Grounds of the Château Noir
c.1900–6
Oil on canvas
90.7 x 71.4 cm
Lent by the National Gallery 1997

Sometimes called 'the father of modern art', Paul Cézanne moved away from the naturalistic painting of the nineteenth century and towards the attention to form that characterised much art of the twentieth century. Despite this, his abiding concern was with the accurate transcription of his experience of nature, a preoccupation he inherited from the Impressionists. While Cézanne retained the high-keyed palette of these painters, in his endeavours to realise his 'sensations', he broke from many of the principles of traditional painting, such as gradated modelling and perspective. He replaced conventional perspective with a freer method of draughtsmanship that allowed him to synthesise 'multiple views' of his subject matter and he substituted traditional modelling of forms with a method of applying patches of colour over the entire surface of the canvas, resulting in a blocky, tapestry-like effect that prefigures some forms of Cubism.

Cézanne also broke from the Impressionists in his concern with design, composition and form. He advised a young painter, Emile Bernard, to look for the 'sphere, the cylinder and the cone' in nature, and while these do not literally appear in Cézanne's paintings, the remark underlines his concern with describing satisfying groupings of forms.

In *The Grounds of the Château Noir c.*1900–6, painted near his home in Aix-en-Provence, Cézanne's concern with both naturalism and design is apparent. He carefully renders the complex forms of the rocky, wooded hillside with a matrix of subtly modulated patches of colour. Framed on either side by the curving trunks of the two foreground trees, this nondescript subject takes on the almost classical sense of balance and airy repose typical of his late works. **(MB)**

Paul Cézanne
1839–1906

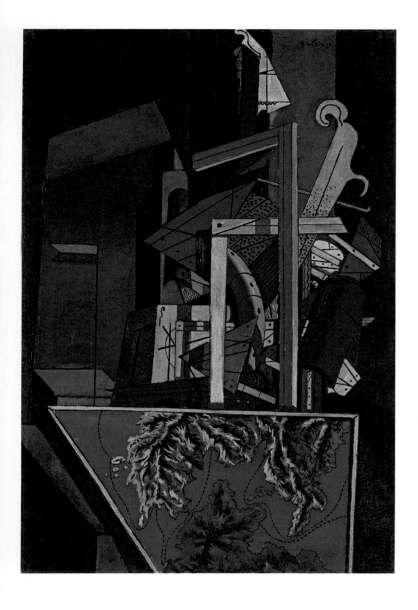

Metaphysical Painting
Metaphysical Painting was short-lived but highly influential. Following the ideas of Nietzsche, de Chirico used the term 'metaphysical' in order to suggest a deeper reality beyond the surface of things in his Parisian paintings of 1913–14. In wartime Ferrara he met Carlo Carrà, one of the founders of Futurism, who was seeking a way back to a reconstructive art based in tradition. It was this view, in tune with a post-war 'return to order' (a return, that is, from avant-garde destructiveness), that prevailed in the Roman periodical *Valori Plastici* (1918–21), dominated by Carrà's art and writing. The publication was also notable for introducing the paintings of Giorgio Morandi. Theoretical differences ensured the swift disintegration of the group, but not before their style had been widely disseminated. Artists in Italy and Germany (such as Mario Sironi and George Grosz) were the first to demonstrate its impact, but it was most profound in the art of the Surrealists Max Ernst, René Magritte and Salvador Dalí. **(MG)**

For much of his career, Giorgio de Chirico's style was slightly out of joint with contemporary taste. He established his reputation in Paris in 1911–15 with paintings showing unexpected objects in mysterious spaces infused with a melancholic atmosphere of loss. Under the influence of the philosopher Friedrich Nietzsche, he called this art 'metaphysical'. *The Uncertainty of the Poet* 1913 captures the eerie sense of potential in the depiction of a classical sculpture and a bunch of bananas set in a slightly disjointed Mediterranean square. During the First World War the painter and his musician-writer brother Alberto Savinio were posted for military service in Ferrara. There de Chirico was only able to paint at night, circumstances that may explain the intensity of *The Melancholy of Departure* 1916. He had long made parallels between the journeys in classical myths and his own displacement from the Greece of his childhood, but here travel takes on a further poignancy under the restrictions of war. Nevertheless, the brothers formed a circle that would bring the disconcerting Metaphysical Painting to wider notice within the context of a post-war return to realism.

De Chirico's early work was acclaimed by the Surrealists, but they rejected his new work of the 1920s. His search for deeper ties to the classical tradition, culminating in his 1940s pastiches of Rubens, set him outside the modernist mainstream. His early work continued to be admired for its disquieting atmosphere but it was only with the diversity of postmodernism that his later career received serious consideration. **(MG)**

Giorgio de Chirico
1888–1978

Left:
The Melancholy of Departure
1916
Oil on canvas
51.8 x 35.9 cm
Purchased 1978

Right:
The Uncertainty of the Poet
1913
Oil on canvas
106 x 94 cm
Purchased with assistance from the National Art Collections Fund (Eugene Cremetti Fund), the Carroll Donner Bequest, the Friends of the Tate Gallery and members of the public 1985

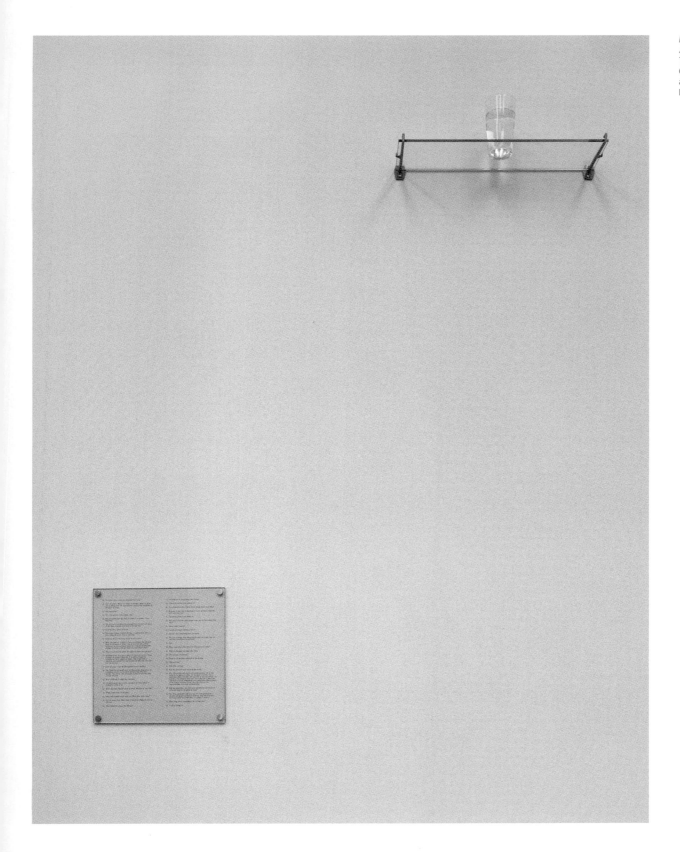

Michael Craig-Martin (born 1941)
An Oak Tree
1973
Glass, water, shelf
and printed text
Lent from a private collection 2000

Conceptual Art

The American art critic Lucy Lippard once commented that there are as many definitions of Conceptual art as there are conceptual artists. Since the late 1960s, when the term was first coined, there has been a general consensus that Conceptual art is concerned primarily with ideas and meanings, and considers the form or representation of those ideas to be of secondary importance. The purpose of this kind of artistic practice is to raise questions in the mind of the viewer, usually in order to draw attention to a particular political, social, cultural or philosophical issue or context. Conceptual art has been produced by numerous artists across the globe, in an extremely wide variety of media (painting, installation, video, photography, found objects, maps, text, etc.) over the past four decades.

While there is some debate about the true origins of Conceptual art, the artist Marcel Duchamp is repeatedly held up by critics, academics and artists as a major influence because of his seminal use of the 'readymade' – an everyday object that is given the status of an artwork through its selection by an artist and placement in a museum, gallery or other art-related context. Although Conceptual art is rooted in an attempt to question and deny accepted categories and conventions, there have been attempts to describe and name its various trends. Lucy Lippard's book *Six Years: The Dematerialization of the Art Object from 1966 to 1972* gathers together documents and texts exploring the artistic practice of a number of artists from this key period. The works created during Lippard's 'six years' are concurrent with the counter-cultural movements of the late 1960s and were often motivated by a desire to side-step the art-market, which relied on the 'object' status of artworks for saleability. They fall roughly into the categories of performance (or action) art, process art, land art, text-based art (words), documentation, intervention and/or readymade.

The American artists Joseph Kosuth, Lawrence Weiner, Sol LeWitt, the transatlantic collective Art & Language and a number of British artists such as Michael Craig-Martin, John Latham and Keith Arnatt all played a major role in the creation and definition of Conceptual art in the late 1960s and early 1970s. Although Conceptual art has since become a broad tendency and a global phenomenon, their influence is clearly apparent in the work of a younger generation of artists from Britain who emerged in the late 1990s, such as Martin Creed and Ceal Floyer.

Joseph Kosuth's *Clock (One and Five), English /Latin Version* 1965, is an example of a conceptual artwork that employs readymade, text-based and documentary elements. A real wall-clock is displayed alongside a life-sized photograph of it and a set of enlarged dictionary definitions for the words 'time', 'machination' and 'object'. The artwork is not merely the sum of the physical objects on the wall. Kosuth is clearly asking us to think about the nature of representation and linguistic definition: 'how do we represent, for example, a clock?' (and therefore, 'what is the nature of all representation?'). Like many Conceptual artworks, Kosuth's *Clock* was one of a series and was issued with a set of instructions. Often, the more information one has about the other works in the series and the artists' intentions or written instructions, the clearer the 'concept' becomes. **(AC)**

Joseph Kosuth (born 1945)
*Clock (One and Five),
English /Latin Version*
1965
Clock, photograph
and printed texts
61 x 290.2 cm
Purchased 1974

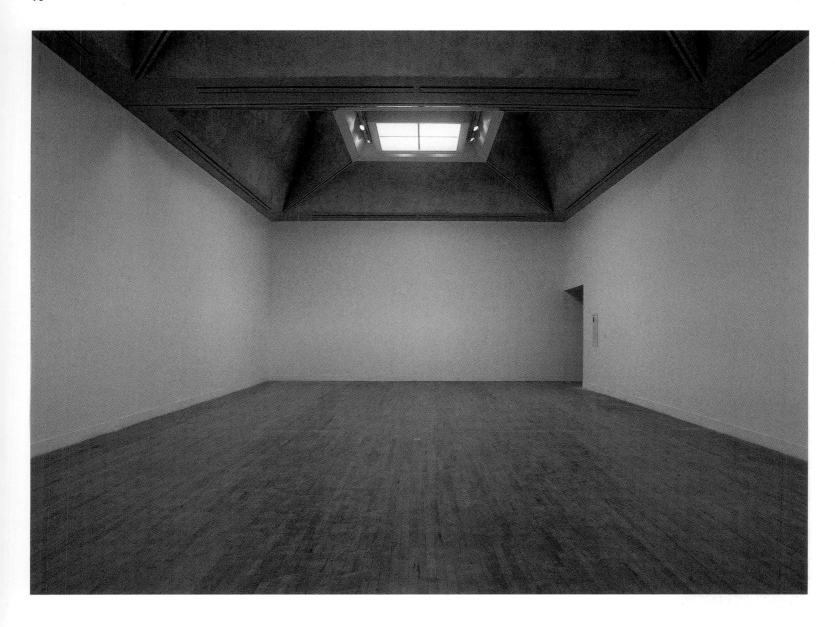

Since 1987, all of Martin Creed's works have been given simple, descriptive titles preceded by a sequential number. This system, which seems straightforward at first, is destabilised by the fact that Creed does not number his works logically. For example, there is no 'Work No. 1'. An important clue to Creed's artistic ideology can be found in Work No. 232, which consists of the statement: the whole world + the work = the whole world. In mathematical terms, this equation gives 'the work' a value of zero, so it can be interpreted as an assertion that all creative endeavour is futile. A more optimistic reading is that any work, no matter how small, can effect and somehow reform the world. For Creed 'nothing' is just as important as 'something', but the meaning of this work can shift with the perception of each viewer. The phrase was conceived by Creed in 1996 whilst he was considering his own artistic practice, and was originally installed in white neon on the facade of a former orphanage, and later on Tate's Millbank building.

Creed's work is informed by Minimalism and Conceptual art, and is often created from everyday elements such as masking tape, Elastoplast, Blu-tack, A4 paper, and even the simple act of switching on and off a light. His subtle interventions aim to maintain the equilibrium of their environments, yet ask fundamental questions about the nature of art, challenging the viewer to re-evaluate the works and the spaces they inhabit.

In 2001 Creed won the Turner Prize. **(CM)**

Left:
Work No. 227: the lights going on and off
2000
Materials and dimensions variable
Installation view, *Turner Prize*, Tate Britain, 2001

Right:
Work No. 232: the Whole World + the Work = the Whole World
2000
Neon tubing
50 x 1550 cm
Presented by the Patrons of New Art (Special Purchase Fund) 2001

Martin Creed
born 1968

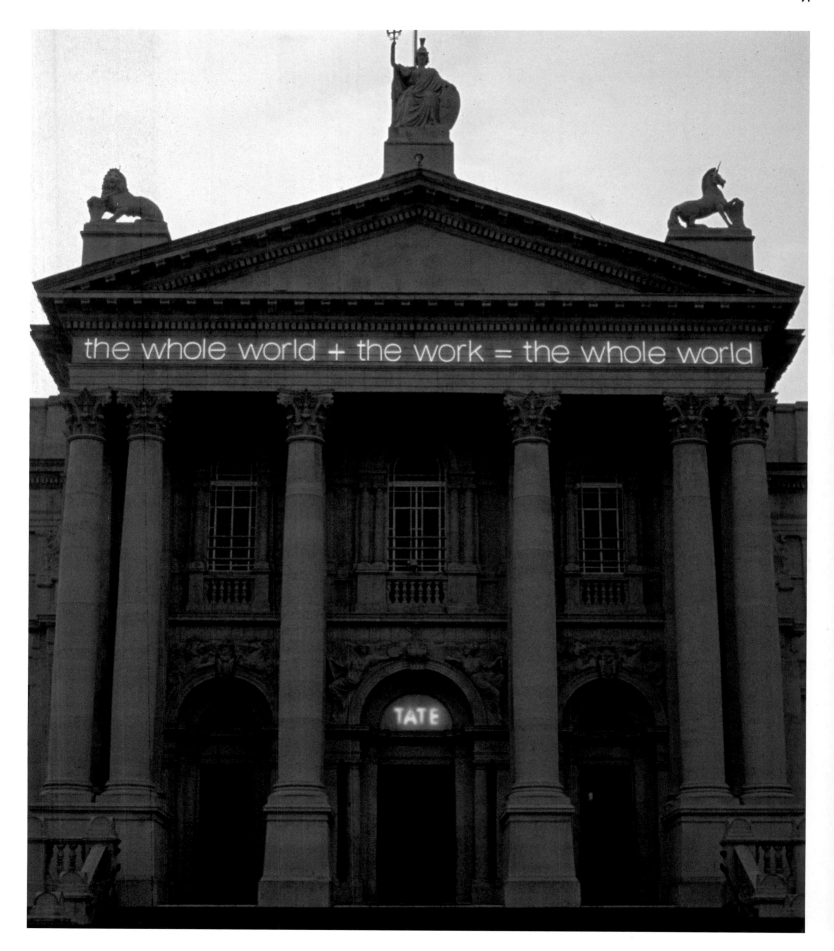

Cubism

It was Henri Matisse who is reputed to have described Georges Braque's 1909 paintings as made of 'little cubes'. Initially intended as an insult, the term stuck since it described the fragmented images as well as alluding to their structural element. This was, however, a simplification that did not encompass the perceptual and conceptual aspects of Cubist practice. The structures of the paintings, initially inspired by the example of Paul Cézanne, aimed at conveying the complex nature of experience while acknowledging the flat canvas. New scientific theories and technological advances that penetrated the fixed surface of matter (such as X-rays and radio-waves), suddenly made the Renaissance convention of perspective inadequate for capturing knowledge of modern life: the fact, for instance, that a bottle is both cylindrical and transparent with a rectangular printed label. This enquiry was also fuelled by the notion of flux, the multi-layered 'simultaneity of experience' proposed by the influential philosopher Henri Bergson.

In a famous collaboration over the five years 1909–14, Braque and Pablo Picasso developed a detailed visual analysis of reality. In their studios in Montmartre, dressed in workmen's overalls (an expression of political identification with manual workers), the two painters began by unravelling the familiar world about them: still-lifes and figures dominate Cubist painting. Cézanne's example influenced the limited colour and build-up of small brushstrokes, while African art (the focus of their earlier primitivist interest) encouraged the simplification of forms as planes or facets. The sophistication of their work reached its apex in 1911–12, when Braque introduced patterned or printed papers into his compositions and Picasso began to construct sculptures. Collage and assemblage – both hugely influential inventions – allowed the direct presence of everyday materials such as newspapers within the composition.

The influence of these works by Picasso and Braque, and later those of Juan Gris, became pervasive in Paris from 1911, although they only showed their work in the gallery of their dealer Daniel-Henri Kahnweiler. Jean Metzinger and Albert Gleizes headed the group of painters who exhibited their Cubist works at the avant-garde Salons and published *Du Cubisme* to explain the movement's theoretical underpinning. This did little to counter the derision that Cubism attracted from the press and public. Nevertheless, in 1912–14, its impact grew internationally, especially with artists whose work emphasised an urban dynamism, from the Italian Futurists and British Vorticists, to the Prague Cubists and Russian Constructivists. The First World War brought a new phase to Cubism, often called 'synthetic', as Picasso and Gris began to assemble their images from fragments of reality. Other recruits included Jacques Lipchitz, who conceived near-abstract sculptures. Cubism's legacy can also be found in the work of painters such as Piet Mondrian.

The impact of Cubism on subsequent art, even that not obviously associated with it, cannot be exaggerated. For some, Cubism was the impetus to abstraction, for others it became one of several means for capturing the experience of the modern world. Later in the century, Cubism was understood to have reinforced the formal, painterly qualities of Abstract Expressionism, and its quotation of urban images was echoed in Pop art. Beyond these particular positions Cubism epitomised the idea of avant-garde experimentation: challenging, controversial and revolutionary. **(MG)**

Above:
Juan Gris (1887–1927)
The Sunblind
1914
Gouache, collage, chalk
and charcoal on canvas
92.1 x 72.7 cm
Purchased 1946

Pablo Picasso (1881–1973)
*Bottle of Vieux Marc, Glass,
Guitar and Newspaper*
1913
Collage and pen and ink
on blue paper
46.7 x 62.5 cm
Purchased 1961

Below left:
Georges Braque (1882–1963)
*Clarinet and Bottle of Rum
on a Mantelpiece*
1911
Oil on canvas
81 x 60 cm
Purchased with assistance
from a special government
grant and with assistance
from the National Art
Collections Fund 1978

Below right:
Pablo Picasso (1881–1973)
Seated Nude
1909–10
Oil on canvas
92.1 x 73 cm
Purchased 1949

Collage

In the early twentieth century, artists began pasting pieces of paper, fabric and even wallpaper to their works, challenging traditional methods of picture-making. Introducing ephemeral material in this way helped to develop the idea of an artwork as an independent object. The term 'collage' comes from the French word *coller* (to glue) and the method was first employed by the Cubist artists Pablo Picasso and Georges Braque, who introduced real items such as newspaper clippings into their *papier collé* (pasted-paper) works. Collage was also employed by Dada artists such as Kurt Schwitters, who coined the nonsense word *Merz* to describe his compositions made up of scavenged scrap items such as bus and theatre tickets. The possibilities of random arrangements of assorted images offered by collage particularly appealed to Surrealist artists, who transformed this idea into painted works to create unlikely associations within a single image. **(LA)**

Right:
Marcel Duchamp (1887–1968)
Why Not Sneeze Rose Sélavy?
1921, editioned replica 1964
Mixed media
11.4 x 22 x 16 cm
Purchased 1999

Below left:
Max Ernst (1891–1976)
Dadaville
c.1924
Painted plaster and cork
laid on canvas
68 x 56 x 6.3 cm
Purchased 1983

Below right:
Man Ray (1890–1976)
New York
1920, editioned replica 1973
Glass, steel, cork and linen tape
25.9 x 6.5 x 6.5 cm
Presented by Lucien Treillard
2002

Dada

'I am writing a manifesto and there is nothing I want', claimed the poet Tristan Tzara in his *Dada Manifesto 1918*; 'and yet', he added, 'in principle I am against manifestos, as I am against principles'. Dada – Tzara reportedly chose the name by inserting a knife into a dictionary – was less an artistic style than an act of defiance. It was witty and disruptive, generated by a disgust with the certainties that had resulted in the First World War (1914–18). Dada emerged at the Cabaret Voltaire in Zurich in 1916. There, and in the neutral havens of Barcelona and New York, artists and intellectuals attacked the status quo through their performances, exhibitions and publications. Their strategies owed much to Futurism but echoed the political radicalism of the 1917 Bolshevik Revolution. In place of technological progress and military might, Dada was satirical, subversive and anarchic. In place of wartime nationalism, it was resolutely international. The range of participants in Zurich alone confirms this: Tzara and Marcel Janco from Romania, the poets Hugo Ball, Emmy Hennings, Richard Huelsenbeck and the painter Hans Richter from Germany, as well as the painters Jean Arp (from disputed Alsace) and Sophie Taeuber, who was Swiss.

Dada works were united in their subversion. Simultaneous poetry and collage, photomontage and object-making undermined high art. In Zurich, Arp adopted chance as a compositional method (gluing down torn paper where it fell), and Ball's sound-poems abandoned words – which he considered corrupted by propaganda – for incantations of sounds. Though the circumstances were quite different, parallel activities flourished in New York, among a group of exiles from Paris and their American friends. There, Marcel Duchamp conceived his 'readymades', manufactured objects identified as art by the artist. He exhibited the most provocative of these, *Fountain* (an inscribed and upturned urinal) in 1917 (p.104). Man Ray made witty photographs and objects inspired by this example, and Francis Picabia – also the driving force in Barcelona – produced the subversive periodical *391* alongside his mechnomorphic paintings.

With peace, Dada exploded in the turmoil of post-war Germany and France. Max Ernst and Kurt Schwitters (who formed his own movement, Merz) found beauty in the fragmentary world of collage and recuperated debris. A group formed around Huelsenbeck in Berlin and allied itself with the revolutionary politics by attacking, in the work of George Grosz and Raoul Hausmann especially, the complacency of the new Weimar Republic. On their arrival in Paris, Picabia and Tzara provided the focus for the convergence of these many strands, along with younger poets, including André Breton and Paul Eluard, who passed into Surrealism.

Essentially indefinable, Dada was a violent counter-blast against conformity. Such incandescence could not be sustained and, in the mid-1920s, it lost its urgency. Nevertheless, its example reverberated through Surrealism to the art of the 1960s and 1990s. Duchamp's Dada provocations and ironic humour remain highly influential, while Picabia's bewilderingly contradictory styles of abstraction and kitsch anticipate postmodernism. 'Dada places doubt', he wrote, 'before action, and above all everything else.' **(MG)**

Kurt Schwitters (1887–1948)
Picture of Spatial Growths –
Picture with Two Small Dogs
1920–39
Mixed media collage on board
97 x 69 cm
Purchased 1984

Surrealist objects
The underlying force of Surrealist objects derived from an idea of the expressive potential of the unrelated. The nineteenth-century poet Isidore Ducasse (writing as the Comte de Lautréamont) had laid down an example that became talismanic: 'the chance encounter of a sewing machine and an umbrella on an operating table'. The Surrealists seized upon the spark of irrational originality in such juxtapositions, liberated from prosaic cause and effect. They found impetus in Marcel Duchamp's 'readymades', the objects of Man Ray (who made *The Enigma of Isidore Ducasse* 1920) and the realism of René Magritte's paintings. However, it was Dalí's enthusiasm for Alberto Giacometti's dream-like sculptures that generated the object-production of the 1930s. At first this resulted in complex agglomerations, but the more powerful works had the potential to infiltrate everyday life: the *Lobster Telephone* 1936 could, conceivably, ring. Like collage, object-making stimulated a rich legacy, from rough scrap materials brought together in the 1950s and 1960s by Pop and New Realist artists to the provocative juxtapositions of artists such as Sarah Lucas and Damien Hirst. **(MG)**

The Catalan painter Salvador Dalí was one of the most controversial and popular artists of the twentieth century. From an early position of achievement – genius, as he would see it – he fashioned for himself a style of remarkable clarity through which his fantasies were depicted with convincing realism. He treated his own biography as the raw material for revelatory sexual and filial obsessions. These fed the works of the late 1920s that secured his entry into Surrealism.

It was through *Un chien andalou*, the film that he made with Luis Buñuel in 1929 (p.222), that Dalí burst upon Surrealism in Paris. His combination of hallucinogenic imagery and Freudian confession reinvigorated the movement at a moment of crisis. The Surrealists' leader, André Breton, allotted him a central role. Dalí renewed the potential of illusionistic painting (together with René Magritte and Yves Tanguy) and introduced Surrealist objects. He based his complex 'paranoiac-critical method' on the parallel realities experienced in paranoia, making layered images in which forms could be understood in multiple ways. His masterly skill is epitomised in the illusionism of *The Metamorphosis of Narcissus* 1937.

Dalí's self-promotion and commercialism irked the Surrealists, especially at the time of their engagement with Communism in the 1930s. Although he produced extraordinary images of the Spanish Civil War in such works as *Autumnal Cannibalism* 1936, his fascination with Lenin and Hitler provoked his expulsion from the movement. He was too closely identified with Surrealism to be jettisoned immediately. Collaborations on Hollywood movies in the 1940s and later explorations of optical illusions secured Dalí's independence. At the same time he cultivated his celebrity. In the end showmanship obscured his considerable achievements, even if he maintained an extraordinary level of popularity. **(MG)**

Lobster Telephone
1936
Plastic, painted plaster and mixed media
17.8 x 33 x 17.8 cm
Purchased 1981

Salvador Dalí
1904–1989

Autumnal Cannibalism
1936
Oil on canvas
6?.1 x 65.1 cm
Purchased 1975

Tacita Dean has used film, photography and drawing to explore the boundaries between fact and fiction, perception and reality. Also fascinated by humankind's desire to conquer the elements, Dean turns a forensic eye onto the atrophied remains of failed visions, such as a utopian house lying derelict and abandoned to the weather, or Robert Smithson's *Spiral Jetty* 1970, a seminal work of Land art now immersed in the surrounding lake.

Dean's film *Disappearance at Sea* 1996 was inspired by the true story of Donald Crowhurst, who took part in the first single-handed yacht race around the world in 1969. Ill-prepared for the voyage, Crowhurst never even made it out of the Atlantic but, unable to admit to failure, he continued to send radio messages charting his now imaginary progress around the world. His boat was eventually found abandoned. Dean makes no direct attempt to depict the events, but instead evokes a sense of dislocation and of time running out by cutting between views of the lenses of a lighthouse and the sun setting across the sea. As the sky darkens, the beam of the lighthouse is seen swooping across the sea, a last glimmer of hope before the screen falls dark. Dean's use of 16mm film is significant. The whirring and the beam of light from the projector echo that of the lighthouse to further enhance the mood.

In *The Roaring Forties: Seven Boards in Seven Days* 1997, Dean constructs an epic narrative of sailors battling the elements in an area of the Atlantic known for strong gales. The unfolding of events is illustrated in the manner of a cinematic storyboard, using chalk on blackboards. The boards are inscribed with wind directions and camera angles, which prevent the viewer from becoming too immersed in the narrative. Areas of the chalk are smudged, hinting at the endless possibilities for reworking the story. **(HS)**

Tacita Dean
born 1965

Left and below (detail):
The Roaring Forties:
Seven Boards in Seven Days
1997
Chalk on blackboards
Each 243.8 x 243.8 cm
Presented by the Patrons
of New Art through the Tate
Gallery Foundation 2000

Edgar Degas is best known as an Impressionist painter, concerned with truthfully capturing the fleeting moments of everyday modern life. However, he was less interested in the effects of light and colour in landscape that mark out the work of the other leading members of the group, such as Claude Monet, Camille Pissarro and Pierre-Auguste Renoir. Degas's great preoccupation was with form, an interest apparent not only in his paintings, but also in a substantial body of drawings and sculptures. His favoured subject matter was the human figure, at rest and in motion, and he found the ideal subject for this interest in the ballet dancers at the Paris Opéra.

His paintings of dancers, often shown rehearsing or resting, have an almost photographic spontaneity and informality. As with most of his work, the sense of spontaneity was contrived, the result of many preparatory studies. This seeming naturalness is also apparent in Degas's sculptures of dancers, which perhaps convey, even better than the paintings, the forcefulness and control of the dancers' movements, and the tension and fatigue evident on their bodies at rest. Despite their quality, Degas showed only one of his sculptures during his lifetime, *Little Dancer Aged Fourteen* 1880–1, a sympathetic portrayal of the self-control, discomfort and strain of the ballerina-in-training. The naturalism of the sculpture is increased by means of a real gauze tutu and a silk ribbon 'tying' the bronze hair. These features echo Degas's original wax model, which was fully clothed in fabric bodice, tutu and slippers, wore a horsehair wig, and had lifelike colour applied to the skin. **(MB)**

Little Dancer Aged Fourteen
1880–1, cast *c.*1922
Painted bronze with
muslin and silk
98.4 x 41.9 x 36.5 cm
Purchased with assistance
from the National Art
Collections Fund 1952

Edgar Degas
1834–1917

Orphism
Named after the mythical lyre-player Orpheus, the term Orphism was coined by Guillaume Apollinaire in 1912 to refer to a group of Parisian painters in whose work he saw a movement towards what he called 'pure painting'. These included Robert Delaunay, Fernand Léger and Francis Picabia. For Apollinaire, music's non-representational quality made it a model of a 'pure' art form; he wanted painting to abandon representation and express itself through form and colour alone. While the artists Apollinaire identified were making influential advances towards abstraction at the time, few shared his particular enthusiasm for pure painting, and some members of the group, such as Picabia and Marcel Duchamp, soon went on to pursue very different interests. **(MB)**

Robert Delaunay was one of the earliest artists to experiment with abstraction, using Cubism as a departure point to move towards a highly abstract, colour-based mode of painting. He was particularly interested in experiments with pigment, and from around 1912 he sought to use colour as a pure means of expression, entirely freeing it from its traditional representational function. It was at this time that Delaunay was named by Apollinaire as a key member of the Orphists, a diverse group of painters whose work was developing towards pure abstraction. From this time onwards, Delaunay typically constructed his compositions using pairs of complementary hues – yellow and violet, green and red, and orange and blue – which when juxtaposed intensify one another, a phenomenon known as 'simultaneous contrast'. Delaunay believed simultaneous contrast could be used to generate a range of effects in painting, including transparency, movement and harmony, and ultimately to convey a sense of personal and universal reality.

Windows Open Simultaneously (First Part, Third Motif) 1912 is a product of these concerns. Here, the Eiffel Tower, one of Delaunay's favourite motifs, is visible as a green wedge at the centre of the painting. Surrounded by buildings and framed by the suggestion of flowing curtains, the tower is melded into a near abstract pattern of complementary coloured forms and planes, creating a shimmering, jewel-like effect. These ideas also gave rise to his most abstract works, based on a disc motif of concentric circles, which he began in 1913. **(MB)**

Windows Open Simultaneously (First Part, Third Motif)
1912
Oil on canvas
45.7 x 37.5 cm
Purchased 1967

Robert Delaunay
1885–1941

Prose on the Trans-Siberian Railway and of Little Jehanne of France
1913
Watercolour and relief print on paper
195.6 x 35.6 cm
Purchased 1980

Russian-born Sonia Terk married the French artist Robert Delaunay in 1910. Around this time she abandoned her Fauvist style of painting and turned instead to the design and making of textiles. Two years later, the Delaunays developed a manner of painting that they termed 'simultaneous', derived from the notion of simultaneous perception. Unlike the Cubists, with whom Robert was associated, they focused on the colours which that came from light, studying the illumination of Paris provided by new electric street-lights. While Cubist paintings depicted multiple view-points of objects and urban landscapes, with a mixture of figurative representation and abstraction, the Delaunays' 'simultaneous paintings' of 1912 devolved into colourful grids of pure abstraction.

A collaboration between Blaise Cendrars and Sonia Delaunay, *Prose on the Trans-Siberian Railway and of Little Jehanne of France* 1913 was hailed as the first 'simultaneous book', conceived to be viewed as imagery and read at the same time. On one side of the two metre-long page, the lines of Cendrars's unpunctuated poem are printed in varying colours and typefaces. Sonia Delaunay supplied a visual complement to the fluctuating rhythm of an interminable train journey recounted in the poem with blocks and streaks of vivid colour. At the base of the page, next to the finishing lines of the poem, she depicted a red Eiffel tower, illustrating the eventual termination of the journey in Paris.

Sonia Delaunay and Cendrars continued to collaborate for several years. Delaunay made further artistic innovations by applying her avant-garde painting ideas to designing posters for artists and commercial products, book covers and textiles as well as creating 'simultaneous outfits' and textiles for interior design. **(EM)**

Sonia Delaunay
1885–1979

The Tree of Fluids
1950
Oil on canvas
116.1 x 89 cm
Accepted by H.M. Government
in lieu of tax and allocated to
the Tate Gallery 1996

Jean Dubuffet spent a lifetime warring against the mainstream, and his importance as an artist, a writer and a collector has been felt both within and beyond the avant-garde. He coined the term 'Art Brut' for art produced by non-professionals working outside cultural norms, such as works by mental patients, prisoners and children, and amassed an important collection of such art. 'Normal means lack of imagination, lack of creativity', Dubuffet argued. 'I, personally, have a very high regard for the values of primitive peoples: instinct, passion, caprice, violence, madness.'

His own artistic output was extensive and varied. The earlier works are generally figurative, although as in *The Tree of Fluids* 1950, his concern is more with the use of texture and gesture to explore bodily fluids than with the employment of line and form to give conventional form to the figure. His work became increasingly abstract in the 1950s as he invested more and more interest in the elaboration of textures. He would often mix materials such as sand, tar and straw into his oil paint. *The Exemplary Life of the Soil (Texturology LXIII)* 1958 is one of a number of works in which he used unconventional methods to portray the textures of soil. For this work, he adapted a technique used by stonemasons to texture newly plastered walls that involved shaking a brush over the painting to scatter tiny droplets of paint across the surface. He was also an accomplished printmaker, and towards the end of the 1960s he began to concentrate increasingly on sculptural and environmental projects. **(SH)**

Jean Dubuffet
1901–1985

Marcel Duchamp's lasting and influential contribution to twentieth-century and contemporary art was to have shifted the focus of artistic practice from the strictly visual to the realm of ideas, engaging the intellect and imagination of the viewer as much as the eyes. Employing a wide range of media including painting, photography and sculpture, his radical and iconoclastic work probes the boundaries of art, its theoretical definitions as much as the institutional framework in which it operates. Especially with his 'readymades', everyday objects he declared to be works of art, Duchamp challenged preconceived categories of taste, beauty and functionality.

Originally trained as an academic painter Duchamp largely abandoned easel painting after 1915 to concentrate on his seminal work *The Bride Stripped Bare by Her Bachelors, Even* 1915–23, a large-scale composition executed in oil and lead on glass, also known as *The Large Glass*. A version of this complex piece was recreated by British artist Richard Hamilton for Tate's major Duchamp retrospective in 1966. The subject of much debate, the freestanding, transparent glass construction is divided into two equal parts: the upper 'female' section of the title's 'bride', and the lower 'male' section of her suitors. The characters are represented as stylised machines whose endlessly repetitive grinding alludes to the frustration of unfulfilled desire. The two sections are destined never to come together, further heightening the sense of disappointment.

From the early 1920s onwards, after an intense creative flurry, Duchamp appeared content to let others further elaborate the ideas implicit in his work and spent most of his time playing chess. Only after his death was it discovered that for the past twenty years he had been working on another major work, the installation *Etant donnés*. **(ABH)**

Fountain
1917, replica 1964
Porcelain
36 x 48 x 61 cm
Purchased with assistance from the Friends of the Tate Gallery 1999

Marcel Duchamp
1887–1968

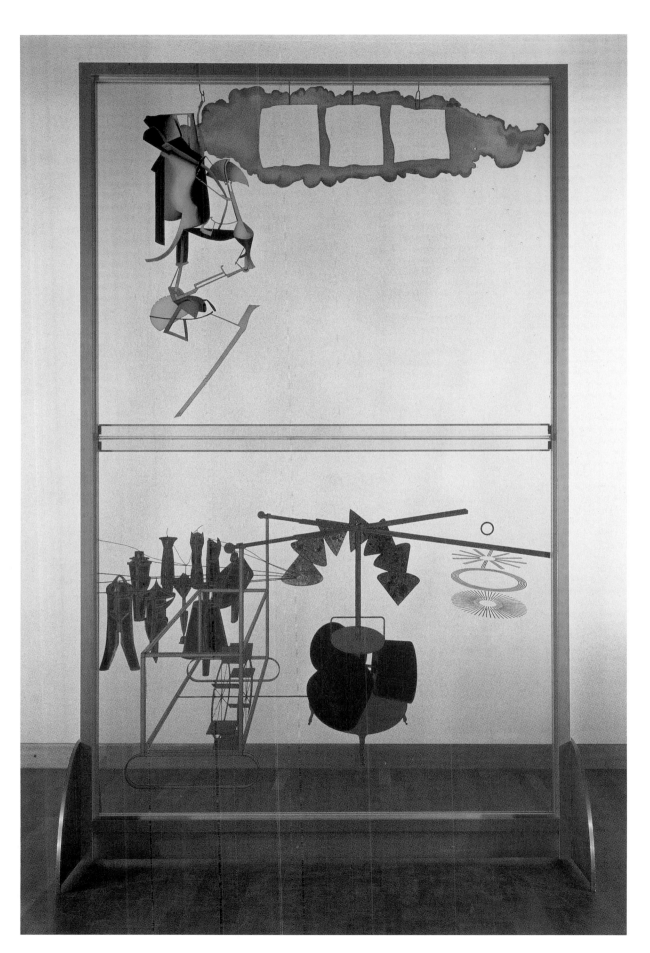

Readymade

In 1917, when Duchamp submitted an ordinary urinal to an exhibition held by the New York Society of Independent Artists, titling it *Fountain* and signing it R. Mutt, he irrevocably changed the course of modern art. Three and a half decades later he remarked that 'readymades' such as this one allowed him to 'reduce the idea of aesthetic consideration to the choice of the mind, not the ability or cleverness of the hand'.

The first pure readymade – that is, an everyday object bearing no trace of modification other than the artist's signature or similar inscription – was a bottle rack that Duchamp had purchased in a Paris department store in 1914. He coined the term to describe this revolutionary strategy two years later. Other readymades include a comb, a snow shovel, a hat rack and a bicycle wheel mounted on top of a wooden stool. Duchamp claimed that he selected these objects on the basis of pure visual indifference. Putting the emphasis on idea and intellect rather than on craft and self-expression, Duchamp's readymades became an important influence on twentieth-century art, especially the art of the later 1960s and 1970s including Pop art, Minimalism and Conceptual art. Duchamp's assertion that what is art is defined by the artist continues to reverberate through much artistic practice until the present day. **(ABH)**

The Bride Stripped Bare by her Bachelors, Even (The Large Glass)
1915–23, replica 1965–6, lower panel reconstructed 1985
Oil, lead, dust and varnish on glass
277.5 x 175.9 cm
Presented by William N. Copley through the American Federation of Arts 1975

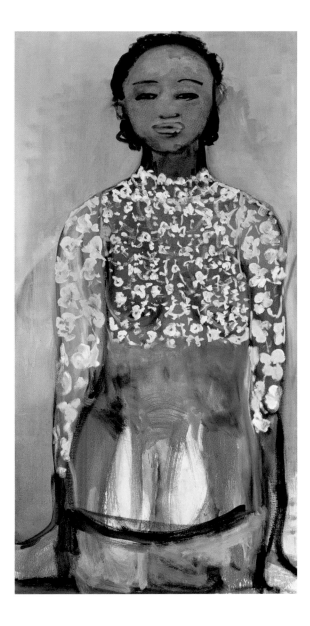

Ivory Black
1997
Oil on canvas
200.4 x 100.2 cm
Purchased 1998

Marlene Dumas is one of the key figures responsible for the revival of painting in the 1990s. Her figurative works rely on imagery drawn from a wealth of sources: newspapers and magazines, as well as art-historical models. While it has been said that she follows in the Expressionist tradition of Francis Bacon or Edvard Munch, her ironic and deconstructive approach to painting and image-making could also be termed neo-Conceptual. Born in South Africa in 1953, she moved to Holland in the mid-1970s.

Dumas's work reveals a highly intelligent awareness of her own cultural, political and social surroundings: race, sexuality, and her role as a female painter within a male-dominated field are all playfully alluded to in the work. Her portraits of young girls and boys, and her images of naked women, often possess a mysterious symbolic power. Perhaps her greatest achievement is the sensual quality of her technique deployed in paintings and drawings that render the human condition with extraordinary tenderness and intimacy. In a sense she has created a sublimated erotics of painting, not merely by using pornography as source material, but by exploring the sensual nature of her chosen medium: thickly applied paint to suggest flesh, or the mordant delicacy of watercolours to evoke fragility and mortality.

Death has been a regular theme in Dumas's work, and recently she has made numerous paintings based on found images of corpses. *Stern* 2004 is a death portrait of Ulrike Meinhof, the German Red Army Faction terrorist who was found dead in her prison cell in 1976. *Lucy* 2004 is based on Caravaggio's painting of 1608 portraying the martyred saint, who was tortured, blinded, burned at the stake and finally stabbed. The open mouths and thrown-back position of each head suggest sexual ecstacy. Dumas also makes the link between art and mortality: 'art is, and has always been, a preparation for death', she has written in a characteristically eloquent rumination on her art. **(ED)**

Marlene Dumas
born 1953

Torso in Metal from 'The Rock Drill'
1913–14
Bronze
70.5 x 58.4 x 44.5 cm
Purchased 1960

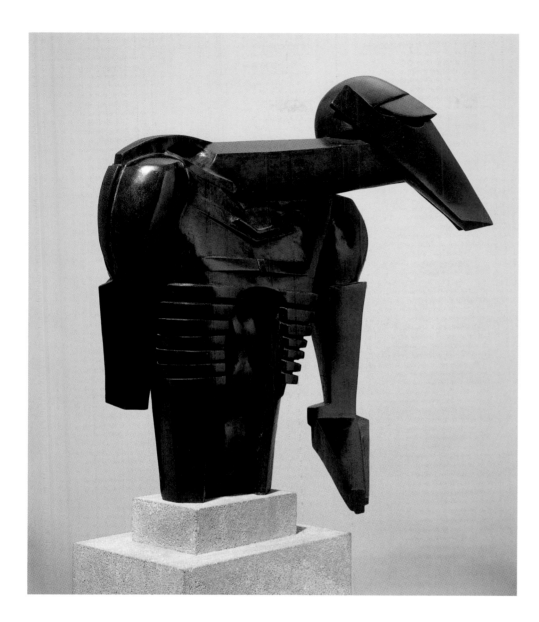

Jacob Epstein was born in New York City of Polish-Jewish parents. He trained at the Art Students League, then in 1902 moved to Paris and in 1905 to London, where he settled, becoming a British citizen in 1907. He was knighted in 1954. Epstein may be said to be the father of modern British sculpture, due both to his introduction of modernist ideas and to the huge fame and notoriety he achieved, the latter as a result of the public controversy aroused by his work from very early on. This controversy stemmed from the modernism of his style and from his bold treatment of

themes relating to procreation, religion and the cycle of life. As Henry Moore later acknowledged, Epstein 'took the brickbats … took the insults … and took them first'. In the years from 1907–16 Epstein produced a substantial group of stone and marble carvings, which constitute an important episode in the early history of modern sculpture, not just in Britain, but internationally. They include a sun god, two large totemic images of Venus, a series of three copulating doves (*Doves* 1914–15) and several images of pregnancy (*Figure in Flenite* 1913). However, in 1913–15 his association with Vorticism saw the production of an exceptional work, *The Rock Drill*. Here his themes of procreation were embodied in the form of a powerful image of modern industrial man, a giant virility symbol consisting of a sculptured plaster humanoid riding a real mechanical drill. This was a pioneering piece of mixed-media art as well as a major expression of a central theme of art at that time – the dynamism of modern life. Epstein later dismantled it and all that remains is the bronze-cast upper part of the figure, *Torso in Metal from 'The Rock Drill'* 1913–14. **(SW)**

Jacob Epstein
1880–1959

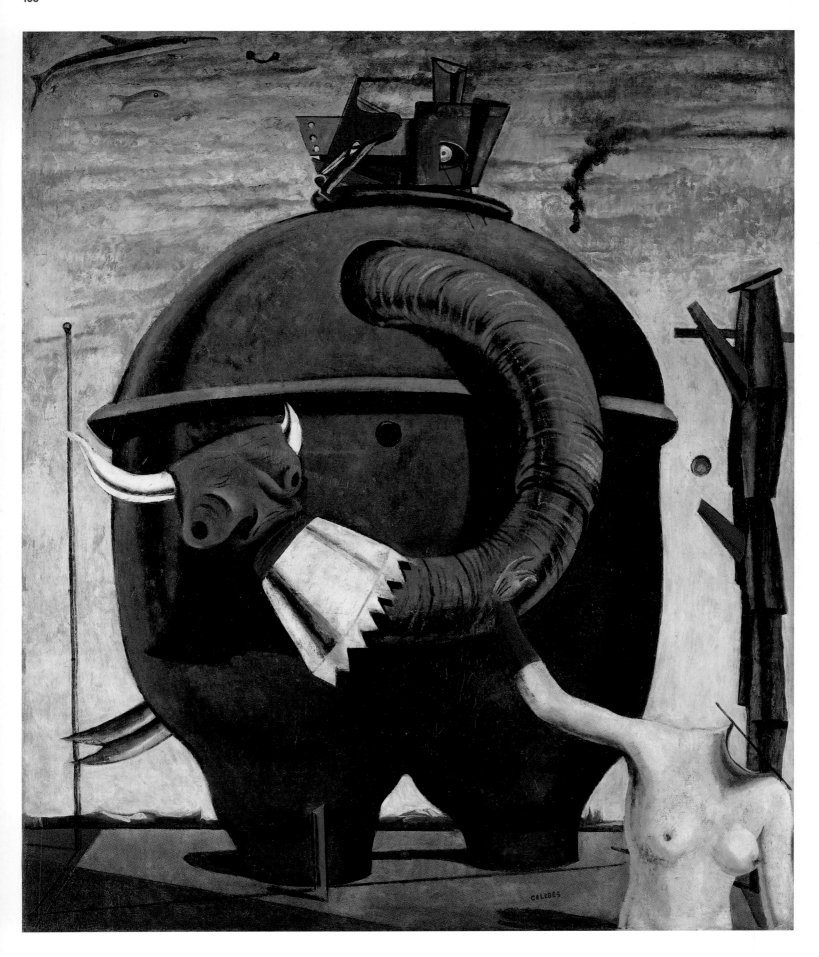

Far left:
Celebes
1921
Oil on canvas
125.4 x 107.9 cm
Purchased 1975

Centre:
Pietà or Revolution by Night
1923
Oil on canvas
116.2 x 88.9 cm
Purchased 1981

Right:
The Entire City
1934
Oil on paper laid on canvas
50.2 x 61.3 cm
Purchased with assistance
from the Knapping Fund 1941

The German artist Max Ernst became involved in Dada following his traumatic experiences fighting in the First World War. He later wrote that 'Max Ernst died on 1 August 1914. He returned to life on 11 November 1918, a young man who wanted to become a magician and find the myths of his time.' By the early 1920s he had moved to Paris to join the artists and writers who formed the Surrealist movement.

The Surrealists had been captivated by his early collages, made from cut-up magazines. He went on to translate the idea of collage into paint, juxtaposing apparently unrelated imagery in works such as *Celebes* 1921 and *Pietà or Revolution by Night* 1923, which has been viewed as one of the first truly Surrealist paintings.

As a key member of the Surrealist group, Ernst became a proponent of their technique of 'automatism', creating images without the intervention of conscious thought. The importance of random encounters led Ernst to experiment with novel methods involving chance, such as *frottage*, in which pigment is rubbed over paper laid on a piece of wood or other textured surface and *grattage*, which involves scraping paint across similar surfaces. These enabled Ernst to discover new and surprising images without having to control the results. *Forest and Dove* 1927 and *The Entire City* 1934 both evolved from such techniques and represent two major themes in Ernst's oeuvre: that of the forest, seen as a metaphor for the imagination by Surrealists, and that of the ruined citadel. **(LA)**

Max Ernst
1891–1976

Expressionism

Expressionism was never a single cohesive movement but, rather, a term applied to the work of a number of different artists' groups and individual practitioners in the early twentieth century. These artists, mostly based in northern Europe and particularly Germany, were seeking a new artistic language to express their sense of spiritual and intellectual dislocation. The philosophy of Friedrich Nietzsche, with its distrust of Western rationalism, was especially influential, encouraging artists to incorporate the instinctive and the irrational in their work.

Perhaps the defining characteristic of Expressionism was the presentation of a deliberately distorted image of the world to convey the artist's own subjective vision. The surfaces of Expressionist paintings were often highly textured with thick, expressive brushstrokes, and their use of boldly contrasting colours was decisively anti-naturalistic. Many artists found inspiration in non-Western and folk art, particularly masks and tribal sculptures from Africa and Oceania, which they believed possessed a rough vitality lacking in European culture.

One of the most significant Expressionist groups was *Die Brücke* (The Bridge), founded in Dresden in 1905, which included the artists Ernst Ludwig Kirchner, Emil Nolde and Karl Schmidt-Rottluff. The name of the group was an image of progress, of crossing from one shore to another, and reflected a belief that art had the power to transform society. This utopianism was manifested in their communal artistic practice, their challenge to sexual taboos, and their rediscovery of nature through retreats to locations such as the nearby Moritzburg Lakes.

In Germany, with the rise of Nazism, the artists associated with Expressionism were condemned as 'degenerate'. Works in public collections were seized and destroyed, and many artists were removed from teaching positions or forced into exile. **(SB)**

Above:
Karl Schmidt-Rottluff (1884–1976)
Male Head
1917
Wood
34.3 x 13.3 x 16.5 cm
Presented by the executors
of Dr Rosa Shapire 1954

Left:
Karl Schmidt-Rottluff
Woman with a Bag
1915
Oil on canvas
95.2 x 87.3 cm
Presented by Dr Rosa Shapire
1950

Emil Nolde (1867–1953)
The Sea B
1930
Oil on canvas
73.7 x 101 cm
Purchased 1966

The Second World War
The final months of the Second World War bought horrific revelations of Nazi death camps and the unleashing of atomic weapons on Japan. European artists such as Alberto Giacometti, Jean Fautrier, Germaine Richier and Francis Bacon made work that was visibly informed by the prevailing mood of dislocation and existential unease. They depicted the human body as wounded, decayed and isolated. Other artists, including Boris Taslitzky and André Fougeron, saw realist styles as the best means to create politically committed works that would engage a mass audience with the grim political realities of the time. In the late 1940s, the onset of the Cold War threatened yet another conflict. In New York, younger painters including Jackson Pollock, Mark Rothko and Barnett Newman responded to the ideological disputes of the time by forging new forms of expressive abstraction that commentators quickly linked to ideas around personal and political freedom. **(SH)**

During the Second World War, Jean Fautrier was associated with the French Resistance. The paintings and sculptures he made during the Occupation suggest the brutal violence of Nazi atrocities. *Large Tragic Head* 1942 is a potent example of such work. The delicate modelling of the eye and gasping mouth contrast with the deep furrows clawed out of the wet clay, obliterating the other features. It is as if the head has been subject to a brutal attack. When this sculpture and other similar works by Fautrier were exhibited after the Liberation, they were seen to memorialise the collective experience of wartime suffering. The writer André Malraux described Fautrier's art as 'the first attempt to dissect contemporary pain'.

In 1943 Fautrier was imprisoned by the SS. He subsequently sought refuge in a sanatorium on the outskirts of Paris. At night, he could hear the Gestapo torturing and executing prisoners in the nearby woods, and over the next two years he made the series *Hostages*. Works such as *Head of a Hostage* 1943–4 suggest the dehumanising of the tortured victim, the pitted and scarred surface of the sculpture being reminiscent of the anonymity of bodies found in mass graves. Versions of the piece exist in bronze, but this cast is made from lead, carrying with it connotations of weight, toxicity and mortality. **(SH)**

Large Tragic Head
1942
Bronze on marble base
38.5 x 21 x 21.5 cm
Purchased 1992

Head of a Hostage
1943–4
Lead and slate
54 x 29.5 x 31 cm
Purchased with assistance from the Friends of the Tate Gallery 1997

Jean Fautrier
1898–1964

Tatlin's Tower
In 1919, not long after the Bolshevik Revolution, the People's Commissariat for Enlightenment invited Vladimir Tatlin to design a *Monument to the Third International*. This was to be part of a new propaganda effort to replace the old symbols of Tsarist power and to herald the advent of a 'modern' chapter in the country's history. Tatlin proposed a glass and steel structure, a double helix spiralling around a diagonal axis, 400 metres high, through which visitors would be moved mechanically past giant screens with flashing messages announcing the latest international news. Outstripping the Eiffel Tower as a symbol of nineteenth-century capitalism, Tatlin's dynamic monument was intended to symbolise the triumph of Communism in the twentieth century. Although the design was shelved for cost reasons and the artist eventually died rejected and destitute, 'Tatlin's Tower' became one of the iconic images of early twentieth-century avant-garde art and its utopian dream of making the world a better place. **(ABH)**

Dan Flavin's name has become synonymous with his bold arrangements of fluorescent lights, which engage in an intimate dialogue with their surrounding architectural space. The first of these was *the diagonal of May 25, 1963 (to Constantin Brancusi)*, a simple gold-coloured tube mounted diagonally on the wall. The neutral geometric forms of Flavin's work, its use of serialisation and reliance on standardised, industrially produced materials, have often been associated with the cool, rational aesthetics of Minimalism, as represented by the artist's contemporaries

Carl Andre, Donald Judd and Sol LeWitt. However, Flavin never subscribed to such notions, referring on occasion to his work as 'maximalist' to redress the balance between its economy of means and its visual exuberance.

The immateriality of the light and the ephemeral nature of the tubes invite readings of Flavin's work as spiritual reflections on a transcendental world. While being influenced by his Catholic upbringing and his time in a priesthood seminary, Flavin always rejected such interpretations stating that his art 'is what it is, and it ain't nothin' else … it is very easy to understand'.

The idiosyncratic formula of Flavin's titles – consistently in lower case, and often with 'untitled' followed by a subtitle in parentheses that often describes the work's inspirational trigger – mirrors the sculptures' dynamic between pure abstraction and the specifics of place, time and source. Many of his works make reference to major figures of twentieth-century art including Henri Matisse, Donald Judd, Ad Reinhardt and Vladimir Tatlin, to whom he dedicated his single most sustained series of 'monuments'. **(ABH)**

'Monument' for V. Tatlin
1966–9
Mixed media
305.4 x 58.4 x 8.9 cm
Purchased 1971

Dan Flavin
1933–1996

Fluxus

Fluxus has been variously described as 'the most radical and experimental art movement of the 1960s' and 'a wild goose chase into the zone of everything ephemeral'. Whichever view one takes, there is no doubt that Fluxus had a profound impact on Minimalism, Performance art, Conceptualism and Mail art, greatly influencing, along the way, the development of artists' co-ops, publishing, music, film and video.

The catalyst for Fluxus was the Lithuanian-born American George Maciunas, who studied fine art, graphics, architecture, art history and musicology in New York and Pittsburgh from 1949 to 1960. Fluxus, which was to be the title of a magazine in 1960, was never a movement, but rather a loose collective of over thirty artists, musicians and theorists who, as one key member, George Brecht, said 'had something un-nameable in common'.

Artists associated with Fluxus admired the work of Marcel Duchamp, John Cage, the Dadaists and Futurists, and created art that, to use Charles Baudelaire's phrase, 'contained at once the object and the subject, the world external to the artist and the artist himself'. Maciunas stressed concretism, humour and functionalism as the three main strands underpinning Fluxus. These ideas were brought to life (often in the street or in unusual locations, using whatever material was to hand, not least the audience) through performance, 'concerts' and film screenings as well as through the medium of small publications, where Maciunas would re-interpret an artist's idea to create a cheap multiple to sell to the masses.

One of earliest manifestations of Fluxus in Britain, *The Festival of Misfits*, took place in London from 23 October to 8 November 1962. At Victor Musgrave's influential Gallery One, Ben Vautier lived in the front window, signing everyday objects as works of art, while his artistic collaborators, such as Robert Filliou, Addi Koepcke, Robin Page, Daniel Spoerri and Emmett Williams, created an interactive maze that visitors could explore. These artists, plus Gustav Metzger, also performed at the *Misfits Fair*, an evening concert held at the Institute of Contemporary Arts. The audience included Richard Hamilton and David Hockney. The next major centre for Fluxus activities was Gallery Ten in Blackheath, run by Brian Lane, who emulated Maciunas as an interpreter of artists' ideas producing beautifully made multiples for sale. Lane also enhanced the performative element of Fluxus through innovative concerts from 1968–70, something that was developed more fully by David Mayor in his extensive exhibition *Fluxshoe*, which toured Britain during 1972–3. The work of ten Fluxus artists appeared in this seven-venue show with over forty other British and overseas artists taking part. The material on display at Tate Modern comes from the papers of Musgrave, Lane and Mayor, now housed in the Tate Archive.

Fluxus artists were incredibly innovative. Counting among their number were a founder of video art (Nam June Paik); an early exponent of electronic music (Takehisa Kosugi); an initiator of 'concept art' (Henry Flynt); the creator of 'events' in which participants were instructed to make or perform what was written on cards (George Brecht); the originator of 'intermedia', where the use of two media leads to the creation of a third – for example drawing and poetry leading to visual poetry, or painting and theatre leading to performance art (Dick Higgins); and a developer of interactive installations (Yoko Ono). Fluxus can thus be seen as a way of life, a veritable art lab, that took Duchamp at his word to make the very act of living into a work of art. **(AG)**

Top:
Performance of Philip Corner's *Piano Activities* by (L–R): Emmett Williams, Wolf Vostell, Nam June Paik, Dick Higgins, Ben Patterson and George Maciunas at the 'Fluxus Internationale Festspiele Neuester Musik', Wiesbaden, September 1962
Photo: Hartmut Rekort, Staatsgalerie Stuttgart, Archiv Sohm

Above:
Carla Liss (born 1944)
Travel Fluxkit 1972
Tate Archive

Below:
George Maciunas (1931–1978)
FluXuS (label) *c*.1966
Tate Archive

Fluxus Collective
VTRE, No. 5 (FLUXUS Vacuum TrapEzoid),
March 1965

Spatialism
While teaching at the Academia de Bellas Artes in his native Argentina, the artist Lucio Fontana drafted with his students the *Manifesto Blanco* (White Manifesto), which was to become the foundation of Spatialism (*Spazialismo*) in 1947. It was followed by a series of other manifestos in collaboration with artists and writers issued until 1952.

Spatialism built on the experience of Futurism, an earlier, utopian Italian movement of which Fontana was a great admirer. The idealistic new movement summed up Fontana's ideas about a fresh aesthetic, the central tenet of which was a 'spatial concept of art'. Movement, colour, time and space were to be the elements of the new art, which sought to transcend the established order and move towards a 'fourth dimension'. This would reveal the potential of art and society to pass through to a new era, where science and art would go hand in hand. **(EB)**

Seeking to supersede the limitations that painting and sculpture imposed on art, Lucio Fontana worked passionately towards the definition of a 'spatial concept of art', hence the titling of many of his works as *Concetti Spaziali* (Spatial Concepts). Fontana sought to re-invest art with a dynamic character, with a fourth dimension going beyond time and space, revealing society's inherent potential for new cultural production and for progress. His vision was channelled through the movement of *Spazialismo* (Spatialism) and his experimentation with a variety of media, including sculpture, painting, ceramics and light installations. The most poignant visual translation of his quest, however, were works made in the 1950s and 1960s, in which he intervened in the canvas's surface, making holes (*buchi*, from 1949) and slashes (*tagli*, from 1959). Carefully premeditated and meticulously executed, Fontana's punctured canvases created both a break between the viewer and the painterly surface, and a level beyond it, leading into the infinite void. The hole was, for Fontana, his greatest discovery, a notion of the incomplete or unfinished, a prelude of what was yet to come, offering a passage through to the 'cosmos'. This created a positive expectancy, expressed in the title of a series of works by the word *Attesa* (Waiting).

Fontana's work had a profound, immediate influence on artists such as Piero Manzoni and Jannis Kounellis, and their repercussions can also be traced in contemporary artists' explorations, such as Anish Kapoor's void and Tatsuo Miyajima's temporal infinity. **(EB)**

Left:
Spatial Concept
1949–50
Canvas
55 x 84.6 cm
Purchased with assistance from the Friends of the Tate Gallery 1985

Right:
Spatial Concept 'Waiting'
1960
Canvas
93 x 73 cm
Purchased 1964

Lucio Fontana
1899–1968

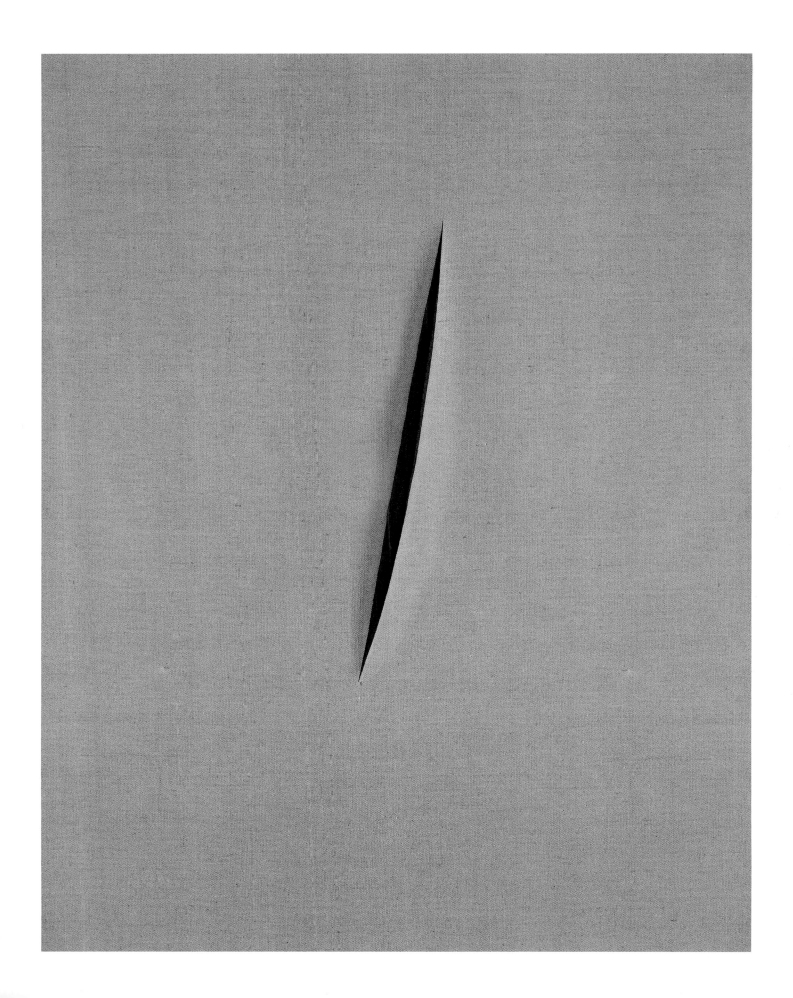

Right:
Giacomo Balla (1871–1958)
*Abstract Speed –
The Car has Passed*
1913
Oil on canvas
50.2 x 65.4 cm
Presented by the Friends
of the Tate Gallery 1970

Below:
Gino Severini (1883–1966)
Suburban Train Arriving in Paris
1915
Oil on canvas
105.1 x 132 cm
Purchased with assistance
from a member of the National
Art Collections Fund 1968

Futurism

The poet and founder of Futurism, Filippo Tommaso Marinetti, was only partly being provocative when he declared: 'Let's kill the moonlight!' His attack was against all romantic notions: from symbolist poetry (through which he had made his name) to the misty-eyed tourism that he felt was strangling his native Italy. In his *The Foundation and Manifesto of Futurism* published in 1909, he attacked the uncritical admiration of the past and found potential instead in the rapid industrialisation that provided a sense of national inventiveness, coherence and modernity. The train, car and plane inspired his boundless admiration for speed and adrenalin-charged action, extending (notoriously) to the declaration of war as 'the world's only hygiene'.

With its genius for provocation, Futurism struck a chord with a whole generation of intellectuals in Italy and beyond, stirring them to radicalism. Most notable among Marinetti's immediate recruits were the painters who signed the *Manifesto of Futurist Painters* in 1910; they included Umberto Boccioni, Carlo Carrà and Gino Severini. Marshalled by the poet, they produced an assault on artistic conventions that only found convincing pictorial form after they had absorbed developments in Paris. As a result, the fragmentary planes of Cubist paintings infused the works in the influential Futurist exhibition that toured Europe in 1912. Unlike Cubist works, however, the shifting experience of modern life was seen in Futurist paintings (much as in Marinetti's poetic *words in freedom*) as dynamic and psychologically charged. In this, the artists were influenced by the philosophy of flux developed by Henri Bergson, giving it form by introducing the 'lines of force' that slice through their compositions. These are evident in the abstracted helixes of Giacomo Balla's studies of a passing car, as well as in Boccioni's sculpture *Unique Forms of Continuity in Space* 1913 (p.76), where planes extend the body into the surrounding space. The idea of mutual interaction was also raised to a wider social level; especially in their riotous performances, the Futurists exploited provocation as a catalyst for change, while they adopted a political position that attacked what they saw as Italy's failed liberal parliamentary system.

It is hardly surprising that the Futurists agitated for Italy's entry into the First World War in 1914. Based on a nationalist rhetoric aimed at the integration of the Italian-speaking lands of Austria-Hungary, they allied themselves with a range of radicals including Benito Mussolini. Success in May 1915 resulted in the Futurists volunteering together, but tragedy was not far off: Boccioni was killed in 1916. Marinetti's genius for organisation ensured that Futurism did not collapse with the war but began to expand into new media: radio, theatre, typography, design. However, the same spirit that had encouraged Balla and Fortunato Depero to propose the *Futurist Reconstruction of the Universe* in 1915 increasingly took on an oppressive tenor in Mussolini's Fascist state of the 1920s. Marinetti enthusiastically supported Fascism, and this association has cast a long shadow over the subsequent appreciation of the movement. **(MG)**

Filippo Tommaso Marinetti
(1876–1944)
Cover of *Zang Tumb Tumb*, 1912
Tate Library

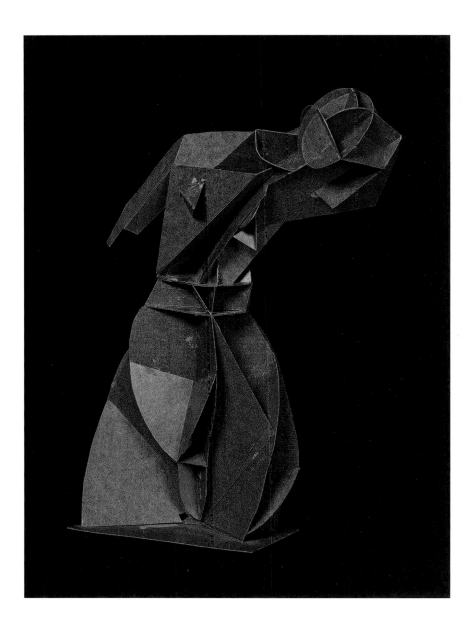

Constructivism
Constructivism is a branch of abstract art founded by Vladimir Tatlin and Alexander Rodchenko in Russia around 1915 and developed by Naum Gabo and his brother Antoine Pevsner. The Constructivists believed that art should reflect the modern world – in method, materials and form. Tatlin was influenced by Picasso's Cubist constructions, which he saw in his Paris studio in 1913. These were three-dimensional still lifes made of scrap materials. Tatlin began to make his own, but they were completely abstract and made of industrial materials. Gabo and Pevsner had also been impressed with Cubism as Gabo's *Model for 'Constructed Torso'* 1917 demonstrates. In 1920 the brothers issued 'The Realistic Manifesto', which outlined the formal aims and aesthetic principals of their constructive technique, as well as articulating the importance of space and time in their art. This manifesto is a refusal of the more utilitarian tendencies in Tatlin's work and theories. Constructivism was suppressed in Russia in the 1920s but was brought to Western Europe by Gabo and Pevsner in the 1930s. **(RL)**

Naum Gabo's interests in science and engineering – space, time, movement and construction – are explored in his sculptures. He employed intersecting solid or strung planes to represent form and volume – a technique developed in line with the Constructivist theories developed with his contemporaries in Russia in the early decades of the twentieth century. Gabo was one of the earliest artists to experiment with kinetic or moving sculpture and his innovative use of man-made, opaque, translucent and transparent materials results in spatial interplay, refracting the light and allowing multiple viewpoints. Gabo used a reduced range of colours – reds, blacks, whites and yellows – which contrasted with the industrial materials he employed.

Many of the maquettes in Tate's collection were given to the gallery on Gabo's death and were reconstructed from component parts found in his attic. These small-scale models were often for monumental public schemes in which sculpture and architecture came together. However, they were rarely realised.

Throughout his life Gabo associated himself with and influenced various circles of artists and artistic movements, moving from Russia to Denmark and Norway at the outset of the First World War, then to Berlin and England, where he stayed for ten years before he left for the United States in 1946. Here he taught at Harvard and eventually died an American citizen. In later years and particularly while in Cornwall from 1939, he began to work with more traditional materials and methods such as stone-carving and print-making. **(RL)**

Naum Gabo
1890–1977

Far left:
Red Cavern
c.1926
Plastic, cork, metal and wood
66 x 51.4 x 27.9 cm
Presented by the artist 1977

Left:
Model for 'Constructed Torso'
1917, reassembled 1981
Cardboard
39.5 x 29 x 16 cm
Accepted by H.M. Government in lieu of tax and allocated to the Tate Gallery 1995

Existentialism
The Existential philosophy of Jean-Paul Sartre, which centred around notions of anguish, abandonment, despair and isolation, influenced a generation of post-war intellectuals and artists. Sartre was good friends with Giacometti whose sculpture *Four Figurines on a Base* 1950/1965, cast *c*.1965–6, exemplifies the key Existentialist sentiments of alienation and loneliness. It relates to Giacometti's memory of four naked women in a brothel in Paris. The tiny size of the figures and the heavy base with sloping sides, which suggests a receding floor, recreates the sense of distance and confrontation experienced by the artist. 'The distance which separated us, the polished floor, seemed insurmountable in spite of my desire to cross it', Giacometti recollected. **(SH)**

'I didn't want to create a figure that looked realistic on the outside, but wanted to experience life and to create only those forms that really affected me', Giacometti said. Born in Switzerland, he moved to Paris in 1920 and quickly became part of avant-garde circles. His early sculptural work was concerned with the uncanny and the erotic and he became an active member of the Surrealist group from 1930 to 1935. It was not until the late 1940s that he started to make the tall, emaciated figures for which he has become best known. These were achieved through an obsessive process of building up the clay, only to cut it away again in an attempt to reach an inner essence. To many observers, these pieces, isolated and strangely remote, seem like metaphors for the disconnected human condition of the modern age. But Giacometti tended to deny the expressive quality in his work. He was always insistent that his art derived from his determination to convey how we perceive the world around us. He often repeated the same subjects over and over again, and asked only those closest to him to be his models, including his brother Diego, who is the subject of the bust shown here. Giacometti's sculptural figures are typically fragmentary, their slender, emaciated forms conveying a vivid but fragile human presence. The French writer Jean Genet commented: 'The resemblance of his figures to each other seems to me to represent that precious point at which human beings are confronted with the most irreducible fact: the loneliness of being exactly equivalent to all others.' **(SH)**

Alberto Giacometti
1901–1966

Far left:
Bust of Diego
1955
Bronze
56.5 x 32 x 14.5 cm
Purchased with assistance from the Friends of the Tate Gallery 1965

Centre:
Standing Woman
1948–9
Bronze
168 x 15.9 x 34 cm
Presented by the artist 1965

Right:
Jean Genet
1954 or 1955
Oil on canvas
65.3 x 54.3 cm
Accepted by H.M. Government in lieu of tax and allocated to the Tate Gallery 1987

Left:
Drains
1990
Pewter
9.4 x 9.4 x 4.2 cm
Purchased 1992

Right:
Untitled 1989–92
Wood, wax, leather,
cotton and human hair
30 x 16 x 51.5 cm
Purchased 1992

 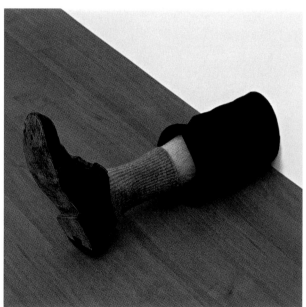

Robert Gober's sculptures and installations take an uncanny look at the desires and fears we project onto everyday objects. His practice has involved meticulously hand-crafting replicas of mass-produced objects including doors, cots and newspapers. These often have a particular metaphorical or biographical resonance for Gober, obliquely referring to his personal history and identity as a gay man in contemporary America.

Untitled 1989–92, a severed leg extending from the gallery wall, is both comic and horrible. The hyperrealism of the leg extends to the sock and shoe on the foot and the real human hairs embedded in the surface of the 'skin'.

Drains 1990 is a handmade copy of a sinkhole installed in the gallery wall. Taking an everyday object out of its ordinary context is a strategy that owes a debt to Surrealism, and the series of works that Gober made in the late 1980s and early 1990s referencing plumbing paraphernalia recalls Marcel Duchamp's infamous *Fountain* 1917 (p.104). However Gober's repeated use of sink and drain imagery suggests a more sustained interest in the political and psychological implications of the pursuit of hygiene in the Western world. *Drains* was made at the height of the AIDS crisis in America and Western Europe. The drain suggests an underworld of bodily fluids and effluvia beneath even the most meticulously cleaned surfaces and may be read as an indictment of the attempts by some political factions to stigmatise the disease at the time. The plug hole also suggests the anus, a point that marks the distinction between the inside and outside of the human body, a site of discharge and of desire. **(RT)**

Robert Gober
born 1954

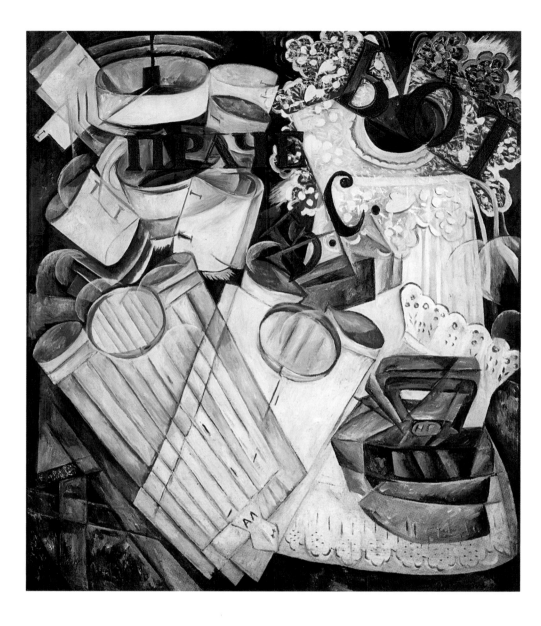

Linen
1913
Oil on canvas
95.6 x 83.8 cm
Presented by Eugène Mollo
and the artist 1953

A leading artist of the early twentieth-century Russian avant-garde, Natalya Goncharova oscillates in her work between the neo-primitive and intensely modern. She was interested in traditional Russian art forms, including iconography, folk art, needlework and popular Russian prints known as *lubki*. She was also influenced, however, by exposure to the paintings of her French contemporaries, including Cézanne, and became concerned with the analysis of form, adopting a style related to Cubism. Together with her lifelong partner and collaborator, the artist Mikhail Larionov, she founded the Rayonist movement, a synthesis of Cubism, Futurism and Orphism. Like the Impressionists, the Rayonists were interested in newly developing scientific theories of vision.

Specifically, their works were concerned with the refraction of light off objects, and they strove to make the painted subject appear to be formed from rays of coloured light.

Dominated by dynamic angles and blocks of harmonious colour, Goncharova's painting *Linen* 1913 is characteristic of her experiments with the beginnings of abstraction and interest in colour and form during this period. The composition bears a resemblance to Cubist collage, featuring shifting viewpoints and segments of Cyrillic text, the most complete of which, *Prache…*, is the beginning of the Russian word for laundry. The gendered underclothes depicted in the work can be read as a symbolic representation of her relationship with Larionov. Often dressing in men's clothing, Goncharova strove to blur the boundaries between masculine and feminine. She held little concern for social conventions, and controversially lived with Larionov out of wedlock, until marrying him late in her life.

While continuing to paint after moving to Paris in 1917, she also worked as an illustrator and became well known as a costume and set designer for classical ballets. **(MB)**

Natalya Goncharova
1881–1962

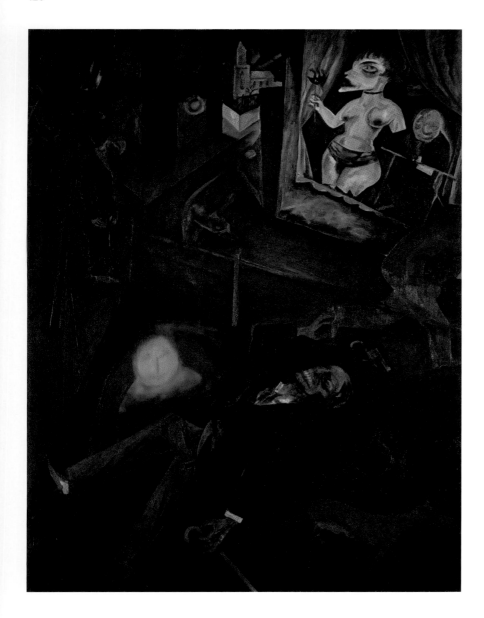

Suicide
1916
Oil on canvas
100 x 77.5 cm
Purchased with assistance
from the National Art
Collections Fund 1976

George Grosz chronicled the corruption and seedy excesses of Berlin during and after the First World War. In his paintings and lithographs, he presented caricatures of snouted, schnapps-swilling officers, prostitutes and sneering capitalists indulging their base pleasures, while maimed veterans beg in the background.

Although born in Berlin in 1893, Grosz grew up in rural Pomerania. He studied in Dresden and Berlin, and spent a few months in Paris. When the First World War broke out, he joined up, but was rapidly disillusioned. Shortly afterwards he was declared unfit and returned to Berlin. Grosz's loathing of the war radicalised his outlook, and his work was filled with contempt for German society. He even anglicised his name from Georg to George to distance himself from his homeland.

Grosz's bitterness is clearly reflected in the red-steeped nightmare of *Suicide* 1916. The painting's intensity and distortions are related to Expressionism, but its portrayal of individual despair is linked to a broader vision of society: a grotesque prostitute and her businessman client survey the street from a window, a criminal scampers away, while far in the background a corrupted church hovers over the scene.

After the war, Grosz became a political cartoonist for a series of left-wing journals, and continued to unleash his bile on the Weimar Republic. Although his tone softened in the late 1920s, he still found himself prosecuted for blasphemy after drawing Christ wearing a gas mask on the cross. In 1933, two weeks before Hitler became Chancellor, he left for New York, taking US citizenship in 1938. He returned to live in Berlin in 1959, but died just a few weeks later. **(SB)**

George Grosz
1893–1959

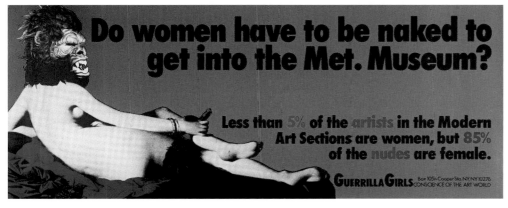

Feminism
Feminist art practice emerged in the 1960s, informed by the radical politics of the Women's Liberation Movement, as well as the Civil Rights, anti-war and students' rights movements. It operated alongside and interpenetrated the radical aesthetics of Pop and Conceptual art, Performance and body art, photography and experimental film and video. From the 1970s to the present day, feminist art history has played a major role in reminding audiences of overlooked and forgotten women artists, and has criticised museums, galleries and other institutions for favouring male artists at the expense of female practitioners. In the 1970s, under the influence of psychoanalytical and poststructuralist theory, female artists such as Jenny Holzer, Cindy Sherman and Barbara Kruger started making works that interrogated the complex relationships between gender, power and representation.

Feminism can now be seen to have had a profound influence on the landscape of late-twentieth- and twenty-first-century art. Yet the need for feminist art practice, like the work of the Guerrilla Girls, continues undiminished, since many issues of inequality with regard to race, age, class, sexuality and disability remain within the art world. **(ED)**

The Guerrilla Girls formed as an anonymous activist group in 1984 to be the 'conscience of the art world', and in particular to protest about sexual discrimination within that field. The initial impetus for their actions was an exhibition in 1984 at the Museum of Modern Art, New York, entitled *International Survey of Painting and Sculpture*, which purported to be an up-to-the minute snapshot of the contemporary art scene, yet from a total of 169 artists featured, only thirteen were women. The Guerrilla Girls hide their real identities behind gorilla masks for public appearances and interviews, and have adopted as pseudonyms the names of deceased female artists and writers such as Kathë Kollwitz, Frida Kahlo and Gertrude Stein, an act that also helps keep these figures in the public consciousness.

The Guerrilla Girls' first public actions in 1985 took the form of acerbic fly-posters, which they pasted up over night in the fashionable New York art district of SoHo. Their ironic use of the language of advertising – like other artists in New York at that time such as Barbara Kruger and Jenny Holzer – exposed some shocking imbalances in the fortunes of male and female artists. Their first targets were their fellow artists and gallerists, but they soon moved on to critique museums, art magazines and other cultural institutions, widening their attacks to expose art-world racism and sexism, as well as other areas of social, racial and gender-based injustice and inequality. *Guerrilla Girls Talk Back* 1985–90 is a portfolio of thirty of these early poster works. One of the best-known, *Do women have to be naked to get into the Met. Museum?*, shows the famous image of Ingres's naked Odalisque sporting a gorilla mask, while the text exposes the lack of women artists versus the preponderance of naked female models on display in the museum. The work first appeared in the form of advertisements on New York City buses, paid for by the Guerrilla Girls themselves, until the bus company cancelled their leasing agreement on the grounds of indecency. **(ED)**

From *Guerrilla Girls Talk Back*
1985–90
Screenprints on paper
43 x 56 cm
28 x 71 cm
Purchased from Jim Kempner Fine Art, New York
(General Funds) 2003

Guerrilla Girls

Philip Guston's career was an impassioned tug-of-war between abstract and figurative painting. Having established himself as one of the leading Abstract Expressionists, he seemed to turn his back on the movement in the late 1960s with his grotesque, bleakly humorous images of isolated objects, disembodied limbs and hooded Ku Klux Klansmen puffing on cigars. Yet this apparently radical shift in his work was, in many ways, a return to his artistic roots.

As a young man in the 1930s, Guston had painted Social Realist murals that reflected the political turmoil of America during the Depression. Living in New York in the 1940s, he came to reject figurative painting. His early abstract paintings were composed of shimmering combinations of short vertical and horizontal brushstrokes in pinks, reds and blues. Gradually, solid forms began to re-emerge, even in a painting as apparently abstract as *The Return* 1956–8. Guston said that the forms were like figures who had been away for some time and who were now returning – jostling each other a little in the process.

With America torn apart by the Civil Rights struggle and protests against the Vietnam War, Guston began to see abstraction as a kind of escapism, shrinking away from the turbulence of contemporary life. He developed a satirical, cartoon-like style by drawing the people and things around him: books, shoes, hands, ashtrays. In his paintings, however, his evident pleasure in depicting 'tangible things' is tempered by a mood of grim anxiety, and familiar objects can become enigmatic or sinister. **(SB)**

Philip Guston
1913–1980

Left:
The Return
1956–8
Oil on canvas
178.1 x 199.1 cm
Purchased 1959

Below:
Hat
1976
Oil on canvas
203.2 x 292.1 cm
Presented by the American Fund
for the Tate Gallery, courtesy of
a private collector 1996

From the late 1940s Richard Hamilton pioneered an art that explored aspects of the environment hitherto largely disregarded by art, and which did so in new ways. In particular, he looked at the burgeoning popular and consumer culture of the post Second World War period, stemming from the USA. In 1957 he produced a famous definition of 'Pop Art' (by which he meant at that time, 'popular culture'): 'Popular (designed for a mass audience).

Transient (short term solution). Expendable (easily forgotten). Low cost. Mass produced. Young (aimed at youth). Witty. Sexy. Gimmicky. Glamorous. Big business.' He proposed to make art with these qualities – all of them anathema to accepted notions of what art should be. The works that he produced are now seen as among the first important manifestations of what by the early 1960s had become known as Pop art and which went on to become a major phenomenon in the USA and Britain, with a parallel movement in Europe under the name of New Realism. Hamilton's early Pop works are complex, allusive and witty, both celebrating their subjects and analysing them. In *Hommage à Chrysler Corp.* 1957, metal foil and other materials are combined with oil paint to create an image based on Chrysler car advertisements. A glamour model caresses the car; she is represented by her bra cup, voluptuous lips and bodily curves, blending with those of the car. The mix of formal complexity and a high degree of abstraction, while never losing sight of the source material, became a key characteristic of the best Pop art. **(SW)**

Towards a definitive statement on the coming trends in men's wear and accessories (a) Together let us explore the stars
1962
Oil, cellulose paint and collage on wood
61 x 81.3 cm
Purchased 1964

Richard Hamilton
born 1922

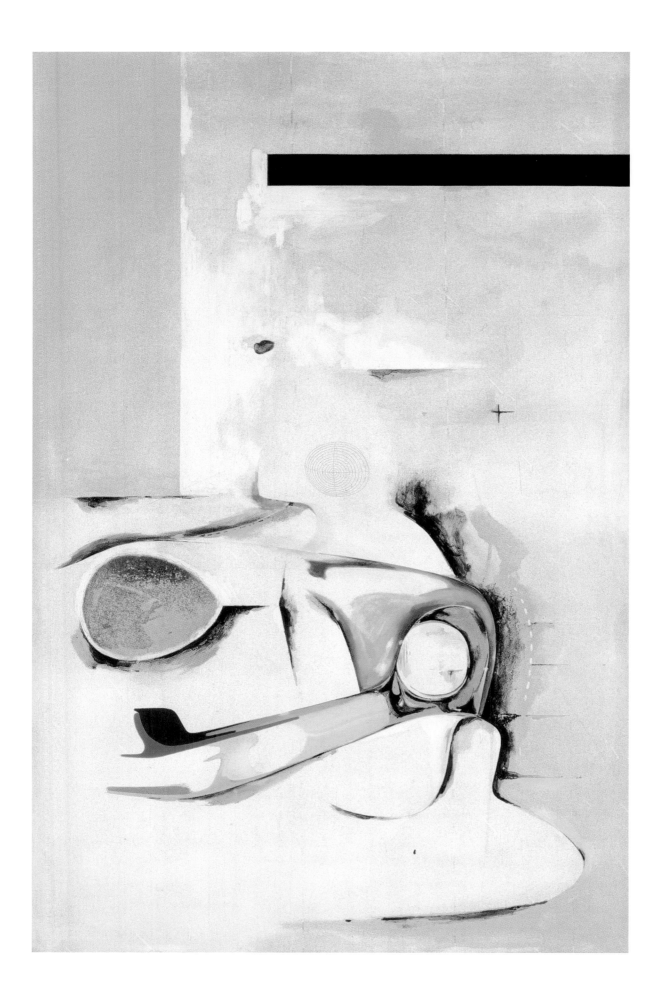

Independent Group

Richard Hamilton was not alone in his interest in popular culture as a subject for serious art. In 1952 he and others formed the Independent Group (IG) within the Institute of Contemporary Art in London (ICA), as a forum for the discussion and promotion of the new approach. The IG included many architects as well as artists. The principal figures beside Hamilton were the artists Nigel Henderson, Eduardo Paolozzi, Victor Pasmore and William Turnbull, and the architects Theo Crosby, Colin St John Wilson, Alison and Peter Smithson, and James Stirling. The architectural and design historian Rayner Banham was also a member of the group. The IG held its first meetings through the winter of 1952–3, and another season took place in 1954–5. At the first meeting, Paolozzi gave a now famous lecture in which he simply projected a large number of images from advertising, the covers of Sci-Fi magazines, comics and the like. Discussions took place on a high intellectual level, and an important influence on the development of Pop art was that of Marcel Duchamp, transmitted through Hamilton. In 1965–6, in collaboration with Duchamp, Hamilton built a replica of his damaged iconic work *The Bride Stripped Bare by Her Bachelors, Even* 1915–23 (p.105). In 1956 the IG organised a ground-breaking exhibition, *This is Tomorrow*, at the Whitechapel Gallery in London. For the poster, Hamilton made what is now seen as perhaps the founding work of Pop art, his collage *Just what is it that makes today's homes so different so appealing?* **(SW)**

Hommage à Chrysler Corp.
1957
Oil, metal foil and
collage on wood
122 x 81 cm
Purchased with assistance
from the National Art Collections
Fund and the Friends of the
Tate Gallery 1995

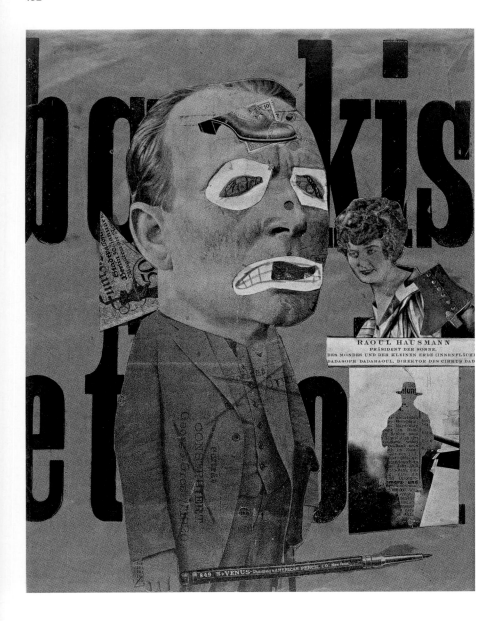

Austrian-born Raoul Hausmann was a founder member of the Berlin Dadaists, whose other members included George Grosz, Hannah Höch and John Heartfield. He was engaged with a diverse range of practices including painting, fashion design, poetry, pamphleteering and publishing. However, he is most celebrated for his innovations in photomontage – combined fragments of photographs and typography often cut from magazines or newspapers. Hausmann defined the power of photomontage as lying in 'its contrast of structure and dimension, rough against smooth, aerial photograph against close-up, perspective against flat surface'. He used the potential for contradiction and paradox afforded by the new medium to lampoon what he saw as the conservativism of contemporary politics, the mass media and the world of fashion. In *The Art Critic* 1919–20 Hausmann vents his biting wit on an archetypal bourgeois critic. The roughly superimposed eyes and mouth suggest that the critic sees with someone else's eyes and speaks with someone else's mouth, while the fragment of a German banknote behind his neck unambiguously suggests financial motivations. Hausmann once said that the average German 'has no more capabilities than those which chance has glued on the outside of his skull; his brain remains empty', a judgement that clearly informed this work and many others by the satirist. **(SH)**

The Art Critic
1919–20
Lithograph and photographic
collage on paper
31.8 x 25.4 cm
Purchased 1974

Raoul Hausmann
1886–1971

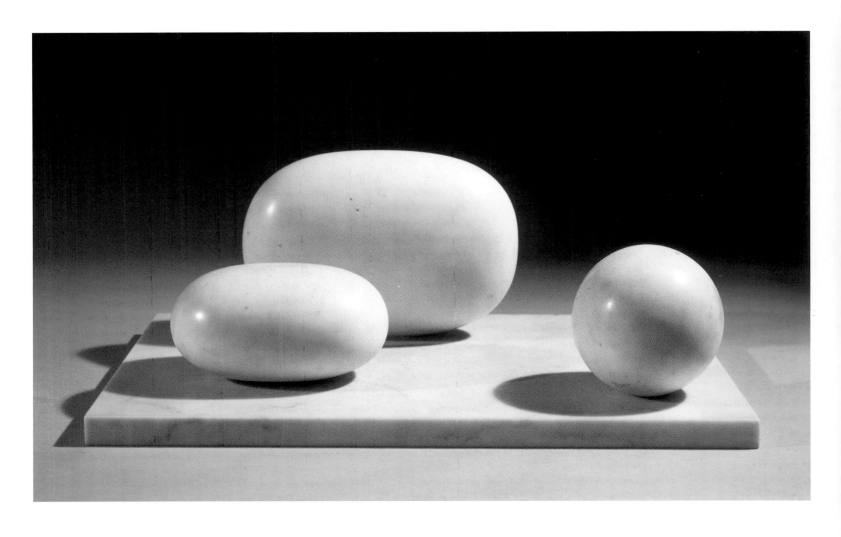

Barbara Hepworth was born in Yorkshire and trained at Leeds School of Art and then from 1921 at the Royal College of Art in London. Following Jacob Epstein, she and her contemporary Henry Moore, also from Yorkshire, became twin pioneers of modern sculpture in Britain. From the mid-1920s Hepworth began to make sculptures of the human, usually female figure, adopting the approach of direct carving (i.e. without a preliminary model) introduced by Constantin Brancusi and in Britain, Epstein. With this went the doctrine of truth to materials, and these works and their successors were made from alabaster, marble, pink ancaster stone, ironstone, African blackwood, rosewood, mahogany, yew and many others. Delicately carved, these sculptures, up to 1934, nevertheless pulse with powerful instinctual feeling and deploy sexual and procreative imagery embodied in increasingly abstract but highly sensual, biomorphic forms, revealing the beauty of the material. In 1931 Hepworth had begun a passionate relationship with the painter Ben Nicholson. In 1934 she gave birth to triplets and she and Nicholson were married shortly afterwards. *Three Forms* 1935 is one of two similar sculptures that were the first she made after recovering from the births and has inevitably been related to her triplets. However, it marks the beginning of a more purely abstract phase of her art, in which she was preoccupied with form itself and the relationships of forms in space. In 1939 she and Nicholson settled in St Ives in Cornwall and her abstract forms became imbued with the spirit of the landscape and seascape of West Cornwall. But her work continued to embrace a human dimension: 'I was the figure in the landscape and every sculpture … contained the ever-changing forms and contours embodying my own response to that landscape.' *Figure (Nanjizal)* 1958 perfectly represents this. **(SW)**

Three Forms
1935
Serravezza marble
21 x 53.2 x 34.3 cm
Presented by Mr and Mrs J.R.
Marcus Brumwell 1964

Barbara Hepworth
1903–1975

WIELICZKA
SALT
MINE

LA MANO PODEROSA

INSIGHT	EYESIGHT
discernment or understanding; penetration; intuition; immediate apprehension or cognition	eyesight; seeing; act of looking; mental view; judgement; observation; scrutiny
the act or fact of seeing or contemplating something not actually present to the eye; mystical or prophetic foresight or understanding; revelation	the action of seeing with the bodily-eye; the exercise of the physical faculty of sight
power or activity of the imagination; inwit	ocular perception
wisdom; intelligence; knowledge	look; view; glimpse; glance; observation

Cabinets of Curiosities

Cabinets of curiosities (also known as *Wunderkammer* or wonder-rooms) were popular in Europe in the sixteenth and seventeenth centuries. These 'cabinets' were in fact usually room-sized collections of natural phenomena collected during overseas expeditions and believed at the time to be rare or marvellous examples of God's creation. Often, they contained a bizarre mix of fact and fiction. For example, the famous curiosity cabinet of Ole Worm, a seventeenth-century Danish physician and antiquary, contained a Scythian lamb, a wooly plant that was thought to be a fabulous sheep-like creature. With its attempt at an encyclopaedic collection of all things, the cabinet of curiosities is often seen as a precursor to the nineteenth-century museum of natural history or other modern-day museums. Collections such as Worm's were, of course, entirely dependent upon the funds and interests of those who were privileged enough to create them.

Artists such as the Surrealist Joseph Cornell, or most recently Mark Dion or Damien Hirst, have created their own small-scale 'cabinets of wonder', revealing an ongoing fascination with the human desire to explore, collect, categorise, name, sort or preserve elements of the world around us – activities that Susan Hiller believes are as intrinsic to the act of making and viewing art as they are to the disciplines of psychoanalysis or archaeology. **(AC)**

Susan Hiller was born in the United States, where she carried out fieldwork during her studies in archaeology and anthropology, before moving to London in 1967. Becoming disillusioned with the disciplines in which she trained, in particular their claims to objectivity, she turned to art as a means to express a more subjective vision. However, her academic background remains evident in many of the works she has produced throughout the last thirty years. Her art often incorporates existing cultural artefacts that have been sorted or classified in some way. *Dedicated to the Unknown Artists* 1972–6 consists of 305 postcards of rough sea views, collected by the artist and accompanied by charts and notes exploring the linguistic and visual descriptions of the seas. Using words and images from both high art and popular culture and a variety of media, Hiller explores ideas about gender, desire, language and memory. Much of her work also relates to her fascination with the unconscious and to 'unnatural phenomena'. Her major installation *Belshazzar's Feast, The Writing on Your Wall* 1983–4 makes reference to the Old Testament account of the appearance of mysterious signs or writings on the wall of Belshazzar, the King of Babylon. Exploring ideas of transmission and interpretation, the installation was also inspired by newspaper stories that the artist had read about ghost images appearing on television.

The carefully labelled archaeological collecting boxes in Hiller's *From the Freud Museum* 1991–6 bring together her collection of private relics and souvenirs. The work was developed after she was invited to create an exhibition at the former London home of the psychoanalyst Sigmund Freud, himself a collector of ethnographic art and artefacts. While Freud's collection reveals much about the accepted taste and cultural preconceptions of his time, Hiller has called her own a deliberate 'archive of misunderstandings, crises and ambivalences'. **(AC)**

Susan Hiller
born 1940

Above and left (detail):
From the Freud Museum
1991–6
Mixed media
220 x 1000 x 60 cm
Purchased 1998

Pharmacy
1992
Mixed media
Purchased 1996

YBA
YBA stands for Young British Artists, a group that emerged in the late 1980s and shook the foundations of British art. The group received public attention for the first time with the *Freeze* exhibition, curated by Damien Hirst, while he was still a student at Goldsmiths College in London. Attended by most of the YBAs and renowned for its influential teachers, such as Michael Craig-Martin, Goldsmiths had in previous years already been shaping new ideas and promoting new forms of cultural production. An overall characteristic of the YBAs was a consistently maintained openness towards the media of art and the form that it could take.

The YBAs came to prominence with a series of exhibitions held at the Saatchi gallery, then housed in a converted factory building in north London. Charles Saatchi subsequently became the most dedicated patron and collector of Britart, as the work of the YBAs was dubbed. The group gained intense media attention and some of them developed their art in tandem with their public personae. They also fostered a new interest in artist-curated shows in disused industrial spaces, something which became a trend in the 1990s and profoundly influenced the making of exhibitions in the following years. **(EB)**

Damien Hirst's work is imbued with his constant preoccupation with life, death, truth, love and art itself. He has, since his graduation from Goldsmiths College in 1989, pushed the boundaries of art, science and the media. A tiger shark suspended in a formaldehyde-filled glass case, the hatching and decay of butterflies, lifeless animals carefully arranged in vitrines and abstract paintings generated by machines, are only some of the means Hirst has employed to express the anxiety surrounding human existence.

Medicine and its by-products is a favourite theme for Hirst, who views it as the agent of resistance to death, our almost desperate attempt to control and temporarily postpone the end. *Pharmacy* 1992 combines much of his trademark elements with the breadth and impressiveness of a large-scale installation. The sterile environment, which emulates a real chemist's shop, envelops the viewer, who is confronted with unquestionably factual symbols – reminders of the unavoidable, such as the prominently suspended fly-zapper in the middle of the room.

The most notorious figure of the YBA generation, Hirst has cunningly interlinked his media-supported celebrity image with his art, thus offering a contemporary continuation of the tradition established by artists such as Salvador Dalí and Andy Warhol. Owing his debt to Francis Bacon, Donald Judd and Joseph Beuys, amongst others, Hirst has developed a signature art that has branded him as one of the most famous, or infamous, contemporary British artists. **(EB)**

Damien Hirst
born 1965

Jenny Holzer is one of a number of artists who emerged in New York in the late 1970s and early 1980s, whose neo-Conceptual stance had a strongly political intent, interrogating the true nature of art, and using appropriation and irony to examine the power structures and myths of late twentieth-century capitalism. She adopted the language-based practice of her male Conceptual art predecessors, but disseminated her texts as messages via the same means employed by advertising, and co-opted the latest developments in technology as her media. She started making her *Truisms* in 1977, when she first arrived in New York, collecting nearly 300 aphorisms or slogans. Initially these infiltrated the public realm as anonymous stickers, appearing on T-shirts or posters. Later she began using electronic media, blazing her messages across the enormous Spectacolor billboard in Times Square, New York, in 1982. By 1984 LED strips had become her hallmark.

Truisms 1984 suggests the world of Big Brother predicted by George Orwell in the novel *Nineteen Eighty-Four*, both the messages and their means of delivery mimicking the authoritative voices of capitalism or mass entertainment. The texts carefully remain gender neutral, the politics or identity of the presumed author or authors being ambiguous, and the sentiments expressed often contradictory. The series raises the matter of social control, and how the unconscious is bombarded every day by subliminal messages and instructions. **(ED)**

Truisms
1984
Metal, plastic and electronic components
16.9 x 153.9 x 16.2 cm
Purchased by the Patrons of New Art through the Friends of the Tate Gallery 1985

Jenny Holzer
born 1950

Performance Art
The term 'Performance Art' denotes work that foregrounds the presence of the live body, often employing a combination of movement, music and theatrical settings, performed in front of a live audience. It has its roots in the provocative Futurist and Dada cabarets of the early twentieth century. These are often regarded as the origins of the genre that developed into Allen Kaprow's Happenings and Fluxus events of the 1950s in New York and Europe. Taking place simultaneously in Europe were Yves Klein's *Anthropometries* – paintings made with the 'living brushes' of nude women covered in blue paint, Piero Manzoni's live models signed as sculpture, and the masochistic body art of the Vienna Aktionists, while in Japan, the experimental work of the Gutai group centred around live performances. By the early 1970s performance had evolved into a primary means for artists to make work that resisted the commodification of art in the commercial gallery system. Its increased popularity in America and Europe during the late 1960s and early 1970s also coincided with the emancipation of the individual from obsolete moral and social conventions.

Key artists associated with performance at this time include Marina Abramovic, Vito Acconci, Yoko Ono, Chris Burden, Rebecca Horn, Ana Mendieta, Bruce Nauman and Gina Pane. Historical examples of the genre include the experimental practice of Yvonne Rainer or Carolee Schneeman at the Judson Theater in New York in the 1960s, and in the following decade the 'living sculptures' of Gilbert & George, the 'Actions' of Joseph Beuys, such as *I like America and America Likes Me* or the combination of live presence and video playback in the work of Joan Jonas. **(CW)**

The German artist Rebecca Horn is well known for surreal, kinetic sculptures and installations, as well as drawings, performances, film and photography, made since the late 1960s. Her work explores the relationships between nature, culture and technology and revolves around recurrent metaphors and motifs such as fragility, alchemy and metamorphosis. A lung condition contracted in 1968 had a profound impact on her practice. A subsequent period of convalescence at a sanatorium inspired a series of sculptures concerned with the body, isolation and vulnerability, using materials reminiscent of bandages and prostheses to make body-extension sculptures.

Horn's sculpture employs a broad vocabulary of objects and materials ranging from the organic – eggs, feathers, butterfly wings – to found items – violins, books or a pair of binoculars. She incorporates liquids such as paint and water, and minerals such as mercury, salt and sulphur into the drawings and assemblages. Mechanical apparatus is frequently used to animate and bind these elements, often appearing to be broken and halting, lending the pieces a melancholic, anthropomorphic quality. The kinetic sculptures relate to her earliest performances in which she considered the ways in which bodily movement might be restricted by costumes and appendages of her own design, and yet might be lent symbolic significance, with references to mythological creatures such as the unicorn.

Work from recent years includes *The Raven's Twin* 1997, a motorised construction displaying two sets of black feathers, and *Book of Ashes* 2002, made as a response to 9/11, in which a golden rod seems to trace words in ash on a mirrored plinth. **(CW)**

Rebecca Horn
born 1944

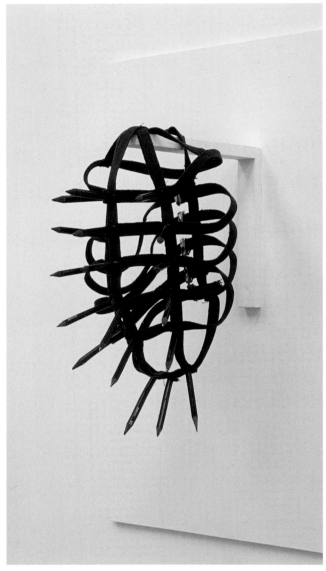

Far left:
Scratching Both Walls at Once
1974–5
Fabric, wood and painted metal
Each 7 x 173.5 x 4.5 cm
Purchased with assistance
from Tate Members 2002

Left:
Finger Gloves
1972
Wood, fabric and metal
33.5 x 96.5 x 35.5 cm
Purchased with assistance
from Tate Members 2002

Above:
Pencil Mask 1972
Mixed media
34.5 x 36.5 x 33 cm
Purchased with assistance
from Tate Members 2002

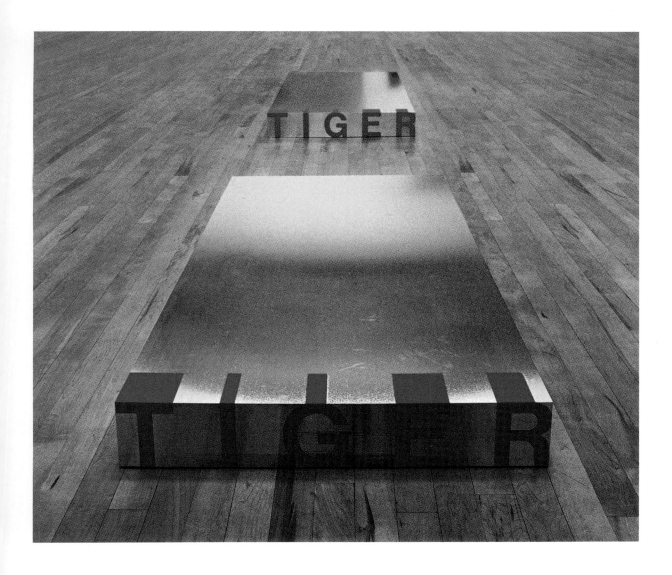

Over the past thirty years Roni Horn has produced drawings, photographs, sculptures, essays and books, in which she seeks to challenge our perceptions and to offer experiences on a range of levels, and to actively engage the viewer with the work. For her sculptures she has often used plain, geometric forms, which is why her work has been linked to that of Minimal artists such as Donald Judd and Sol LeWitt. However, in Minimalism sculpture is seen in terms of space, whereas for Horn it represents the 'physicality of a symbol'.

Nature and language are her principal interests, and symbolism, mythology and metaphor are central to her work. In *Thicket no.2* 1990 two solid, polished aluminium rectangles are embedded with yellow plastic letters which refer to William Blake's words 'Tyger tyger burning bright' from *Songs of Innocence and of Experience*. The poem appears to refer to the Creation and to extol the Creator: 'What immortal hand or eye/Dare frame thy fearful symmetry?' Horn has been working with paired objects since 1980. For her, presenting identical objects in pairs is not about geometrical symmetry, but a way of exploring identity and difference. Horn has said that her interest in pairings, as well as the way in which she explores so many different idioms, relates to her own androgyny. **(EB)**

Thicket No.2
1990, reconstructed 1999
Aluminium and plastic
11.5 x 66 x 367.7 cm
Presented by Janet Wolfson de Botton 1996

Roni Horn
born 1955

0 through 9
1961
Oil on canvas
137.2 x 104.8 cm
Presented by the Friends
of the Tate Gallery 1961

'I tend to like things that already exist', Jasper Johns has said of his subject matter. A leading figure of American Pop art, he is known for using maps, flags, targets, numbers, and other iconic and instantly recognisable subjects as the basis of his paintings, prints and sculptures. He was influenced early in his career by Marcel Duchamp's 'readymades' – found objects presented as works of art – and has consistently undermined conventional ideas of artistic originality by borrowing existing imagery from popular culture and other artists. His work combines simplicity and contradiction, and is best understood in relation to his love of poetry, psychology and philosophy, particularly the work of Ludwig Wittgenstein. 'Sometimes I see it and then paint it. Other times I paint it and then see it', he has remarked.

0 through 9 1961 is a highly characteristic work. Johns let the process of superimposing the sequence of numbers 0 to 9 dictate the structure of the painting. This allowed him to concentrate on the material qualities of the paint, building up a rich and complex surface as if making an abstract work. Johns's life-long interest in processes of mark-making have also informed his extensive output in screen printing, lithography and etching. In printmaking he found a medium whose emphasis on repetition suited both his interest in popular imagery and his love of experimentation. He is now recognised as one of the most innovative printmakers of the late twentieth century. **(SH)**

Jasper Johns
born 1930

Donald Judd began making three-dimensional objects in order to pursue his interest in volume, space and colour. Rejecting the traditional European values of composition and representation, he wanted to eradicate all trace of the artist's hand, and was one of the first artists to have his work industrially manufactured. Concentrating on a limited number of forms, strikingly rendered in contrasting materials and colours, Judd created an astonishing range of visual effects.

In *Untitled* 1972 the austerity of form is in marked contrast to the sensuous effect of light hitting the red enamel base and reflecting on the copper interior walls of the open box structure. By encouraging concentration on the volume and presence of the structure, as well as the space around it, Judd's work draws attention to the relationship between the object, the viewer, and its environment.

In the 1980s Judd began to make works composed of metal units bolted together. In most of these pieces the individual components are enamelled in intense colours, which Judd carefully arranged so that no two components of the same colour would adjoin each other. Some formed large-scale floor pieces, whilst other smaller works such as *Untitled (DJ 85-51)* 1985 were designed to be hung at a specific height on the wall. *Untitled* 1989, Tate's floor piece, is one of a number of works of identical shape and size, but the only one entirely composed of galvanised iron.

Judd also engaged with philosophy, architecture, design and politics. His extensive writing and legacy of work has greatly influenced succeeding generations of artists and designers. **(HS)**

Untitled (DJ 85-51)
1985
Painted aluminium
30 x 300 x 30 cm
Presented by Janet Wolfson de Botton 1996

Donald Judd
1928–1994

Untitled
1972
Copper, enamel and aluminium
91.6 x 155.5 x 178.2 cm
Presented by the American Fund
for the Tate Gallery 1992

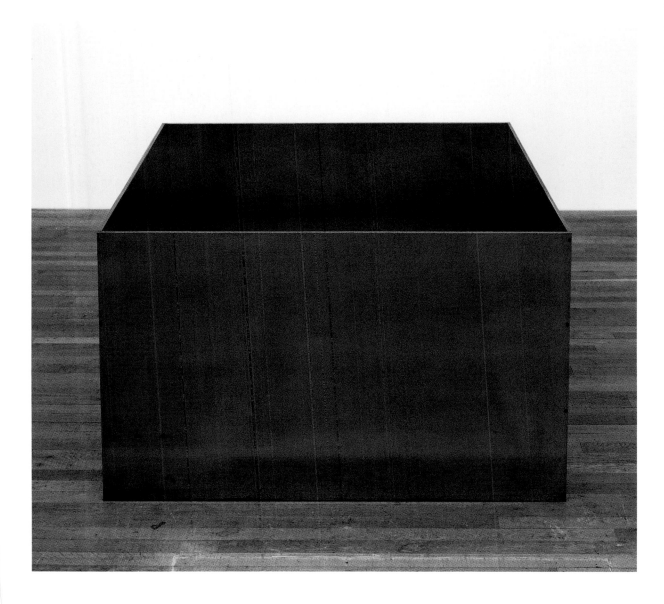

Seriality

From the 1960s many artists associated with Minimalism experimented with seriality, using predetermined systems such as a simple mathematical progression or the repetition of a standard modular unit to structure their work. This approach to making art was anticipated in the serial production methods of Abstract Expressionist painters such as Mark Rothko, Jackson Pollock and Willem De Kooning, and can be traced back even further to Monet's series of paintings of individual motifs such as haystacks. However, by using industrial methods of production and operating according to a predetermined methodical system, artists of Judd's generation were able to avoid making intuitive or compositional decisions during the art-making process, thus making work that existed entirely in its own right, and not as an expression of the maker's thoughts. By making works consisting of a number of identical components arranged at equal intervals from each other, Judd draws the viewer's attention to the intervening spaces. He also produced series of subtle variations on basic forms, emphasising the dramatic changes of effect that may arise when using different materials or making minor alterations to the form. Robert Morris's four mirrored cubes (*Untitled* 1965/71, p.182) are arranged so that the viewer can walk around them, setting up a complex series of reflections. **(HS)**

Synaesthesia
'Synaesthesia' is a term used to describe both a neurological condition and an artistic device. From the Greek *syn* meaning 'union' and *aesthesis* meaning 'sensation', it refers to the literal or artistic overlapping of the senses. A synaesthete may be able, for example, to see sounds, hear colours, or taste a tactile sensation.

In the early decades of the twentieth century, the composer Alexander Scriabin was creating experimental orchestral works that synthesised sound and coloured light. Around the same time, Wassily Kandinsky and the Futurist Filippo Tommaso Marinetti were devising their own synaesthetic systems. Kandinsky is said to have experienced synaesthesia from a young age. Early in his career, he created abstract stage productions, also using coloured light, with titles such as *The Yellow Sound* and *Green Sound*. He was influenced by the music of Wagner and Schoenberg, as well as the theosophical writings of H.P. Blavatsky. His most widely known paintings – his 'Improvisations' or 'Compositions' – make clear reference to music and use colour and line in a free way to express 'inner necessity' or spirituality. **(AC)**

Wassily Kandinsky was one of the pioneers of abstract art. In his distinctive path towards non-figuration, he used the symbolic power of colour and the directional thrust of line to create fully abstract paintings before the First World War. By reducing the descriptive details of recognisable motifs – frequently, castles on hills or horseback riders – he stripped away superfluous elements, leaving calligraphic lines as structuring devices within his compositions. Kandinsky conceived of his art as an alternative pathway to a spiritual realm, made more powerful by not being tied to the observed world. The essential qualities of sound, its unfolding through time, and the structures and tonalities of musical orchestration became critical analogies for his experiments in painting. To underline these links to the abstract characteristics of music, he titled many of his works 'compositions' and 'improvisations'.

Kandinsky's path toward abstraction was gradual and incremental. Early on, his imagery was inspired by folklore scenes and icons he encountered in Russia. Other influences were the heightened natural colours of the Fauvist art he saw in Paris in 1905–6, and the landscape of southern Germany, where he lived and painted with the artist Gabriele Münter in the early years of the twentieth century. When the First World War broke out, he returned to Russia, soon becoming involved in the artistic activities of the fledgling Bolshevik State. After a short-lived return to figuration in a rococo style, his paintings gradually evolved towards a more centred, contained and linear expression in response to the work of other artists such as Malevich and El Lissitzky. Becoming disenchanted with an increasing political control over artistic expression, he left Russia for Berlin in 1921, and was invited to join the Bauhaus, where he remained until the National Socialists closed the school in 1933. He settled in Paris in 1933, where he continued to work until his death in 1944. **(SR)**

Wassily Kandinsky
1866–1944

Cossacks
1910–11
Oil on canvas
94.6 x 130.2 cm
Presented by Mrs Hazel McKinley 1938

In the past three decades Anish Kapoor has challenged the boundaries of sculpture. Polarities such as place and placelessness, darkness and light, substance and emptiness have been central to his work and are expressed through a wide spectrum of materials. His early, powder-pigment coated sculptural groups were followed by works that explored the void, either as freestanding objects or as architectural interventions in the museum space. A continuous passage from convex to concave and from matt to polished surfaces is characteristic of his work, as are visual references to ancient art combined, however, with a bold exploration of abstract forms and unorthodox materials.

Kapoor's enigmatic forms induce in the viewer a heightened awareness of his or her own presence and perceptions. In *Ishi's Light* 2003 the egg-shaped sculpture's outer shell is rough, gradually shading into the sharply contrasting, highly polished interior, thus creating a smooth transition from the tangible to the intangible. The dark, deep colour of the sculpture's reflective interior concavity magnetically invites the viewer inside the work, where one's presence suddenly seems to hover in silence, experiencing emptiness not as nothingness, but as a transition towards a different perception of space and time. **(EB)**

Ishi's Light
2003
Fibreglass and lacquer
310 x 225 x 258 cm
Presented by Tate International
Council 2005

Anish Kapoor
born 1954

Left:
White Curve
1974
Painted aluminium
161.9 x 513.1 cm
Purchased 1980

Right:
Broadway
1958
Oil on canvas
198.1 x 176.8 cm
Presented by E.J. Power
through the Friends
of the Tate Gallery 1962

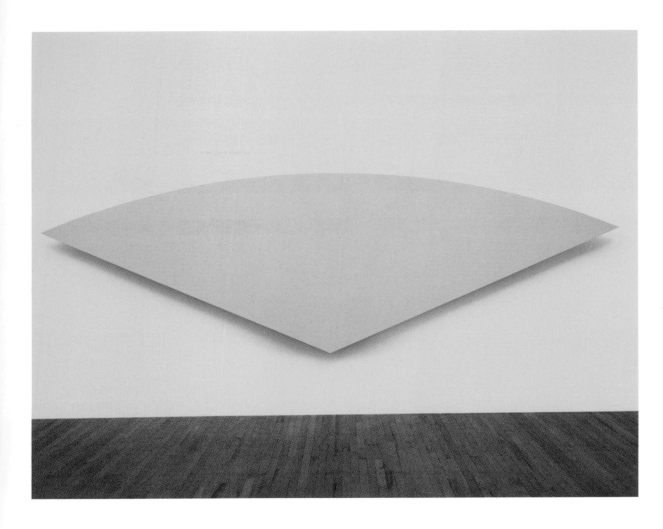

Ellsworth Kelly's work engages with the act of looking in a direct way. His paintings and sculptures are intended to heighten the viewer's awareness of 'pure experience' in physical and visual dimensions. Since the 1950s Kelly has based his art on simple things observed in the real world – small fragments of everyday life such as the spaces between buildings or the shadows cast by trees. He develops and refines what he sees through a series of drawings and collages before arriving at the final abstract motif.

In the late 1940s Kelly went to Paris, where he was influenced by Romanesque and Byzantine architecture as well as Surrealism and Neo-Plasticism. On moving to New York in 1954 he was associated with the Abstract Expressionist movement, although his work emphasises the flat surface of the picture plane through the use of simplified form and dominant monotone colour, which are more usually associated with Minimalism. *Broadway* 1958 is one of a series of paintings made in New York when Kelly was experimenting with the relationship between figure and background. The red form dominates through its flat physical presence while the white segments surrounding it suggest a perspectival view.

Kelly continued to reduce the painted background until, by the late 1960s, he had entirely jettisoned the rectangular backdrop support in favour of the literal background space of the wall. A frequent form is the fan shape featuring in *White Curve* 1974, a monochromatic painting made on sheet aluminium, which hangs at a distance from the wall, occupying a place between painting and sculpture in its relation to the architectural space. **(EM)**

Ellsworth Kelly
born 1923

Ernst Ludwig Kirchner aimed to create paintings that expressed freedom from social and artistic conventions in both style and subject matter. His jagged brushwork and often garish palette were common features of *Die Brücke* (The Bridge), the artistic group he co-founded in Dresden in 1905. Influenced by the Parisian art world and inspired by non-European art, Kirchner's loose handling of paint exemplified a shift towards an Expressionist mode of representation.

The nude was a crucial motif for *Die Brücke* artists and Kirchner frequently depicted models relaxing in his Dresden studio or frolicking in the countryside, at one with the natural world. Against the backdrop of a growing cult of nature and nudist movements, associated in Germany with a specifically national ideal, Kirchner was in some senses invoking a conventional subject. However, in works such as *Bathers at Moritzburg* 1909/26 the openly sexualised depiction of interaction between men and women took what was a mainstream notion into more shocking territory. In particular, the reclining female figure at the right and squatting woman in the centre appear to turn provocatively towards the viewer. Living on the margins of bourgeois society, Kirchner's explicit breaking of moral codes can be equated with his ambitions for artistic liberation.

Die Brücke was short-lived and by 1913 Kirchner had shifted his focus to the decadence of the modern era. In a series of celebrated urban street-scenes made in Berlin, his increasingly taut and angular style seems to anticipate the tensions of the First World War. **(LA)**

Bathers at Moritzburg
1909/26
Oil on canvas
151.1 x 199.7 cm
Purchased 1980

Ernst Ludwig Kirchner

1880–1938

During his brief but influential career, Yves Klein sought ways to evoke the immaterial or invisible in his art, what he called the 'void'. As a teenager he had once day-dreamed of signing 'the far side of the vault of heaven' and thus claiming it as his 'greatest and most beautiful artwork'. He devoted his career to attempting to render the void tangible.

Uninterested in the traditional values of representation, Klein believed that colour could be a subject in itself, and in the late 1940s he painted his first 'monochrome', a flat field of a single, vibrant colour. Fascinated by the effects of the colour blue, which he saw as giving 'rise to a sense of immersion in a space greater than infinity … the blue is the invisible becoming visible', he developed a technique of combining pure pigment with synthetic resin to make a distinctive and intense colour, which he patented as 'International Klein Blue'. He produced nearly 200 monochrome canvases of varying textures, including *IKB 79* 1959, and went on to apply the pigment to three-dimensional objects, including sponges, a globe and replicas of iconic statues.

Klein also introduced a performative aspect into his work. In 1960 he conducted performances in which nude models were painted blue then instructed by the artist to press themselves against the canvas, creating an imprint of their torsos and thighs, the areas of the body in which Klein felt the creative energy of the universe could be found. In another series known as the *Fire Paintings*, a flame thrower was used to create images on specially treated cardboard. **(HS)**

IKB 79
1959
Paint on canvas on wood
139.7 x 119.7 x 3.2 cm
Purchased 1972

Yves Klein
1928–1962

Franz Kline began his career painting urban landscapes of New York and of the mining region where he was raised. After a short spell in London, he settled in New York and came into contact with Willem De Kooning, Jackson Pollock, and other artists associated with Abstract Expressionism. By 1950 he was making vigorous, large-scale abstract paintings in black and white, and soon became recognised as a central figure in the movement.

Meryon 1960–1 is a classic example of Kline's mature work. Great bands and wedges of black paint form a rough grid that seems to push at the edges of the frame, with an awkwardness and strength that Kline relished. The sense of space and insistence on flatness evident here are the result of Kline's interest in Japanese art. Many of his works have an almost calligraphic feel. The marks in *Meryon* also have strong architectural connotations, and it has been suggested that the work relates to an engraving of a clock-tower by the nineteenth-century French artist Charles Meryon. While this might seem to be at odds with a pure abstraction, Kline explained: 'I don't have the feeling that something has to be completely non-associative as far as figure form is concerned'. Although he used colour in some of his later paintings, it is for the austerity, force and scale of his black-and-white works that he is best remembered. **(SH)**

Meryon
1960–1
Oil on canvas
235.9 x 195.6 cm
Purchased 1967

Franz Kline
1910–1962

Jannis Kounellis's quasi-theatrical installations, which incorporate materials as diverse as iron, cotton, coal, coffee, wood, fire, stones, plaster, earth, sacks, plants and live animals, challenge with their boldness of realisation and depth of meaning. His name has been inextricably linked with the Arte Povera movement.

Originally from Greece, Kounellis moved to Italy to study art in the late 1950s and has been living there ever since. He often invests his work with references to history, architecture and myth. *Untitled* 1979 brings together these interests with potent symbols, such as smoke, a reference to erasure and regeneration, and birds, which signify hope and freedom of imagination. It looks back to his very early works, made in the 1950s, featuring large stencilled letters and symbols on paper, but also foreshadows his large-scale installations of the 1980s and the 1990s, where he employed industrial materials such as coal and iron combined with symbols alluding to human presence, such as fire. **(EB)**

Untitled
1979
Charcoal, paper, arrows
and stuffed birds
360 x 500 cm
Purchased 1983

Jannis Kounellis
born 1936

Lee Krasner was the only female painter associated with the first generation of Abstract Expressionists. Like many American artists forging a career during the Depression era, she initially depended mainly on government work, and was involved in a number of public art projects. Although her early paintings were figurative, after studying at the Hans Hofmann School of Fine Arts in the late 1930s, she started to explore vigorous and expressive forms of abstraction. In 1945 she married the artist Jackson Pollock and together they moved out of New York City to a rural village in Long Island. Although the period that followed was a productive one for Krasner, her reputation was largely eclipsed by Pollock's extraordinary rise to fame.

In interviews, Krasner insisted that her life and work were inseparable, and it was immediately after Pollock's death in a car accident in 1956 that she created her most memorable paintings. *Gothic Landscape* 1961 is characteristic of her work during this period, its violent brushstrokes suggesting an outpouring of grief. At the time of making the work, Krasner was suffering from insomnia and was mainly painting at night. This may explain the limited palette of blacks, whites, ochres and browns. Although it is essentially an abstract painting, the thick vertical lines in the centre can be seen as trees, and in the later 1960s and 1970s Krasner worked with more and more nature-derived imagery. In the fifty years during which she was active, Krasner experimented with an extraordinary range of styles, and was influenced by artists as diverse as Henri Matisse and Piet Mondrian. **(SH)**

Gothic Landscape
1961
Oil on canvas
176.8 x 237.8 cm
Purchased 1981

Lee Krasner
1908–1984

The son of a psychoanalyst, child-prodigy artist Guillermo Kuitca studied theatre in the early 1980s and directed experimental plays. His relationship with the theatre strongly influenced his paintings of this time, many of which suggest stage sets with the atmosphere of a traumatic aftermath. He began using beds in his art in 1982, a year in which he was particularly depressed. Since this time, the symbolic ground evoked by beds in his work has evolved from that of refuge to wider territories – apartments, cities, landscapes and the internal worlds of memories, dreams and nightmares. The most vulnerable, intimate and private of places, a bed in Kuitca's visual language evokes public arenas, places where individuals connect through many social processes.

Of Russian descent, Kuitca grew up and still lives in Buenos Aires, from where he looks towards European culture. As a result of this, the use of maps in his work signifies cultural displacement, beginning with the journey of his grandparents to Argentina and expanding to encompass movement in all its forms. Maps are also systems for understanding the world and the roads that appear on them represent facilitators of communication.

Untitled 1992 is one of several works in which Kuitca unites beds with maps. Twenty child-sized beds stand side by side, like a group of small protagonists. European road maps painted on every mattress are punctuated by buttons serving as markers for major cities – the places where people intersect. In his more recent paintings, the human element is almost completely absent and beds take on a central role as signifiers of loneliness and absence. **(EM)**

Untitled
1992
Mixed media
Each object 40 x 60 x 120 cm
Purchased with assistance from the Latin American Acquisitions Committee and the Estate of Tom Bendhem 2004

Guillermo Kuitca
born 1961

Still Life with a Beer Mug
1921–2
Oil on canvas
92.1 x 60 cm
Purchased with assistance
from the Friends of the
Tate Gallery 1976

Fernand Léger was apprenticed to an architect in his native Normandy before moving to Paris in 1900, where he worked as a draughtsman while studying at the École des Arts Decoratifs and the Académie Julian. He soon befriended Robert Delaunay and Albert Gleizes, and started exhibiting at the Salon d'Automne from 1907, the year of Cézanne's posthumous retrospective, which left a lasting influence on his work. From 1909, he played a part in the development of Cubism, but his rounded, tubular style led a critic to call him a 'tubist'. He had his first one-man show at Galerie Kahnweiler, Paris, in 1912. While serving in the French army in 1914–18, he developed a passion for machines and industrial design. Around 1920, he met Le Corbusier and Jean Ozenfant, and both architect and painter encouraged his interest in mechanical forms. In the early 1920s, Léger's work became more precise and mathematical, as is evident in works such as *Still Life with a Beer Mug* 1921–2. The geometric patterns and flat, schematic depiction of the subject-matter shows the influence of the 'call to order' that swept through the Parisian avant-garde at the time. In the late 1920s, he began to introduce natural forms into his paintings, such as the curving lines and organic shapes in *Leaves and Shell* 1927. During the Second World War, he took refuge in the United States, teaching and painting sporadically in San Francisco, New York and Quebec. Upon his return to France, evidence of his love for modernity, everyday street life and workers began to emerge in more loosely composed canvases such as *The Acrobat and his Partner* 1948. By the time of his death in 1955, he had created one of the more recognisable and popular styles in twentieth-century art. **(CB)**

Fernand Léger
1881–1955

The Acrobat and his Partner
1948
Oil on canvas
130.2 x 162.6 cm
Purchased 1980

Wyndham Lewis
1882–1957

Wyndham Lewis had a turbulent private life and his career as an artist and writer was rarely free from controversy. His role as founder of Vorticism in the years immediately preceding the First World War, however, cast him as a great innovator, and a key figure in the history of modern British art. He was an extremely fine draughtsman, and his painted works in oil and watercolour show a fascination and ability with colour and a keen eye for design.

After a period studying in continental Europe in the early years of the twentieth century, Lewis began experimenting with his own brand of modernism. Although no oil paintings survive from this period, existing drawings of abstracted figures show his understanding of Cubism and a particular stylistic debt to Futurist artists such as Umberto Boccioni, whose work was exhibited in England around 1912.

In 1913, Lewis was temporarily associated with the London-based Bloomsbury group, contributing designs in their craft-based Omega studio. However, following a disagreement with the group, Lewis embarked on his own venture of Vorticism, creating works characterised by a bold, near-abstract style that reflected his complex attitude to the modern world. The urban metropolis is evoked through dramatic, angular compositions peopled with automatons and dominated by skyscrapers. The composition of *Workshop c.*1914–15 suggests both the physical interior of the artist's studio and his inner, creative space. The painting has also been linked to the popular Victorian view of Britain as the 'Workshop of the World', a view supported by Lewis. The deliberately brash palette and uncomfortable, claustrophobic geometry reflects Lewis's confrontational approach and relentless attack on tradition. **(LA)**

Workshop
*c.*1914–15
Oil on canvas
76.5 x 61 cm
Purchased 1974

Sol LeWitt is seen as a leading figure in both Minimal and Conceptual art. Since the 1960s he has created a distinctive idiom and produced a wide range of work including site-specific wall drawings and paintings, sculpture, design objects, drawings and prints. Reacting against what he and many of his contemporaries considered the emotional extremes of Abstract Expressionism, LeWitt looked for inspiration to the legacy of German and Russian Constructivism. His interest in structures and rejection of the subjective led him to define a personal vocabulary based on simple geometrical forms, particularly the cube and the grid, which he employed to construct his highly individual, complex works. Sculptures such as *Five Open*

Geometric Structures 1979 are impersonal works made by assistants according to his instructions. Challenging to the eye and mind, these are based on systems that may seem logical, since they are meticulously organised following a carefully premeditated idea. They are, however, as the artist himself has commented, intuitive, purposeless, and not illustrative of theories.

LeWitt started making wall drawings in the late 1960s. Drawn by competent draughtsmen on a prepared wall from a set of instructions, they explore combinations and permutations of lines and colours. They are devised in such a way that they can be carried out in almost any space, within reason, and will fit that space. They are thus to a degree site-specific. Although they are fundamentally explorations of two-dimensional surfaces, the site-specificity of the drawings obliges the viewer to perceive them as part of the three-dimensional space in which they are installed. *Six Geometric Figures (+Two)* 1980–1, drawn with white chalk on black paint, has been installed on all four walls of a gallery at Tate Modern, creating a complete environment. **(EB)**

Five Open Geometric Structures
1979
Painted wood
92 x 672 x 91.4 cm
Presented by Janet
Wolfson de Botton 1996

Sol LeWitt
1928–2007

Roy Lichtenstein is best known for his distinctive cartoon style in which bold black outlines and areas of regular dots imitate scaled-up areas of mechanical printing. He developed this signature style in the early 1960s, producing his first paintings based on characters from comic strips in 1961. Rejecting the personal, expressive style of Abstract Expressionism, Lichtenstein turned to the clichéd content of commercially produced comic strips, challenging what had previously been acceptable as art. Comic strips were ideal material for the new Pop movement, which, like Cubism earlier in the century, focused on common objects and experiences. Lichtenstein

appropriated comics for their ability to express highly charged emotional subject matter in a manner that is stylised and obvious, distancing them from their content. He saw them as an ideal means to reflect what he believed to be the dominant visual culture in America at that time.

Formal concerns are central to Lichtenstein's comic-strip paintings, which are not simple copies but are carefully adjusted for maximum aesthetic impact, combining flat, graphic simplification with the monumentality of classical archetypes. For Lichtenstein, cartoons were a contemporary version of the ideal forms represented in classical art. He compared his reduction and distillation of his source material to the processes employed by Picasso, in which stylised features become emotive symbols. The double-canvas work *Whaam!* 1963 typifies this approach. In 1962–3 Lichtenstein made many paintings based on war comics, in which violent acts feature as aestheticised and stylised motifs. Other comic-strip paintings depict intimate moments in the home, the speech bubbles expressing thoughts and feelings at once banal and reassuringly human. **(EM)**

Whaam!
1963
Acrylic and oil on canvas
172.7 x 406.4 cm
Purchased 1966

Roy Lichtenstein
1923–1997

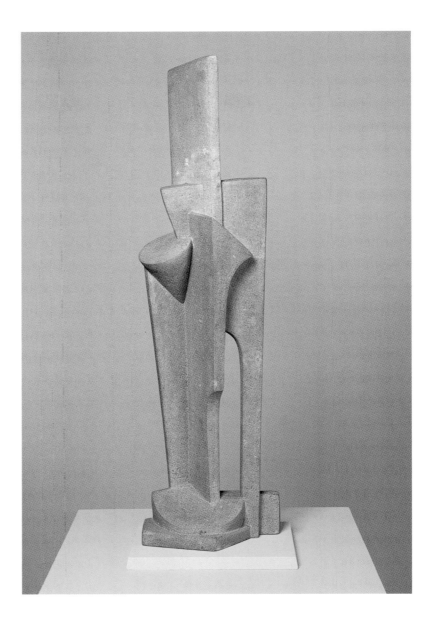

Sculpture
1915–16
Limestone
98 x 28 x 18 cm
Purchased with assistance
from the Friends of the Tate
Gallery, Mrs Jack Steinberg
and the Rayne Foundation 1982

One of the most significant Cubist sculptors, Jacques Lipchitz developed Cubist ideas on the analysis of form throughout his career. While his earliest sculptures were naturalistic representations of the human figure, after being introduced to the work of Cubist painters, including Pablo Picasso, Lipchitz began experimenting with the application of the principles of Cubism to the sculpted object. Attempting to engage the imagination of the viewer, he explored novel ways in which form could be represented. Some works from this period depict the 'negative space' around the object by rendering it as solid and incorporating the resultant form into the sculpture.

Sculpture 1915–16 is one of Lipchitz's earliest Cubist works, developed from his assemblages made the previous year. While the work appears entirely abstract, it in fact represents a figure seated at a table, rendered from a characteristically Cubist grouping of intersecting geometric forms. The totemic structure also bears a close relationship to architectural forms, exaggerated by its rendering in carved stone (from a clay model).

Concerned that the forms were not recognisable in his sculptures, Lipchitz soon began to make his work less rigorously abstract. His investigations into space developed with a series of dynamic pictorial constructions called 'transparents'. In his later period, his work is dominated by semi-abstracted, muscular human figures, often illustrating religious and mythological subjects. Despite their stylistic differences from sculptures made during his high Cubist period, these works too have an ambiguity and simplification of form that Lipchitz maintained was informed by Cubist principles. **(MB)**

Jacques Lipchitz
1891–1973

René Magritte played on perceptions of reality, producing apparently recognisable images in disconcerting and unfathomable narratives. Initially involved with a group of Brussels-based intellectuals, Magritte was drawn into the Parisian Surrealist group in the mid-1920s. As with many Surrealist artists, he found inspiration in the metaphysical painting of Giorgio de Chirico. He developed a deadpan, hyper-real painting style through which he aimed to examine 'the naked mystery of things'. In contrast to the biomorphic abstraction found in Yves Tanguy's work, Magritte composed his paintings from a vocabulary of objects taken from the everyday world.

Many of these objects have symbolic meaning, often derived from the writings of the psychoanalyst Sigmund Freud. The bowler hat and candle found embedded in the lead plaque in *The Reckless Sleeper* 1928 (p.223), for example, represent the female and male sexual organs. While living in Paris between 1927 and 1930, Magritte became immersed in the Surrealist preoccupation with dreams and the subconscious, which can be seen manifested in this work, in which a sleeping figure is depicted in a coffin-like structure, evoking uneasy associations.

The Annunciation 1930 is one of Magritte's largest canvases. The magisterial and strangely quiet landscape includes an odd assortment of objects, including two bilboquets, a term Magritte used to describe the sculptural objects reminiscent of chess pieces or wooden balustrades which appear regularly as anthropomorphic figures in his paintings. The title invokes a religious subject, but has also been seen as a provocative strike at André Breton for his anti-Catholic attack on Magritte's wife for wearing a crucifix. **(LA)**

Left:
Man with a Newspaper
1928
Oil on canvas
127.9 x 94 cm
Presented by the Friends
of the Tate Gallery 1964

Above:
The Future of Statues
1937
Painted plaster
33 x 16.5 x 20.3 cm
Purchased 1981

René Magritte
1898–1967

The Annunciation
1930
Oil on canvas
113.7 x 145.9 cm
Purchased with assistance
from the Friends of the
Tate Gallery 1986

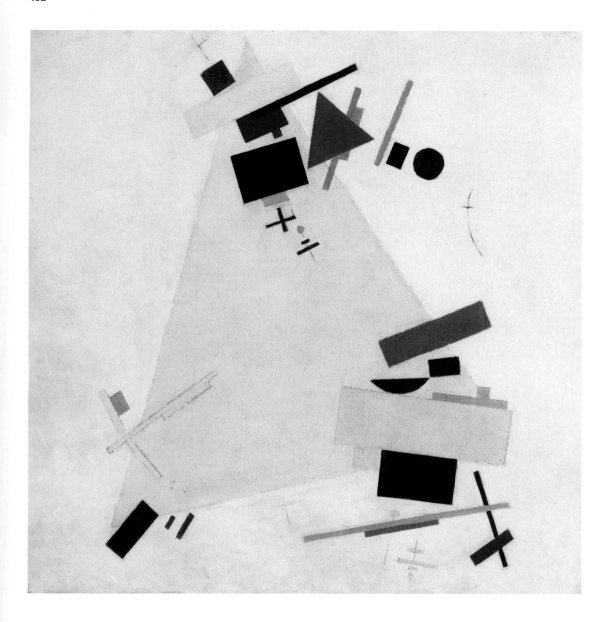

Kasimir Malevich was the founder of Suprematism, a pioneering abstract art movement that he described as an attempt 'to free art from the dead weight of the real world'. Writing in 1927, he went on to proclaim that 'Art no longer wants to serve the State and Church, it no longer wishes to illuminate the history of manners, it wants to have nothing further to do with the object as such, and believes that it can exist in and for itself without "things".'

Born in Ukraine, Malevich was in his mid-twenties when he moved to Moscow to study art. He quickly absorbed the lessons of Impressionism, Cubism and Futurism, producing paintings that combined the formal innovations of the French avant garde with the strong colours and stylised figures of peasant folk art and icon painting.

In 1915 he launched Suprematism with an exhibition in St Petersburg. The signature painting was a black square against a white background, which he placed high in the corner of the gallery, the position traditionally occupied by the icon in Orthodox homes. This gesture reflected his belief in the spiritual, even mystical qualities of abstract art.

From the simple static forms of the early Suprematist paintings, Malevich began to create works such as *Dynamic Suprematism*, in which an array of geometrical shapes appear to be in flux, clustering together or drifting apart. The asymmetrical tilt of the white triangle provides a restless background to the composition, which keeps a fine balance between order and disintegration.

After the October Revolution, Malevich was increasingly absorbed in teaching, writing and developing architectural projects. He went back to painting in the late 1920s, partly returning to figuration. Many of these late works depict the peasant culture that was now threatened by Stalin's policies of collectivisation. **(SB)**

Dynamic Suprematism
1915 or 1916
Oil on canvas
80.3 x 80 cm
Purchased with assistance from the Friends of the Tate Gallery 1978

Kasimir Malevich
1878–1935

Man Ray (born Emmanuel Radnitsky) was a painter, photographer, draughtsman, film-maker, and maker of Dada and Surrealist objects. Along with Marcel Duchamp and Francis Picabia, he was involved in the anarchic Dada movement in New York, which emphasised the illogical and the absurd, and encouraged the use of chance in artistic production.

When Man Ray moved to Paris in 1921, he was quickly accepted by André Breton and joined his circle of followers, who later became the Surrealists. Inspired by Freud, they tried to tap into the creative powers of the subconscious mind, using bizarre juxtapositions to trigger hidden ideas. They endeavoured to produce work that, in the words of writer Isidore Ducasse, was 'as beautiful as the chance encounter of a sewing machine and an umbrella on an operating table'. Man Ray explored Surrealist ideas of chance, desire and dream-states through new photographic techniques. By placing objects on sensitised paper and exposing them to light he created 'Rayographs', camera-less photos that made familiar objects seem mysterious and strange. Together with Lee Miller, he also produced 'solarised' photographs, in which the tones of shadows are inverted, making figures appear to float in thin air. However, it was his objects that became iconic symbols of Dada and Surrealism. *Cadeau* 1921 rendered a domestic iron useless, while endowing it with a new bizarre, humorous and poetic aspect. *Indestructible Object* (p.222) is one of many replicas of *Object of Destruction*, first created in 1922–3 and smashed to pieces by Man Ray himself. By creating a plethora of replicas throughout his career, Man Ray challenged the notion of the artistic 'original' in a true Dada spirit of subversion. **(CM)**

Cadeau
1921, editioned replica 1972
Iron and nails
17.8 x 9.4 x 12.6 cm
Presented by the Tate
Collectors Forum 2002

Man Ray
1890–1976

Artist's Shit
1961
Tin can with paper wrapping
with unidentified contents
4.8 x 6.5 x 6.5 cm
Purchased 2000

The Abject

The abject has been a central concept in contemporary art, particularly since the beginning of the 1990s. The theory of the abject was developed by Julia Kristeva in her 1980 book *Powers of Horror*. Partly influenced by the writings of Georges Bataille, Kristeva elaborated the abject as elements of the body or bodily functions that are impure and potentially threatening to our cleanliness, propriety and, eventually, order. Excrement, menstrual blood, even the skin on a cup of hot milk are signs of the abject, but Kristeva's primary example is the corpse, which traumatically reminds us of our own mortality. She wrote: 'A wound with blood and pus, or the sickly, acrid smell of sweat, of decay … refuse and corpses *show me* what I permanently thrust aside in order to live.' For artists, the purpose of drawing attention to the abject may be said to be to combat more idealising and complacent views of human nature and existence.

A complex notion, the abject has been adopted by many artists and in numerous ways, including in a feminist context (the abjection of female bodily functions within a patriarchal order) and as the basis of a culture of shock and disgust. Piero Manzoni, Cindy Sherman, Louise Bourgeois, Paul McCarthy, Gilbert and George, Kiki Smith, Robert Gober and Jake and Dinos Chapman are some of the artists whose work manifests the abject. **(EB)**

Piero Manzoni was one of the most innovative and influential artists of the twentieth century, and is seen as a founder of what came to be known as Conceptual art. In his tragically short life he sought to establish an 'imageless' art and to challenge the traditional artistic order. His *Achromes*, a series of reliefs comprising a base covered in white material such as chalk, cotton, fur, bread or polystyrene, were an early expression of his approach, followed by provocative performances staging his ideas, such as marking eggs with his thumbprint and then eating them.

His most notorious works, however, fetishised his own body and bodily functions, for example *Artist's Breath* 1960, one of a series of works in which he blew up a balloon and sealed it to a wooden base.

Artist's Shit 1961 belongs to the same period. Manzoni created ninety industrially sealed and labelled cans containing (as far as we know) his own excrement. The cans were intended to be sold for the weight of their contents in gold (30 grams). The artist said that the contents of the tin was 'the most intimate' thing by an artist that one can own, thus commenting on the desire of collectors for the most authentic possible work of an artist, and beyond that on the value of the artwork, on the art market and economic systems in general. *Artist's Shit* also foreshadows the near-obsessive exploration of the self that characterises a great deal of contemporary art. **(EB)**

Piero Manzoni
1933–1963

Achrome
1958
China-clay on canvas
100.3 x 100.3 cm
Purchased 1974

Sampling
Sampling describes the method of creating a new sound composition by assembling fragments of pre-existing recordings, similar to the visual strategy of collage. This is typically done with a sampler, most often a program on a digital computer, but is also possible with tape loops or vinyl records on a phonograph. Samples often consist of a short section of a song, such as a particular drum beat or guitar riff, that is then used much like a musical instrument to play its part in a complex new arrangement. Though there are examples dating back as far as the 1940s, sampling only became popular in the 1980s as part of the emerging hip-hop and rap scene in the United States. In its reliance on 'found' material and its subversion of conventional models of originality, sampling is akin to the readymade, placing a similar emphasis on the artist's selection process and on rendering the familiar unfamiliar. **(ABH)**

Christian Marclay subverts and transcends traditional boundaries between art and music. He began his career as a musical performer in the late 1970s, when he pioneered the use of records and turntables as media for performance and improvisation, often including scratched, broken or otherwise altered records in his concerts. He works in a wide variety of media including vinyl records, album covers, musical instruments, magnetic tape, photography and video, and his use of 'found' materials, as well as wit and humour, can be traced back to the legacy of Marcel Duchamp's 'readymades'.

Similar to musical recordings made by sampling, Marclay's installation *Video Quartet* 2002 is entirely made up from the visual and musical work of others, mostly Hollywood movies, edited together with Final Cut Pro software on a standard home computer. Marclay has created a kaleidoscopic tapestry of nearly 700 carefully selected clips from films such as *Psycho* (1960), *The Sound of Music* (1965), *Barbarella* (1968), *Poltergeist* (1982), *Back to the Future* (1985) and *Captain Corelli's Mandolin* (2001). *Video Quartet* astutely plays with the common hierarchy between seeing and hearing. Whereas it is possible to absorb the soundtrack as one coherent sensory impression, due to the scale of the projection one is not able to take in all four screens at any one time. Thus the customary importance given to image over sound as the driving force of cinematic film is reversed. **(ABH)**

Video Quartet
2002
Four-screen projection, found Hollywood film clips transferred to colour video, audio track, 14 min
Presented by the Film and Video Special Acquisitions Fund 2003

Christian Marclay
born 1955

In 1957 Agnes Martin moved from New Mexico to New York for a ten-year period, becoming part of the Abstract Expressionist group. Although she shared with its members, particularly Mark Rothko and Barnett Newman, an urge towards quasi-religious transcendentalism, her paintings are also inspired by her reading of the ancient Chinese philosophy of Taoism. The bare desert landscape of New Mexico, to which she returned in 1967, remaining there until her death in 2004, is also an important source. Since the early 1960s she has made paintings of identical format, the seventy-two-square-inch canvas providing the ground for her meditative expression. In common with Minimalist works, Martin's paintings are characterised by geometric abstraction, repetition and reductive simplicity. However, unlike Minimalist works, which celebrate impersonal industrial processes, they are made with a delicate hand-drawn line, suggesting emotional states.

For Martin, perfection, the Platonic ideal, has no place in the real world but may only be imagined. The purpose of art, she believed, is to create a visual language that approaches the expression of this perfection, not by being it, but by evoking it. This perfection may also be understood as 'abstract emotion', the kind of sublime, wordless emotion conjured by music and by art rather than the common feelings triggered by events in people's lives. *Morning* 1965 is one of a group of paintings whose titles name things in nature that may arouse a sense of perfect beauty. Its grid of fragile rectangles on white canvas evokes a day in its earliest moments of becoming. **(EM)**

Morning
1965
Acrylic and pencil on canvas
182.6 x 181.9 cm
Purchased 1974

Agnes Martin
1912–2004

Throughout his long career, Henri Matisse explored the expressive and decorative qualities of colour and form, always drawing inspiration from nature, whether in near-abstract works, or in the arcs and arabesques of landscapes, still lifes and interiors. As a leading member of the Fauve group between 1905 and 1907, his early work was characterised by an animated handling of pure, non-naturalistic colour, inspired by the Mediterranean light.

By 1914 Matisse had simplified his method, limiting his palette and paring down forms in works which approach abstraction. *Trivaux Pond* was made around the time Matisse returned to more literal representation and is one of several landscapes he made in 1916 and 1917 in the Bois de Meudon, a park close to his Paris home. With its linear arrangement of verticals, lyrical blending of motifs and controlled use of greens and blue, the work presents an image of harmony in nature, while retaining something of the more muted quality of his preceding works.

Made some thirty years later, *The Snail* shows Matisse exploring colour and form through very different means. A dynamic example of his late work, Matisse used cut-out painted paper to create bold, decorative images. Based on the curving form of a snail's shell, the roughly torn paper is arranged according to contrasting colours. Despite the obvious differences between this and his earlier painting, Matisse maintained that 'there is no separation between my old pictures and my cut-outs, except that with greater completeness and abstraction, I have attained a form filtered to its essentials … I have preserved the sign which … is necessary to make the object exist in its own form.' **(LA)**

Left:
Trivaux Pond
1916 or 1917
Oil on canvas
92.7 x 74.3 cm
Bequeathed by C. Frank Stoop
1933

Right:
The Snail
1953
Gouache on paper,
cut and pasted on paper
mounted on canvas
286.4 x 287 cm
Purchased with assistance
from the Friends of the
Tate Gallery 1962

Henri Matisse
1869–1954

Steve McQueen belongs to a young generation of British artists working in film and video. He has developed, since the early 1990s, an original practice, which challenges the conventions of cinema and furthers the possibility of his medium. Extreme uses of techniques such as editing, close-ups and framing endow his works with a dramatic character, while repetition, the position of the camera and a focus on details and the action of the protagonists lend his films ambiguity and tension.

McQueen's early works were predominantly black and white, without sound. *Drumroll* 1998 marks a shift to colour and is his first film to use sound. It is a triptych of projected images documenting the rolling of a metal oil barrel down the streets of Manhattan. Cameras affixed to the edges and centre of the barrel reproduce rotating images of shop fronts, the traffic in the streets and flashes of the sky, while the soundtrack is composed of the traffic din, the clatter of the barrel rolling on the pavement and the artist's own voice apologising for the disturbance he is causing to passers-by. The viewer is thus placed in the centre of the artwork; the experience of watching it becomes almost equivalent to being in the interior of the barrel, taking in the action from the three fixed camera points. *Drumroll* exemplifies the importance of the human body in McQueen's practice. It also brings together other recurring themes in his art such as journeying, movement, dislocation and exile. **(EB)**

Drumroll
1998
Video installation, 22 mins, 8 secs
Lent by Pamela and Richard Kramlich and the American Fund for the Tate Gallery, fractional and promised gift, 2000

Steve McQueen
born 1969

Cildo Meireles is often considered a pioneer of installation art. Born in 1948 in Rio de Janeiro, he was influenced early in his career by a slightly older generation of Brazilian artists, such as Lygia Clark or Hélio Oiticica, who had developed a Neo-Concretist style – a type of art that involves the viewer in more than the act of distanced observation. Meireles has made works that vary greatly in scale, material or subject matter, though he is perhaps best known for the creation of a number of large-scale environments incorporating sound, smell, or touch and inviting the perceptual engagement of the viewer. His work is often motivated by a strong socio-political consciousness.

Meireles's major installation *Eureka/Blindhotland* 1970–5 makes explicit the non-visual properties of objects – in particular, volume, weight and density, which are normally considered only as implicit aspects of sculpture. The work consists of a number of elements, including 200 black rubber balls of the same size but varying weights, which are placed in a theatrical, spot-lit area surrounded by nets. Visitors are encouraged to feel the weights of the different balls, while a soundtrack plays a series of recordings of the balls being dropped from various heights. *Eureka* (meaning 'I have found it') is the word famously exclaimed by the Greek mathematician Archimedes when he entered his bathtub and, observing the displacement of water, discovered the means of determining the proportion of base metal in King Hiero's golden crown. The title of the work thus makes reference to the mathematical principles and physical properties with which the artist is fascinated, and to the reciprocal impact of a body entering a given space. **(AC)**

Eureka/Blindhotland
1970–5
Mixed media
Lent by the American Fund for the Tate Gallery 2003

Cildo Meireles
born 1948

Carl Andre (born 1935)
Venus Forge
1980
Steel and copper plates
0.5 x 120 x 155.5 cm
Presented by Janet Wolfson
de Botton 1996

Minimalism

Minimalism is an extreme from of abstract art and one of the strongest cultural manifestations of the idea that art should have its own reality and form rather than try to represent the world. Also referred to as 'Minimal art', it emerged in New York during the early 1960s. The artists who are usually grouped together under the term – Frank Stella, Donald Judd, Dan Flavin, Carl Andre, Sol LeWitt and Robert Morris among them – had no common programme, but all of their work is characterised by cubes, right-angled forms, industrial and manufactured materials, and symmetrical or grid-like arrangements. Many of their ideas were derived from the Russian Constructivists and Suprematists such as Kasimir Malevich, whose paintings were arrangements of abstract, geometric forms. The term 'Minimalism' started to become widespread after the philosopher and art writer Richard Wollheim wrote, in 1965, that there was a wave of contemporary work with 'minimal art content'. Although he was discussing Marcel Duchamp's readymades, Robert Rauschenberg's combine paintings and Ad Reinhardt's black paintings, the term was soon applied to Judd, Flavin, Andre and others, as well as to a whole range of wider cultural tendencies, from music to interior design.

Frank Stella's *Six Mile Bottom* 1960 (p.221) pre-dates the use of the term 'Minimalism' by a few years, but his artistic aims reflect those of Judd and others. To paint the work, Stella used an ordinary house-painter's brush, working with commercial paints taken straight from the can. He wanted to eliminate any representational reading of his work, commenting in 1964 that 'my painting is based on the fact that only what can be seen there is there'.

Carl Andre's *Equivalent VIII* 1966 (p.61), a precise arrangement of 120 firebricks, is an iconic work of Minimalist art. A sculpture of extreme simplicity and purity, it invites the viewer to focus on the materials and the context of its presentation. Dan Flavin admired Vladimir Tatlin's proposal for the *Monument to the Third International* 1919, a revolving spiral structure that would have been taller than the Eiffel Tower, and his *'Monument' for V. Tatlin* 1966–9 (p.113) demonstrates the Minimalist debt to the Russian Constructivists. As with all Flavin's sculptures, his homage was made using manufactured fluorescent tubes. As a writer, Donald Judd was Minimalism's best apologist and he also became its best-known practitioner. However, he preferred the term 'specific objects' to describe his work, a description that reflects his desire to eliminate any factor that might interfere with the physical qualities of a self-sufficient sculpture. He wrote that 'a shape, a volume, a colour, a surface is something in itself'. The clean lines and industrial materials of *Untitled* 1990 make the sculpture an exemplary piece of late Minimalism. Contemporary artists such as Martin Creed, David Batchelor and Anish Kapoor continue to explore Minimalism's legacy. **(CB)**

Above:
Donald Judd (1928–1994)
Untitled
1990
Anodised aluminium,
steel and acrylic
Dimensions variable
Presented by the American
Fund for the Tate Gallery 2002

Left:
Sol LeWitt (born 1928)
*Two Open Modular Cubes/
Half-Off*
1972
Enamelled aluminium
160 x 305.4 x 233 cm
Purchased 1974

Biomorphism
The concept of biomorphism is most commonly linked to evocative but abstract organic forms created by artists during the twentieth century. It is particularly associated with Surrealism, and the term was first used in this frame of reference by the American critic and art historian Alfred H. Barr in 1936. The transformative power and strangeness of biomorphic forms appealed to Surrealist artists, who recognised that though dislocated from reality, this abstracted imagery evoked the cyclical rhythms of the natural world. Joan Miró's compositions involved configurations of floating amoebic shapes set against flat expanses of colour, while Yves Tanguy populated his canvases with non-human creatures, which appear to have derived from early evolutionary organisms. **(LA)**

Joan Miró held his first exhibition in Paris in 1925, marking his 'tumultuous entrance' into Surrealism. He was viewed by the movement's leader, André Breton, as the exemplary Surrealist painter and his working practices, particularly his advocacy of automatic drawing and the important role that poetry held in his work, were in keeping with Surrealist concerns.

In spontaneous, abstract compositions, Miró dislocated forms into separate signs that acted as visual metaphors. These ambiguous symbols often represent body parts, sometimes referring to human reproductive processes, such as the black breast-like form that appears to feed a strange, amoebic organism in *Painting* 1927. This work may have been based on Guillaume Apollinaire's 1917 poem 'The Breasts of Tirésias'. Miró frequently used poems as starting points for his work, incorporating his own writing into *tableaux-poemes* (picture-poems), the first of which date from the mid-1920s. He returned to this form in the 1930s in works such as the lyrically titled *A Star Caresses the Breast of a Negress (Painting Poem)* 1938, in which dancing words and images form linguistic and visual rhymes. In his late works, Miró again used colour-fields as the backdrop for compositions of complex, abstracted signs. *Message from a Friend* 1964 evolved from an image of an upward-facing arrow inscribed on a letter sent to Miró by the artist Alexander Calder. Over several years, Miró made numerous drawings on the theme. By the time he came to paint Tate's version, the arrow had turned downwards, transformed into a great black mass, which penetrates the lower section of the painting. **(LA)**

Painting
1927
Tempera and oil on canvas
97.2 x 130.2 cm
Purchased 1971

Joan Miró
1893–1983

Message from a Friend
1964
Oil on canvas
262 x 275.5 cm
Purchased with assistance from
funds bequeathed by Miss H.M.
Arbuthnot through the Friends
of the Tate Gallery 1983

Tatsuo Miyajima creates works that focus on the concept of time. Having started by making performances in the early 1980s, he has sought, since 1987, to render his art more tangible and enduring, though still performative. To this end he employed LED (Light Emitting Diode) technology for his now famous installations, where sequences of the numbers 1 to 99 and back are presented by digital counters, each working at a different pace. His earlier, relatively static installations of the late 1980s gave way to more animated works during the course of the 1990s. In these, counters are arranged in basic geometrical shapes or in grids, causing the numbers to run in parallel lines and create a variety of rhythms. In *Lattice* 1990, for example, time appears to be moving in all directions.

For Miyajima time is 'organised freedom', continuous, infinite and inconceivable. He is influenced by Buddhism, and the circularity of Eastern time. As a result, spirals, which represent time in Oriental culture, figure prominently in his works. For him, the LED counters, keeping score in groups of ten and excluding zero, a state of nothingness and unused potential energy, represent the human being, as in Buddhist philosophy. But spirals also relate to chains such as DNA. European philosophy as well as the linearity of Western time are equally important elements in his work. He established his core concept early in his career: 'keep changing, connect with everything, continue forever', continuously striving towards 'one art of all'. **(EB)**

Lattice
1990
Light emitting diode counters
Presented by Janet Wolfson de Botton 1998

Tatsuo Miyajima
born 1957

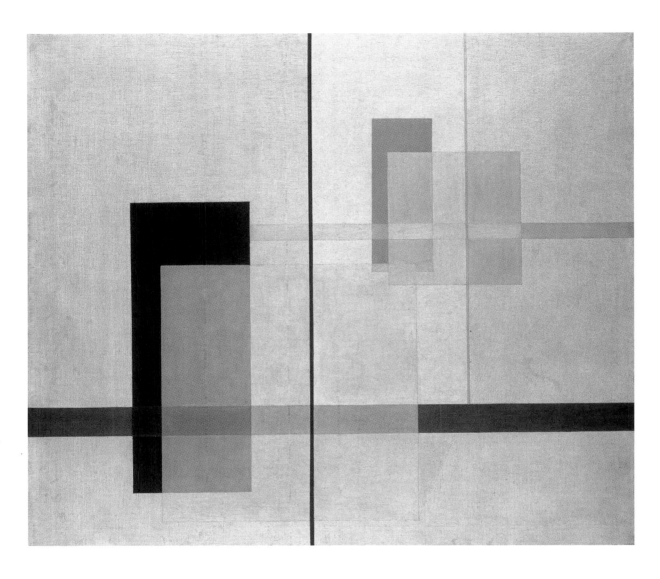

Bauhaus
Mention art education and the conversation will inevitably turn to the Bauhaus, the most influential art and design school of the twentieth century. Founded in 1919 by the architect Walter Gropius, the school counted amongst its teachers some of the best-known artists and architects of its time, including Wassily Kandinsky, Paul Klee, Oskar Schlemmer, Josef Albers, László Moholy-Nagy and Mies van der Rohe. Like many avant-garde practitioners, the Bauhaus masters firmly believed in art as a force of positive social reform: good design for a better world.

Having originally advocated a new unity of art and craft, much in the spirit of the craftsmen working anonymously on Medieval cathedrals, from 1923 onwards the school began to concentrate on designs for industrial production. Bauhaus classics include Marcel Breuer's bent-steel chair, 'Wassily', and Marianne Brandt's semi-spherical silver teapot.

Having left its purpose-designed dwellings in Dessau in 1932, the following year the school was closed by the Nazis. By this time, however, the majority of its most famous teachers had already left, disseminating the utopian Bauhaus ethos across Europe and the United States. **(ABH)**

Rejecting traditional boundaries between high and low culture László Moholy-Nagy's work encompasses a cornucopia of media including painting, photography, sculpture, film, stage sets and graphic design. Born in Hungary, in the early 1920s Moholy emigrated via Vienna to Berlin, then the Mecca of the Eastern European avant garde. From 1923 until 1928, he headed the metal workshop and the preliminary course at the Bauhaus. His appointment coincided with the reorientation of the school from handicrafts towards the machine aesthetics of industrial production with an emphasis on clean lines and functional forms.

Originally trained as a lawyer, Moholy had little formal artistic education, initially being drawn to poetry. Deeply shocked by the horrors of the First World War, he embraced the leftist-orientated avant-garde notion of art as a force for social change. This utopian ambition found its visual expression in a rigorously abstract language that broke with art-historical traditions to be democratically accessible to all. Inspired by Russian Constructivism and its insistence that art had to be pure and void of any representational references, paintings such as *K VII* 1922 are characterised by Moholy's idiosyncratic emphasis on transparency and light. Built from opaque areas of colour, the geometric shapes seemingly float above each other to create pictorial depth without spatial illusion.

Following the rise of the Nazis, in the mid-1930s Moholy moved to Amsterdam and London before finally settling in Chicago to set up the New Bauhaus (subsequently the School of Design in Chicago and from 1944 onwards the Institute of Design). His teachings and books such as the posthumously published *Vision in Motion* played a seminal role in the transition of modernist ideas from Europe to post-war America. **(ABH)**

K VII
1922
Oil on canvas
115.3 x 135.9 cm
Purchased 1961

László Moholy-Nagy
1895–1946

De Stijl
De Stijl (The Style) was a Dutch collective of artists, architects and writers led by Piet Mondrian and Theo van Doesburg that promoted the social and moral function of art, architecture and design. Its theories were put forward in the journal *De Stijl*, first published in 1917. During the 1920s De Stijl became increasingly international, exerting influence on abstract movements and design schools across Europe. Visually, De Stijl is characterised by strictly geometric forms composed of horizontal and vertical lines, which confine themselves to the three 'pure' primary colours – yellow, blue and red – against neutral tones of white, grey and black. This abstract style was intended to express a utopian ideal in which life and art would be integrated harmoniously to renew society, and reflected the important spiritual aspect of De Stijl. Mondrian left the group in 1924 following a dispute with van Doesburg. The *De Stijl* journal continued to be published until 1932. **(LA)**

Piet Mondrian's discovery of Cubism, first in Amsterdam and later in Paris in 1912, had a profound effect on his subsequent career. In contrast to the colourful post-Impressionist paintings he had previously made, he began to incorporate the visual principles of Cubism into his work by reducing his palette to pale monochromes and paring down forms to sequences of intersecting lines and planes. His interest lay in the abstract quality of line, and he explored this in paintings such as Tate's *The Tree A* 1913, one of a series of works in which he investigated leafless branches. Driven by a desire to unify the picture surface and to seek out the 'essence' of painting, Mondrian gradually suppressed the subject in favour of a concentration on the formal elements of picture-making. By 1916 he had eliminated all motifs from his work, and by 1920 he had returned to Paris and published his theory of abstraction, termed 'Neo-Plasticism', reflecting his concern with the 'plastic' or material attributes of painting and form.

In his Neo-Plastic works, Mondrian aimed to create harmony between line and colour in order to represent essential universal relationships such as male/female, mind/body, and so on. *Composition B/(No.II), with Red* 1935 characterises this geometric abstraction. The tension created by the horizontal and vertical lines, which form asymmetrically arranged rectangles, is countered by a single pure, red square. After the mid-1930s, Mondrian incorporated parallel lines painted closely together to create more energetic arrangements such as *Composition with Yellow, Blue and Red* 1937–42, intended to reflect the grid of the modern city. **(LA)**

Composition B/(No.II), with Red
1935
Oil on canvas
80.3 x 63.3 cm
Accepted by H.M. Government in lieu of tax with additional payment (General Funds) made with assistance from the National Lottery through the Heritage Lottery Fund, The National Art Collections Fund, the Friends of the Tate Gallery and the Dr V.J. Daniel Bequest 1999
© 2006 Mondrian/Holtzman Trust c/o hcr@hcrinternational.com

Piet Mondrian
1872–1944

Claude Monet is one of the best-known painters of the late nineteenth and early twentieth century, and as the principal pioneer of Impressionism he had a vital impact on the subsequent history of modern art. Rather than focusing on the grand traditions of history or religious painting, he depicted landscapes and images of the contemporary world, working directly from nature. The term Impressionism was first coined after his landscape *Impression: Sunrise* (now housed in the Marmottan Museum, Paris) was exhibited in 1874. In such works, Monet aimed to capture sensations produced in fleeting moments, concentrating on the means through which paint could be used to evoke light and shadow. He used pure colours in small, rapid brushstrokes to recreate the atmosphere of a particular time of day, or the fog of the modern industrialised city.

Claude Monet
1840–1926

In the 1890s Monet embarked on a project in which he painted subjects repeatedly in order to capture changing light and weather effects through dawn to sunset, often painting several canvases during a given day. This method was to influence subsequent artists in the early twentieth century, such as Piet Mondrian and Wassily Kandinsky, who recognised that by working in series, subject matter could become less important than the formal qualities of the painting itself – that is, the paint, the canvas, colour, line and form. This idea eventually led to elimination of the motif altogether, and in this sense Monet's work may be viewed as a forerunner of abstraction. An abstract quality is evident in his late series of water-lily paintings, which he produced in his studio at Giverny from 1914 until his death in 1926. Many of these expansive canvases create a sense that colour is dissolving across the canvas. However, despite the vast scale and fluid handling of paint, Monet's subject never entirely recedes, and we remain aware of the bright yellow lily-pads floating on the rippling pond, and the suggestion of clouds and sky reflected in the water. **(LA)**

Water-Lilies
after 1916
Oil on canvas
200.7 x 426.7 cm
Lent by the National Gallery 1997

Henry Moore was born in Yorkshire. Following army service in the First World War he trained at Leeds School of Art and then from 1921–4 at the Royal College of Art in London. Following Epstein, he and his contemporary Barbara Hepworth, also from Yorkshire, became twin pioneers of modern sculpture in Britain. From the mid-1920s Moore began to make sculptures of the female figure, adopting the approach of direct carving (without a preliminary model) introduced by Brancusi and in Britain, by Epstein. With this went the doctrine of 'truth to materials', the idea that the material should be worked in such a way as to respect and reveal its innate properties. This partly accounts for the simplified forms and uncluttered surfaces of his work. But Moore was also affected by non-European sculpture, particularly pre-Columbian and African works. From 1924 he made a series of mother and child groups, which express with great force this fundamental theme. In 1929 he made the first of his recumbent female figures, intense statements of the mystery of the feminine that increasingly related the female body to the forms of landscape, creating earth-mother images. By 1938 he had begun to pierce these, introducing new elements of spatial and thematic complexity into his work (*Recumbent Figure* 1938). He stressed that 'a hole can have as much shape meaning as a solid mass' and he spoke of the 'mystery of the hole – the mysterious fascination of caves in hillsides and cliffs'. At the same time, some of his work became highly abstract, but with powerful biomorphic forms (*Composition* 1932). This dual path continued after the Second World War. He pursued the mother and child theme and began to work in plaster for casting in bronze, which enabled him to make much larger and more spatially complex works. *Upright Internal/External Form* 1952–3 was, said Moore, 'based on this idea of one form being protected by another … I suppose in my mind was also the Mother and Child idea and of birth and the child in embryo.' **(SW)**

Henry Moore
1898–1986

Upright Internal/External Form
1952–3
Plaster
195.6 x 67.9 x 69.2 cm
Presented by the artist 1978

Both as an artist and as a critic, Robert Morris played a central role in defining three artistic movements of the 1960s and 1970s: Minimalist sculpture, Process art, and Earthworks. In his 'Notes on Sculpture' published in the journal *Artforum* in 1966 he attempted to define an absolute essence of sculpture, describing it as 'scale, proportion, shape, mass'. To reveal these essential properties, he advocated using simple forms such as cubes, pyramids and regular polyhedrons. Like other Minimalist sculptors including Donald Judd and Carl Andre, Morris believed that paring the artwork down to simple shapes allowed for a more direct relationship between the viewer and the work. He strove to create sculptural 'situations' in which 'one is aware of one's own body at the same time that one is aware of the piece'.

Morris's interest in the interaction between the spectator of an artwork and the environment in which it is situated owed much to his early engagement with dance. In fact he created his earliest Minimalist objects as props for dances performed by the Judson Dance Theater (whose members included his wife Simone Forti). The untitled sculpture of 1965/71 exemplifies Morris's interest in the relationship between moving bodies and still objects. The work consists of four large cubes of mirror glass placed at the corners of a square. As the viewer walks between the cubes, their mirrored surfaces produce a series of complex and shifting interactions. **(SH)**

Untitled
1965/71
Mirror plate glass and wood
Each 91.4 x 91.4 x 91.4 cm
Purchased 1972

Robert Morris
born 1931

Commonly regarded as one of the fathers of Expressionism, Edvard Munch used his own life as the source material for his work, a radical development in the evolution of modern art. Early tragedies – the death of his mother and elder sister from tuberculosis during his childhood and adolescence – haunted his adult life. *The Sick Child* 1907 is the fourth version of a painting that Munch made after visiting the house of an ailing child with his doctor father. It combines memories of the red-haired child Munch encountered there with the protracted trauma of his sister's sickbed. He regarded the first version of this picture as heralding a new departure in his art. Both in the style of painting – flattening perspective – and in its subject matter – physical vulnerability and grief – *The Sick Child* challenged contemporary fashions and was harshly criticised in Oslo art circles. However, Munch's approach was better appreciated abroad, particularly in Germany, where he began to exhibit regularly.

In common with the work of the German Expressionist artists, Munch's portrayal of the darker sides of human existence was perceived as highly threatening by the Nazi Party, who believed that art should serve the purpose of exalting the idealised Aryan way of life. In 1937 Nazi officials purged German museums of works that were considered by the Party to be 'degenerate', including eighty-two paintings by Munch. A selection of these works was exhibited under the title *Entartete Kunst* or Degenerate Art, demonstrating the perceived moral turpitude of those who did not subscribe to their political beliefs. Many of those included in this exhibition are now considered to be the greatest modern artists. **(EM)**

The Sick Child
1907
Oil on canvas
118.7 x 121 cm
Presented by Thomas Olsen 1939

Edvard Munch
1863–1944

Juan Muñoz was a figurative sculptor who first gained attention in his native Spain during the late 1980s. Much of his work addresses the dynamics of architectural and public space, highlighting the potential of sites to provide the backdrop for interpersonal dramas. His smaller-scale sculptures often feature recurring architectural motifs such as balconies, banisters and railings, placed in unlikely situations in the gallery.

Muñoz's larger installations are overtly theatrical, often consisting of large-scale, site-specific scenarios in which the viewer is confronted with monochrome, cast-resin figures including dwarves, ventriloquist's dummies and ballerinas. These installations typically elicit an unsettling, ambivalent response in the viewer. In *Towards the Corner* 1998, seven hysterically laughing figures with Oriental features sit or stand on a set of benches facing towards a corner of the gallery. This placement encourages the viewer to move around the sculpture to see the figures from the front. Their extreme jollity in the absence of any apparent cause provokes a series of reactions in the viewer, from initial amusement or bemusement to a more uncomfortable and anxious response. In front of the benches, the viewer moves from feeling complicit in the figures' mirth to sensing that he or she is the object of their derision.

Muñoz was also known as a draughtsman and made a series of delicate drawings of interiors known as 'Raincoat drawings' because he composed them with chalk on sections of black fabric used for the commercial manufacture of macintoshes. **(RT)**

Towards the Corner
1998
Wood, resin, paint and metal
210 x 378.5 x 113 cm
Purchased with assistance
from Tate Members 2003

Juan Muñoz
1953–2001

Bruce Nauman has worked in a vast range of media since the late 1960s, including sculpture, neon, performance, text, installation, film, video and photography. He originally studied mathematics at college, and his practice has the character of scientific enquiry: an open-ended investigation into the stuff of the world, its materials, the body, language and emotions. 'To every rule, I also try to find the opposite, to reverse it', he has said.

The studio and the body of the artist have always been at the core of Nauman's practice, and early in his career he developed the notion that everything the artist did in the studio was art, thereby redefining art as an activity rather than a product. The realisation that he spent most of his time in the studio pacing up and down led to his seminal film, video and photographic works of the late 1960s, in which he repeats various physical activities for the camera: walking, dancing, playing the violin, putting on make-up, making faces. He has continued to use video throughout his career, developing numerous disturbing works with actors, who are often dressed as clowns, seemingly trapped in repetitive linguistic or physical situations, as in *Double No* 1988.

In the 1970s Nauman developed a series of empty spaces, cages and corridors that placed the spectator in tense or claustrophobic physical surroundings. These works were often augmented by texts, video or closed-circuit TV. During the 1980s, in direct response to the widespread use of imprisonment and torture by many South American regimes, he made a series of works from chairs and steel girders suspended by taut cables from walls and ceiling. These were further developed when he started using taxidermist's moulds to create hanging sculptures of disfigured animal carcasses, as in *Untitled (Three Large Animals)* 1989. **(ED)**

Untitled (Three Large Animals)
1989
Aluminium and wire
120 x 300 x 300 cm
Presented by the Froehlich
Foundation, Stuttgart 2000

Bruce Nauman
born 1941

Newman, who was the son of Polish-Jewish immigrants to America, first established himself as a critic rather than a painter. Although a committed anarchist, in 1933 he offered himself as a candidate for Mayor of New York City. It was not until after the Second World War, when he became a key member of the group of artists known as the Abstract Expressionists, that he developed his signature artistic style.

Adam 1951–2 and *Eve* 1950 are typical of Newman's mature work. They are characterised by large expanses of one colour interrupted by vertical bands of another that literally split the composition into sections. For Newman these 'zips' created a tension between simplicity and complexity, solidity and fragility. He wanted viewers to stand close enough to his paintings to experience all their nuances of colour and structure, and to undergo feelings of heightened self-awareness. As the titles of these two works indicate, he was preoccupied with the Jewish myths of Creation. He was also greatly troubled by the aftermath of the Second World War, especially in relation to the Holocaust. 'I felt the issue in those years was – what can a painter do?', he wrote. In spite of the pared-down appearance of his works, he saw them as addressing 'life', 'man', 'nature', 'death' and 'tragedy'.

Newman always insisted on the rich emotional and spiritual content of his work, but for most of his life it met with incomprehension. It was not until he was nearly sixty that he began to be recognised as one of America's foremost artists. His influence on the development of Minimalist painting and sculpture since the 1960s is now undisputed. **(SH)**

Adam
1951–2
Oil on canvas
242.9 x 202.9 cm
Purchased 1968

Barnett Newman
1905–1970

With the sculptors Barbara Hepworth and Henry Moore, the painter Ben Nicholson completed a trio of pioneering modernist British artists in the 1920s and 1930s. Like them, after the Second World War he became an established figure, opening the way for a younger generation of abstract artists. On a visit to Paris in 1921 Nicholson saw a Cubist painting by Picasso and was deeply struck by it. Over the next ten years he developed a highly sophisticated appreciation of the new pictorial freedoms and possibilities offered by Cubism. With this went a technique and painterly sensibility of outstanding delicacy and refinement. He also became increasingly interested in exploring surface texture, preparing his paintings with a freely brushed ground,

sometimes thickened with marble dust. Over this he would paint extremely thinly, frequently scraping away the surface or incising into it. In 1932–3 he made several month-long trips to Paris, visiting the studios of Picasso, Brancusi, Mondrian and other leading modern artists. Following this, his paintings became increasingly abstract and his interest in surface led him to work in relief. From 1933 he produced a series of abstract reliefs, which he painted white. As a group they make a major contribution, on an international level, to the whole idea of an art of pure, universal beauty that was central to art at that time. His concerns in these works were with creating subtle relationships between two elementary forms of opposite character – the rectangle and the circle – and then adding complexity by extending this relationship into three dimensions in a series of shallow relief levels or planes. Nicholson stressed that this geometric art was not cold or mathematical: 'A square and a circle are nothing in themselves and are alive only in the instinctive and inspirational use an artist can make of them in expressing a poetic idea.' **(SW)**

1934 (relief)
1934
Oil on wood
71.8 x 96.5 x 3.2 cm
Purchased 1978

Ben Nicholson
1894–1982

Nouveau Réalisme

In May 1960 the critic Pierre Restany published a manifesto that proclaimed the arrival of Nouveau Réalisme (New Realism) in France. A joint declaration was signed by the artists Arman, François Dufrêne, Raymond Hains, Yves Klein, Martial Raysse, Daniel Spoerri, Jean Tinguely and Jacques Villeglé, stating their vision of 'new perceptual approaches to reality'. This group and a number of others in their circle shared an interest in exploring their immediate, urban environment in a direct manner. They incorporated objects such as automobile parts, posters, fabrics, dishes and cans into their work. Often seen as a counterpart to American and British Pop art, Nouveau Réalisme also adopted the Dadaist idea of the *objet trouvé* (found object) and extended the medium of collage. By including and transforming everyday objects into art, these artists ask the viewer to reconsider the value and shape of all things ordinary, overlooked, mass-produced, or trashed.

The artist known as Arman (Armand Fernandez) started to present rubbish as art in 1959 in a number of works to which he referred as the 'poubelles'. These were similar to his 'accumulations', in which identical objects were presented in a given format. Two works by Arman in the Tate Collection, *Condition of Woman I* 1960, and *Bluebeard's Wife* 1969, include items one would normally find in a household bathroom cabinet. In both works the objects are encased within resin or glass and presented on a plinth or pedestal, elevating them to the status of art. Similarly, 'objects found in chance positions, in order or disorder' were fixed to their base (a table, tray, box or drawer) and mounted vertically on the wall by the artist Daniel Spoerri. César (César Baldaccini) made sculptures and reliefs from compressed car parts. His compressions, which could be regarded as collage or assemblage, turned functional objects into what look like blocks of scrap metal, rendering them useless while simultaneously giving them a new role as a work of art. While Arman, Spoerri and César took their materials from the factory floor or domestic space, Jacques Villeglé found his 'readymade' canvases in the streets of Paris, where he removed large sections of torn, multi-layered fly-posters in order to re-present them in the gallery.

Perhaps the most famous artist of the group, Yves Klein was less interested in everyday, mass-produced or readymade objects than his peers, choosing rather to focus on what Villeglé had called 'distance from the act of painting' through his experiments with process and his interest in the universal or transcendental properties of a material or colour. Klein died prematurely, in 1962, at the age of thirty-four, but although his career was cut short he had been remarkably influential on the development of several strands of artistic practice that were to become more fully formed later in the century, including performance and Conceptual art. The Bulgarian artist Christo (Christo Javacheff) was also associated with Nouveau Réalisme in the early 1960s, when he began to wrap objects in plastic and rope, thus transforming them and drawing attention to their shape and contours. Christo's wrapped objects, the soft-sculptures of Gerard Deschamps and the early works of Niki de Saint Phalle also show the influence of Nouveau Réalisme, as well as Surrealism. Equally, it is possible to see the legacy of Nouveau Réalisme in work produced during the 1990s by the 'Young British Artists' such as Tracey Emin, Sarah Lucas and Michael Landy, who are concerned with the stuff of everyday life and the cultural assumptions and by-products of today's throw-away society. **(AC)**

Arman (1928–2005)
Condition of Woman I
1960
Mixed media, metal,
wood and glass
192 x 46.2 x 32 cm
Purchased 1982

Below:
Jacques Mahé de la Villeglé
(born 1926)
Jazzmen
1961
Torn posters mounted on canvas
217 x 177 cm
Presented by the Friends
of the Tate Gallery 2000

Right:
Daniel Spoerri (born 1930)
Prose Poems
1959–60
Mixed media on wood
60 x 54.2 x 36.1 cm
Purchased 1982

A central figure in the development of American Pop art, Claes Oldenburg is best known for his soft sculptures and massive public installations based on comically enlarged domestic and everyday objects. Inspired by signs, billboards and objects in the windows he passed on the way to the studio, in 1961 Oldenburg opened *The Store*, a shop furnished with an array of his scaled-up, expressively sculpted and painted consumer goods, including clothes and food. Such works as *Counter and Plates with Potatoes and Ham* 1961 (p.00) were offered for sale, fusing art objects with commercialism. This conflation of artistic creativity with commerce represented a seminal moment in the development of Pop art. Similar sculpted objects were also used as props in Oldenburg's 'Happenings', a series of multi-media performance events staged between 1960 and 1966. In contrast to his soft sculpture, which transformed hard objects into soft, body-like entities, Oldenburg's Happenings depersonalised the participators and objectified their bodies.

Oldenburg has produced several works on the theme of drainpipes, suggested to him by the letter T and an advertisement in a Swedish magazine for a drainpipe that had curves and bends. Putting the two together, Oldenburg created *Soft Drainpipe – Blue (Cool) Version* 1967 and its alter-ego, *Soft Drainpipe – Red (Hot) Version*. The dimensions of the blue version may be altered by adjusting the pulley from which it hangs against the wall, varying the human and animal body parts it evokes (a penis, an elephant's ears and trunk, a crucified figure). The red version is made of red vinyl cut from the same pattern and filled with Styrofoam pellets, resulting in a more solid, unvarying stuffed form. **(EM)**

Soft Drainpipe –
Blue (Cool) Version
1967
Acrylic on canvas and steel
259.1 x 187.6 x 35.6 cm
Purchased 1970

Claes Oldenburg
born 1929

Cornelia Parker, who was nominated for the Turner Prize in 1997, is best known for appropriating objects and subjecting them to acts of violence. But in her careful manipulation and subsequent display of the remnants, she exposes layers of meaning within them.

To make *Thirty Pieces of Silver* 1988–9, Parker scoured junk shops and boot sales to collect hundreds of silver objects no longer wanted by their owners. She then laid them out on a road and arranged for them to be run over by a steamroller. The contorted remains are shown suspended in thirty disc-like formations, hovering a few inches above the gallery floor, which gives them an ephemeral, fluid appearance. As in many of her works, Parker was interested in the metamorphoses of form and meaning that objects may undergo. Most silver objects have sentimental or commemorative value over and above their material worth – the sports-day trophy, for example, or the wedding present of best cutlery – and yet they eventually turn up in junk shops. The biblical reference implicit in the title suggests a betrayal, but whether this might allude to Parker's act of 'cartoon violence', or to the former owners' relinquishment of the objects, is open to conjecture.

The history of an object can trigger associations that may transform its value. In 1998 Parker visited the Tate conservation studios and was shown a number of canvas liners that had been removed from paintings by J.M.W. Turner. Intrigued by the fragile beauty of the liners, Parker subsequently displayed them with an adjacent label to indicate from which painting they had been removed. They have since been accessioned into the collection, thus transformed by Parker from discarded remnants to artworks in their own right. **(HS)**

Thirty Pieces of Silver
1988–9
Silver and metal
Purchased with assistance from
Maggi and David Gordon 1998

Cornelia Parker
born 1956

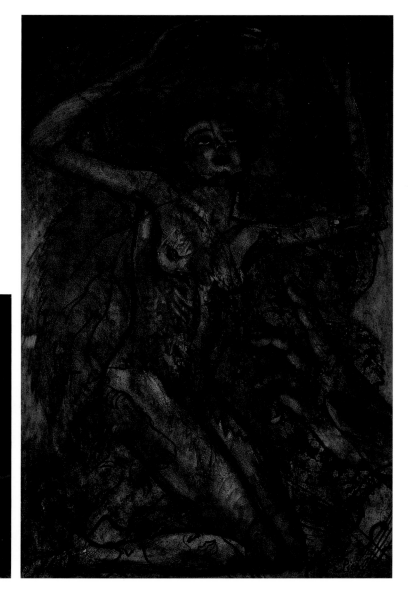

Kitsch
The German word for trash, 'kitsch' is often used to describe images considered to be cheap and tawdry, in bad taste, or reflecting stereotypes in popular culture. The word was first used in relation to art in the late 1930s, when 'kitsch' was discussed as the very opposite of high art. However, artists began to integrate 'low' forms of imagery into their work, often as an act of defiance against traditional notions of beauty. Francis Picabia based his female nudes of the 1940s on photographs of rouge-lipped, Hollywood-type pin-ups from popular magazines or mildly pornographic sources. In the 1960s Pop artists drew on seemingly vulgar commercial imagery to make statements about the growing consumer market. Kitsch became an important source for many strands of postmodernist art during the 1970s and 1980s and artists such as Jeff Koons, John Currin and Paul McCarthy continue to engage with notions of kitsch to this day. **(LA)**

Francis Picabia
1879–1953

Francis Picabia adopted an iconoclastic approach to making art, in which he regularly destroyed or painted over his canvases, eliminating previous styles in order to avoid repetition. Known for his extravagant lifestyle, love of parties, fast cars and boats, he was a larger-than-life figure who continually defied stylistic conformity. Despite his participation in the Dada movement in Paris and association with Surrealism, his highly individual approach ultimately separated him from affiliation to any specific avant-garde movement.

Three of Tate's five works by Picabia were radically altered by the artist, and each of these is known in its previous state through photographs. He painted *The Fig-Leaf* 1922 over his mechanomorphic painting *Hot Eyes*, a work based on a technical drawing of an air-turbine brake that had caused great scandal when exhibited in 1921. By resubmitting the canvas in its new guise, with the connotations of censorship implied by its new title, Picabia made a pointed statement about the conservatism, as he saw it, of the established art world.

In around 1929 Picabia began a series of works known as the 'transparencies', which evolved out of figurative paintings he had made in the 1920s. Often associated with Surrealist preoccupations with the interior life of the subconscious, they feature linear figures, animals and foliage, super-imposed in layers suggesting fragmentary and ambiguous space. The ethereal, sub-aquatic quality of *Otaïti* 1930 is typical of these works, and its motifs such as the ram's head and double mask appear in other 'transparencies'. The central female figure appears to prefigure Picabia's kitsch nudes of the following decade. **(LA)**

Far left:
The Handsome Pork-Butcher
c.1924–6, c.1929–35
Oil and mixed media on canvas
92.4 x 73.7 cm
Accepted by H.M. Government in lieu of tax and allocated to the Tate Gallery 1996

Centre:
Otaïti
1930
Oil on canvas
194 x 130.3 cm
Purchased 2005

Right:
The Fig-Leaf
1922
Household paint on canvas
200 x 160 cm
Purchased 1984

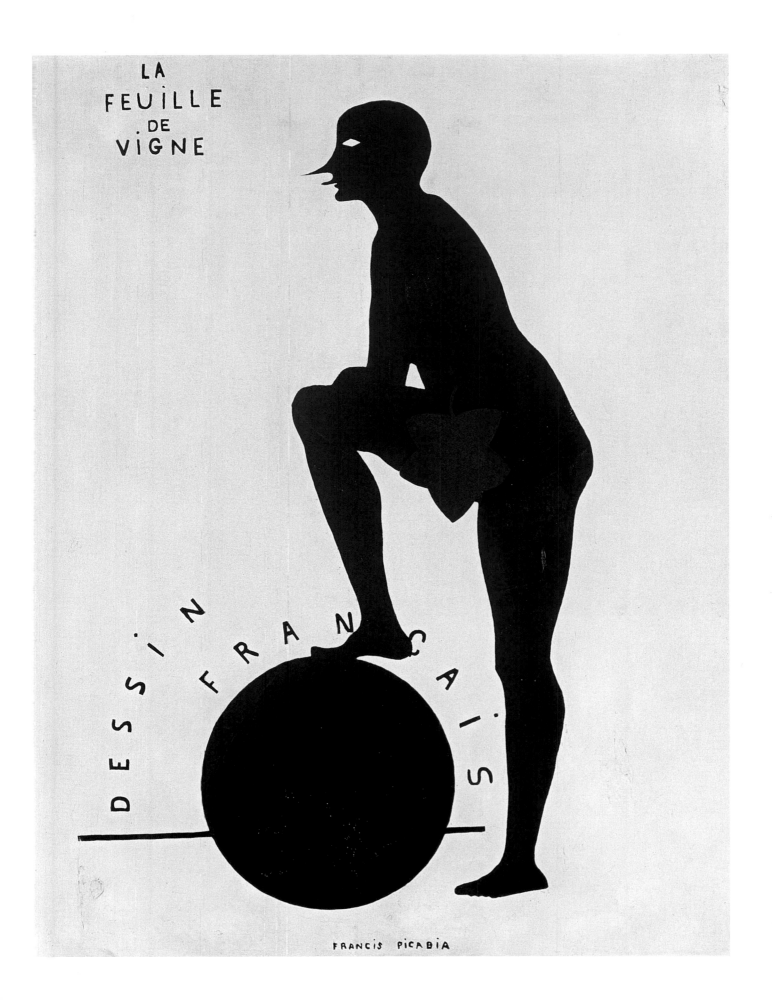

Weeping Woman
1937
Oil on canvas
60.8 x 50 cm
Accepted by H.M. Government in lieu of tax with additional payment (Grant-in-Aid) made with assistance from the National Heritage Memorial Fund, the National Art Collections Fund and the Friends of the Tate Gallery 1987

Pablo Picasso is perhaps the most famous and important artist of the twentieth century, known both for his celebrity persona and complex personal relationships as well as for his virtuosity. In a career spanning over seventy years, his artistic inventiveness led him to work in an unparalleled variety of styles: from the melancholic 'blue period' (*Girl in a Chemise c*.1905), through the great innovations of Cubism, to monumental, neo-classical paintings and works featuring deformations of faces and bodies to express heightened emotion (*Weeping Woman* 1937).

Picasso's innovation also lay in his manipulation of unlikely materials. The wooden relief *Still Life* 1914 could be described as a Cubist collage in three dimensions. The knife, glass, piece of cheese and slice of sausage that rest on a table are all made in wood, as is the decorative dado rail behind. The still life becomes an object in itself, and the piece of upholstery fringe used to represent the tablecloth plays on our perceptions of what is real and what is artifice.

Still Life was shown in the *Exhibition of Surrealist Objects* in Paris in 1936. Picasso had exhibited with the Surrealists from the mid-1920s following his shift from neo-classicism towards a violently expressive style in which he distorted and metamorphosed the human figure. *The Three Dancers* 1925 was made at this moment of transition, and is considered one of his most important works. The exuberance and joy of dance is undermined by the aggressive manner in which the figures are depicted, particularly the sharp-toothed female at the left, whose exposed breasts and twisted body represents woman as femme fatale. **(LA)**

Pablo Picasso
1881–1973

The Three Dancers
1925
Oil on canvas
215.3 x 142.2 cm
Purchased with a special Grant-in-Aid and the Florence Fox Bequest with assistance from the Friends of the Tate Gallery and the Contemporary Art Society 1965

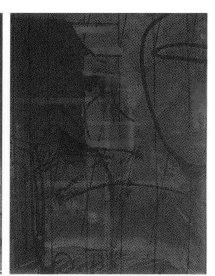

Sigmar Polke's work may be understood as an analysis of the mark-making central to two-dimensional representation. From his earliest practice, he emphasised a dynamic tension between expressive gesture – often humorously subverting its traditional subjectivity – and mechanical reproduction. His paintings combine found printed images with more organically made marks. He used half-tone photography from newspapers and magazines, enlarging and reproducing it on canvas, often corrupting the original beyond recognition. From 1964 he began overlaying imagery on printed fabrics, creating a double layer of patterning and undermining the traditional relationship between subject and background. Latterly he painted on transparent fabric, through which the structural support of the wooden stretchers was clearly visible. *Triptych* was made in this manner. Volumes of white, green and red paint were poured onto a base of translucent resin on the three transparent canvases and caused to flow in different directions resulting in pools and expressive dribbles. The final layer of imagery is based on a greatly enlarged black and white half-tone grid, taken from a found illustration. The painting was conceived when Polke was working on a series of 'Printing Errors' (1996–8), which examined the minute ink slippages and spillages that read as errors on the printed page.

Because of his use of mass-media imagery Polke is commonly associated with the Pop movement. In particular, his use of benday (printing) dots connects him with American Pop artist Roy Lichtenstein. Polke's work may be understood as an investigation into the codes by which knowledge is structured and communicated in our age of mechanical reproduction. The tension between various types of mark-making and between figurative imagery and abstraction are central concerns of his art. **(EM)**

Above, and right (detail):
Triptych
2002
Three panels
Mixed media on fabric
397.9 x 299.7 cm
Purchased with assistance from Tate Members, Noam and Geraldine Gottesman, Harvey Shipley-Miller and private donors courtesy of the American Patrons of Tate 2004

Sigmar Polke
1941–2010

Jackson Pollock was a key member of the group of American artists known as Abstract Expressionists, and arguably one of the most revolutionary painters of the twentieth century. His methods flew in the face of traditional artistic practices and he became renowned for making paintings by dripping paint onto a canvas on the floor. 'On the floor I am more at ease', he explained. 'I can walk around … and literally be in the painting.'

Pollock's practice was particularly influenced by Native American art, Mexican mural painting and Carl Jung's theories of the unconscious, of which he became aware during treatment for a mental breakdown in his mid-twenties. In 1944, he was talent-spotted by the influential art critic Clement Greenberg, who thought he made 'some of the strongest paintings I have yet seen by an American'.

Consistently wild and rebellious, Pollock's life was always troubled by alcohol and depression. In spite of widespread recognition, it is possible to interpret anger and frustration in his work, as in *Yellow Islands* 1952, in which he threw huge quantities of black paint over the canvas. In 1956, he was killed in a car crash. He quickly became immortalised as a symbol of creative freedom and risk-taking, and in this exerted a strong influence on the rising cult of individualism in American and European art. As a result of his 'Action Painting', the emphasis he placed on the physical act of art-making, and its relation to the artists' inner impulses, his legacy has been seen as particularly important for the development of Performance art in the 1960s. **(SH)**

Jackson Pollock
1912–1956

Drip Painting

Pollock invented his 'drip' paintings around 1947, and gained an international reputation in 1949 when *Time* magazine ran a piece about 'Jack the Dripper', asking, 'Is He the Greatest Living Painter in the United States?' *Summertime: Number 9A* 1948 is exemplary of this radical technique. Pollock made the work by dripping and pouring household paint over two large canvases placed flat on the ground. The resulting painting has a complex, rhythmic structure, in which overlapping skeins of paint record the artist's dramatic physical gestures. Pollock's choreography as he circled around his canvases was famously captured in a film and a set of photographs made by Hans Namuth in 1950. **(SH)**

Summertime: Number 9A
1948
Oil, enamel and house paint on canvas
84.8 x 555 cm
Purchased 1988

Right:
Claes Oldenburg (born 1929)
Counter and Plates
with Potato and Ham
1961
Painted plaster
11.7 x 107.3 x 57.8 cm
Presented by EJ Power
through the Friends of
the Tate Gallery 1970

Below:
Richard Artschwager (born 1923)
Table and Chair
1963–4
Melamine laminate and wood
Two objects:
75.5 x 132 x 95.2 cm
114.3 x 43.8 x 53.3 cm
Purchased 1983

Pop Art

The term Pop art came into wide use in the early 1960s to describe a distinctively new approach to painting and sculpture that had developed more or less simultaneously in Britain and the USA from the mid-1950s. The name derived from the new art's exploration of source material drawn from popular and commercial culture ranging from junk food and its packaging to advertising, pop music, Hollywood movies, fairgrounds, tabloid newspapers, comics, sci-fi, crime and girlie magazines, and street signs. A parallel development took place in Western Europe under the name of Nouveau Réalisme (New Realism). Consciously referring to nineteenth-century theories of Realism, the name signalled a wider scope of subject matter than that implied by the name Pop art: that is, any aspect of reality hitherto deemed inappropriate as the basis of ambitious art, including art itself. It also emphasised a key characteristic of Pop art: that this new subject matter was being treated in new ways.

Pop art and Nouveau Réalisme emerged from a combination of aesthetic and social revolt. The aesthetic revolt was against the idea of abstract art and in favour of a new engagement with the everyday world. With this went a rejection of a political and social conservatism that had reached an apogee in the immediate post-Second World War period before being exploded in the 1960s.

In Britain what became Pop art was pioneered by the Independent Group, whose leading figures included Richard Hamilton and Eduardo Paolozzi. From 1956 Hamilton produced a series of founding works of Pop art, among them *Hommage à Chrysler Corp.* (p.131) and *$he*. These were based on American advertising for, respectively, automobiles and refrigerators and point up a fascination with American consumer culture characteristic of British Pop. Both address the use of women in advertising and in the case of *$he*, the social construction of woman as housewife. In Hamilton's work the source images are typically highly processed, resulting in formal and technical complexity and a degree of allusiveness. Nevertheless, the flavour and vividness of the source is preserved. This complex interplay between source and formal structure, worked out in different ways, is fundamental to Pop art. At about the same time Peter Blake, ten years Hamilton's junior, began to make paintings and collages from specifically British pop sources. He became a prominent figure among a group of slightly younger Pop artists who emerged at the 1961 *Young Contemporaries* exhibition in London, among them David Hockney.

In the USA Pop art was pioneered from the mid-1950s by Jasper Johns and Robert Rauschenberg in collage and assemblage works using found materials, often combined with painting. Johns's *Flag* paintings, made from 1955, established a key aspect of US Pop art: the use of a two-dimensional source image in such a way that the distinction between the source and the art object was blurred, questioning the dividing line between art and life and therefore the nature of art itself. From this premise Roy Lichtenstein and Andy Warhol went on to create great and radical bodies of work, mainly in painting, although both also produced three-dimensional pieces. Claes Oldenburg worked in three dimensions from the start and may be considered the principal Pop sculptor. Perhaps his most important contributions were his soft sculptures of everyday objects made in fabric, often stuffed with kapok, and displayed so that they took on extraordinary metamorphic shapes. His *Soft Drainpipe* (p.190) is a perfect example of this. Capable of being manually reconfigured, it offers multiple readings in addition to its source, a drainpipe and length of guttering: male genitals, elephants ears and trunk, Mickey Mouse head, hammer, letter T and so on. Richard Artschwager also played interesting games with his source material. *Table and Chair* 1963–4 is clearly a work of art – a mediated representation of real objects. Disconcertingly however, it could, just, be used as furniture. Furthermore its forms, two rectangular boxes and a rectangular slab, are those of the Minimal art that flourished in parallel with Pop.

In its heyday in the 1960s Pop art was often condemned as brash and superficial. But it had roots in earlier phases of twentieth-century art, notably Dada and Surrealism, and its influence has been lasting and pervasive. **(SW)**

Above:
Richard Hamilton (born 1922)
$he
1958–61
Oil, cellulose paint
and collage on wood
121.9 x 81.3 cm
Purchased 1970

Below:
Andy Warhol (1928–1987)
Black Bean
1968
Screenprint on paper
88.9 x 58.7 cm
Purchased 1978

Postmodernism

Fiona Rae (born 1963)
Night Vision
1998
Oil and acrylic on canvas
244 x 213.5 cm
Purchased 1998

'Postmodernism' describes a broad range of cultural tendencies that emerged as a reaction to modernism during the second half of the twentieth century. The term 'Modernism' itself is applied to a vast and diverse group of art and artists, many with competing or contradictory characteristics, and this is equally true of postmodernism. Yet there are important differences, and perhaps architectural history provides the clearest illustration of the transition between the two eras. In 1966, the American architect Robert Venturi poked fun at the modernist motto 'Less is more' – shorthand for the clean lines and unadorned architecture of the Modern Style – with the phrase 'Less is a bore'. His comment was meant more as a witty epigram than a call to arms, but it helps to point out many of the cultural changes that were brewing at the time. While modernism could be partly characterised by utopian ambitions, high seriousness and a deep concern with form, postmodernism revels in a broadly pluralist approach, celebrating outmoded genres, art-historical parody, surface decoration and up-front social commentary.

Postmodernism's playful approach to tradition and art history is fuelled in part by scepticism about cultural progress, a tendency that has led some critics to accuse postmodern artists of relinquishing culture to the capitalists. Many postmodern artists, moreover, set out to collapse the distinction between high and low culture. Pop art, with its love of consumerism and tawdry, everyday things, could perhaps be seen as the first form of postmodernism, and emerged in New York at about the same time as Minimalism, which might be called the last gasp of modernism. Roy Lichtenstein's *Whaam*! 1963 (p.158) revels in the vivid graphics of American comics and is one example of how postmodernist art assailed the highbrow aims of modernism. Other artists who practised what might now be considered a precursor to postmodernism are the Americans Jasper Johns, Robert Rauschenberg and Cy Twombly, who reacted to the high seriousness of Abstract Expressionism with work that was witty, socially engaged and called upon a broad range of references, from recent history to ancient poetry.

During the 1970s and 1980s, many American artists – including Barbara Kruger, Richard Prince, The Guerrilla Girls and Jenny Holzer – created art that was socially and politically demanding. Yet an element of celebration was also important to postmodernism, and many artists, such as Jeff Koons, pursued kitsch and consumerism in their work. In *Three Ball Total Equilibrium Tank (Two Dr J Silver Series, Spalding NBA Tip-Off)* 1985, Koons suspended a trio of commercial basketballs in an aquarium as if they were precious relics. In the 1980s, painters David Salle and Julian Schnabel combined layered imagery with bombastic themes, and their work has become synonymous with 1980s postmodernism in New York. Since the late 1970s, Cindy Sherman and Jeff Wall have explored the area between documentary and fiction in photography, and their work has become enormously influential. Bruce Nauman's *Double No* 1988, a looped video installation of two clowns bouncing on pogo sticks – with one television placed upside down on top of the other so that the clowns seem to be banging heads – is just one example of video art, a medium that became increasingly popular with postmodernist artists at the end of the twentieth century.

Contemporary art continues to be touched by a postmodernist ethos. Fiona Rae's *Night Vision* 1998, for instance, blends elements of hard-edge geometric abstraction reminiscent of modernism with expressive smears of pigment that disrupt the flat surface of the painting as if the artist were 'sampling', like a DJ, the history of abstract art. Similarly, Christian Marclay's *Video Quartet* 2002 (p.166) samples footage from Hollywood films to create a structure that is fractured, with a collage of seemingly discordant sounds and images, and yet creates a coherent whole from this diverse range of found material. **(CB)**

Left:
Jeff Koons (born 1955)
*Three Ball Total Equilibrium
Tank (Two Dr J Silver Series,
Spalding NBA Tip-Off)*
1985
Mixed media
153.6 x 123.8 x 33.6 cm
Purchased 1995

Below:
Jeff Wall (born 1946)
*A Sudden Gust of Wind
(after Hokusai)*
1993
Photographic transparency
and illuminated display case
250 x 397 x 34 cm
Purchased with assistance from
the Patrons of New Art through
the Tate Gallery Foundation and
from the National Art Collections
Fund 1995

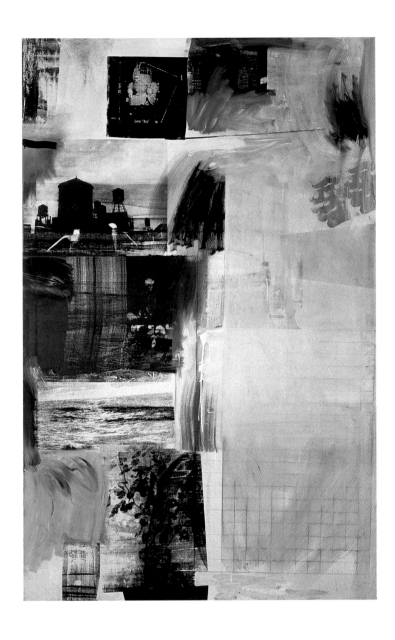

Robert Rauschenberg's career has been long and varied, and although he is seen as an important historical figure in performance art, set design and experiments with art and technology, he is best known as a leader in bridging the period between Abstract Expressionism and Pop art. One of his best-known works is the *Erased de Kooning Drawing* of 1953, a small work on paper made from the marks remaining after rubbing out a drawing by the Abstract Expressionist Willem De Kooning. Often seen as a rebuff to the preciousness associated with the artist's gesture, Rauschenberg's conceptual experiment with what he called 'the simultaneous unmaking of one work and the making of another' also relates to the monochrome paintings he had been making while studying with Joseph Albers at Black Mountain College in North Carolina.

By the late 1950s, Rauschenberg had begun to incorporate found imagery from newspapers and magazines into his drawings, prints and paintings. *Almanac* 1962, made by silk-screening found images in a loose, poetic manner, and then overlaying them with painterly brushstrokes, is characteristic of his work at this time. Among his most celebrated achievements are the so-called 'combines' he made from 1954 to 1962, which integrated aspects of painting and sculpture and often included bizarre objects such as stuffed animals, street signs or bedding. There is rarely a specific meaning or narrative in Rauschenberg's works; rather, viewers are invited to make their own interpretations from the visual flux of media, subjects and gestural marks. **(SH)**

Almanac
1962
Oil, acrylic and
silkscreen on canvas
244.3 x 152.4 cm
Presented by the Friends
of the Tate Gallery 1969

Robert Rauschenberg
1925–2008

Monochrome
Often mistakenly described as a 'blank canvas', monochrome painting is the term applied to works of art that are made up of a single colour or tone. The practice of monochrome painting was a surprisingly resilient one throughout twentieth-century American and European avant-garde art. At times the attraction for artists was nihilistic, at others more spiritual.

Paradoxically, monochrome works were executed in different historical contexts both to criticise and to reaffirm the value of painting. The origins of the practice lie with the work of Kasimir Malevich and Aleksandr Rodchenko in Russia in the 1910s. Monochrome painting then flourished in the United States in the 1950s and 1960s, when it was closely related to Minimal sculpture, dance and filmmaking. Important practitioners from this period included Robert Rauschenberg, Ad Reinhardt, Brice Marden and Robert Ryman, as well as Piero Manzoni and Yves Klein in Europe. Contemporary artists including Gerhard Richter and Anish Kapoor have continued to experiment with the monochrome, finding in it endless possibilities for exploring and contesting artistic values. **(SH)**

Ad Reinhardt was a purist. His life-long search was for 'art as art and as nothing else'. He expressed this idea both in his paintings and his writings as a series of negations. 'No lines or imaginings, no shapes or composings or representings, no visions or sensations or impulses, no symbols or signs or impastos, no decoratings or colourings or picturings, no pleasures or pains, no accidents or ready-mades, no things, no ideas, no relations, no attributes, no qualities – nothing that is not of the essence', he wrote in 1962. Though he never swerved from a rigorous abstraction, it was not until the last years of his life, when he limited himself to making square black paintings, that he seemed to have achieved his goal. Although the black paintings, of which Tate's *Abstract Painting No. 5* 1962 is exemplary, appear at first to be completely monochrome, close examination reveals an underlying grid of very subtly coloured squares. Each of the colours was mixed with black oil paint to give a matt surface quality. Because of these paintings, and his deep interest in Eastern philosophy, Reinhardt was sometimes referred to as the 'black monk' of the New York art scene. He is widely recognised as an important early figure in Minimalism and his influence as a teacher and writer is evident in the work of many American artists of the 1960s and 1970s. **(SH)**

Abstract Painting No. 5
1962
Oil on canvas
152.4 x 152.4 cm
Presented by Mrs Rita Reinhardt through the American Federation of Arts 1972

Ad Reinhardt
1913–1967

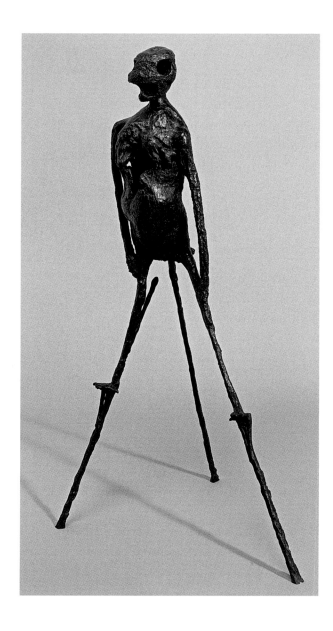

Shepherd of the Landes
1951, cast 1996
Bronze
149 x 89 x 60 cm
Lent from a private collection 1998

Germaine Richier's early work was classically figurative. After the Second World War, she began to use bronze in a more expressive way, and frequently incorporated objects from the natural world, such as driftwood, into her sculptures, creating an array of disturbing creatures. *Storm Man* 1947–8 and *Hurricane Woman* 1948–9 are typical: their pitted and scarred surfaces, as well as their mutilated facial features, suggest intense human suffering. In her sometimes brutal treatment of her working material Richier can be likened to Alberto Giacometti. For both artists the atmosphere of violence and destruction in post-war Europe determined the direction of their work. Richier believed that in order to be effective, art should not 'withdraw from expression', since 'we decidedly cannot conceal human expression in the drama of our time'.

Richier's works frequently suggest the metamorphosis of humans into animals. In *Shepherd of the Landes* 1951, a shepherd has merged with the stilts he uses to help see over long distances of grazing territory, to create a hybrid creature. *Chess Board (Large Version)* 1959, Richier's final work, consists of five oversized playing pieces that are as horrific as they are playful. The King brandishes a set of sculptor's calipers. The Queen, who has a horse-like head, raises her arms, as does the Knight, while the Castle stands on three legs. The bishop is a hunched figure wearing a three-cornered hat. Richier's half-human, half-animal forms exerted a significant influence on the post-war generation of British sculptors, including Reg Butler, Kenneth Armitage and Lynn Chadwick. **(SH)**

Germaine Richier
1902–1959

In the early 1960s, the German artist Gerhard Richter began to make paintings based on photographs. While some of these were taken from newspapers and magazines, they also included amateur and family snaps. Richter was drawn to the awkwardness and lack of sophistication of such images: 'There was no style, no composition, no judgement', he has said. 'It liberated me from personal experience. There was nothing but a pure picture.' He often exaggerated the blurred quality of his source material, as if to emphasise that he was painting an object – a photographic print – rather than the person or landscape it depicted. This approach enabled him to maintain an ironic, questioning distance from his subject matter: the prosaic reality of life in post-war Europe, encompassing city scenes, portraits, advertisements, the cultural heritage of the past and the political turbulence of the present.

Abstraction became a significant part of Richter's output during the 1970s and 1980s. The acid colours and dense surface of these works were built up in successive layers, each one scraped back then painted over again with a range of different brushes and thick spatulas. These techniques, eradicating the artist's original intentions to create something unforeseen, can be understood as another strategy for removing his personality from the work. *St John* 1988 belongs to a series called the 'London Paintings', each named after one of the chapels at Westminster Abbey. However, the titles are not intended to be descriptive, nor should this be taken as a religious work. In contrast to earlier artists such as Wassily Kandinsky or Mark Rothko, Richter insists that abstract paintings do not embody spiritual values or the transcendent sublime – they're just paintings. **(SB)**

St John
1988
Oil on canvas
200.5 x 260.5 cm
Presented by the Patrons of New Art through the Friends of the Tate Gallery 1988

Gerhard Richter
born 1932

Editioned Sculpture
The term 'editioned sculpture' refers to casts of an original sculpture produced in limited quantities during an artist's lifetime or posthumously authorised by an estate. Auguste Rodin was one of the first artists to produce multiple casts of work in this way for the mass market. He made numerous versions of his works in different materials and cast them in varying numbers depending on demand. Before his death, he authorised the French government to make copies of his works from the original plaster casts, which have subsequently been released as editioned bronzes. A work is considered an original edition if it is an authorised cast from the artist's model, and is generally numbered in a similar manner to an editioned print. Editions produced posthumously, however, can be controversial. None of Edgar Degas's sculptures, for example, were cast in bronze during his lifetime, and some critics argue that he never intended them to be more than working models in wax. **(MB)**

Auguste Rodin, perhaps the greatest of nineteenth-century sculptors, is renowned for his vigorous and expressive rendering of the human form. He was originally trained as an ornamental mason, and his ability to capture the subtleties of the human figure was so extraordinary that when he exhibited an early work, *The Age of Bronze*, in 1877, he was accused of casting his work from life. Rodin was, however, concerned with the articulation of ideas over form, and many of his works appear incomplete or intentionally fragmentary as a result. With its free treatment of form, usually to dramatic or emotive ends, Rodin's work is especially valued as a precursor of pure expression, as well as Expressionism more specifically.

While *The Kiss* features two of Rodin's more idealised figures, the lack of inhibition conveyed by their pose

Auguste Rodin
1840–1917

captures the essence of human sexual intimacy. As with many of Rodin's groups of figures, *The Kiss* was originally conceived as part of *The Gates of Hell*, a larger, unfinished commission begun in 1880, which illustrated scenes from Dante's *Inferno*. The depicted couple are Francesca da Rimini and her husband's brother, Paolo Malatesta, the thirteenth-century adulterous lovers doomed to the second circle of hell in Dante's work. Rodin shows the lovers at the moment of their first impassioned kiss, before they are discovered – and subsequently murdered – by Francesca's husband.

The work in Tate's collection is one of three full-scale marble versions carved during Rodin's lifetime, although he also created several smaller versions of the work in clay, plaster and bronze. Rodin encouraged the reproduction of his works, and further editions of many of his sculptures have been produced posthumously.

Cornelia Parker used Rodin's sculpture as the basis for her intervention *The Distance (A Kiss with added string)* 2003, wrapping the work in a mile of string to express the claustrophobic nature of intense relationships. **(MB)**

Left:
Cornelia Parker
The Distance
(A Kiss with added string)
2003
Installation view, *Tate Triennial of British Art*, 2003

Right:
Auguste Rodin
The Kiss
1901–4
Pentelican marble
182.2 x 121.9 x 153 cm
Purchased with assistance from the National Art Collections Fund and public contributions 1953

Left:
Untitled c.1950–2
Oil on canvas
189 x 100.8 cm
Presented by the Mark Rothko
Foundation 1986

Right:
Seagram Murals 1958–9
Installation view, Tate Modern,
March 2006

Mark Rothko
1903–1970

Mark Rothko's style of painting refers both to the simplified compositions and flat areas of colour used by artists such as Matisse and to the Abstract Expressionist work of his American contemporaries.

His *Seagram Murals* were originally commissioned to enhance the decor of the Four Seasons restaurant in the Seagram Building in New York. But after a meal there in 1959, Rothko suddenly withdrew from the commission and returned the money. Instead, he gave the *Seagram Murals* to the Tate in the late 1960s. His main concern was that they should be displayed in a compact space under reduced light. The murals arrived at the gallery in 1970 – the year the artist committed suicide.

Through his use of pillar and window forms and flat colour planes, Rothko alludes to classical and renaissance architecture – in this case to the blind windows and the deliberately oppressive atmosphere of Michelangelo's Laurentian Library in Florence – as well as to Roman villas and Grecian temples. When interviewed about the commission, Rothko later claimed that by referring to these previous empires, he intended to challenge the power of the burgeoning American empire and its elites by confronting diners with his paintings.

Whereas Rothko's earlier works draw on a brighter palette of intense colour, here it is the sombre blacks, reds and maroons, as well as their manner of display, that promote quiet, meditative contemplation for some viewers and claustrophobia in others. **(RL)**

Niki de Saint Phalle is probably best known for her figurative sculptural works, including a fantastical kinetic fountain made in collaboration with her husband Jean Tinguely, commissioned by the City of Paris for a site adjacent to the Centre Georges Pompidou.

However, her 1961 exhibition of 'shooting pictures' was a radical departure from her earlier work and marked her acceptance into an influential circle of artists (dubbed the Nouveau Réalistes by critic Pierre Restany) who were working in Paris in the late 1950s and early 1960s. The Nouveau Réalistes offered a critique of modern life by incorporating mundane objects into collage and sculpture. These artists were also beginning to introduce performative aspects into their work. De Saint Phalle had the idea of putting bottles or bags of paint behind plaster, creating a white, textured surface. The work would then be hung on the wall of the gallery and visitors would be encouraged to shoot at it. The paint was released on impact, creating a splattered effect that gently parodied the gestural painting style of the Abstract Expressionists, whom de Saint Phalle admired. The opening of her exhibition at Galerie J, Paris, was attended by Robert Rauschenberg and Jasper Johns, both of whom participated in the shooting of Tate's painting.

After two years of making shooting pictures, de Saint Phalle felt that the process was becoming addictive and decided it was time to stop, but was keen to retain an interactive element in her work. She began to make large-scale archetypal female figures, which she called 'Nanas'. In 1966 she collaborated with Jean Tinguely and Per Olof Ultlvedt on *hon-en katedral* for the Moderna Museet, Stockholm – a gigantic, reclining 'Nana' that could be entered via the vagina. **(HS)**

Niki de Saint Phalle
1930–2002

Shooting Picture
1961
Plaster, paint, string, polythene and wire on wood
143 x 78 cm
Purchased 1984

Colombian artist Doris Salcedo makes sculptures and installations in response to her extensive research into the experiences of those affected by violence and conflict, particularly by the ongoing civil war in her native country. Travelling to remote areas, she interviews ordinary people, hearing their stories and witnessing the catastrophic effects of traumatic events on their daily lives. Although inspired by individual testimonies, Salcedo avoids explicit references in her sculpture and instead attempts to capture something of the essence of human suffering.

Unland: Audible in the Mouth 1998 is one of a series of sculptures based on simple wooden tables of a type that might be found in any home. Salcedo invented the word 'Unland' to convey the condition of dispossession and displacement resulting from war. Before making the series, she interviewed children who had witnessed the murder or abduction of their parents. Although the table is a symbolically loaded object, associated with sustenance and often the focal point of domestic life, Salcedo wanted to disrupt this familiarity. The legs have been sawn off at one end and the two tables joined together awkwardly to form disjointed, weakened structures, suggesting dysfunction. Salcedo and her assistants then painstakingly drilled countless tiny holes into the surface of the structure, through which they sewed human hair and thread. The delicate web appears to grow from the table, lending it an anthropomorphic quality. In this sense it resembles a prostrate body, lying exposed and vulnerable. **(HS)**

Unland: Audible in the Mouth
1998
Wood, thread and hair
80 x 75 x 315 cm
Presented by the Patrons
of New Art through the
Tate Gallery Foundation 1999

Doris Salcedo
born 1958

Two Women
1912
Oil on canvas
76.5 x 84.5 cm
Presented by the executors
of Dr Rosa Shapire 1954

Karl Schmidt-Rottluff was one of the leading painters of German Expressionsim. Through his friend Erich Heckel, he met Ernst Ludwig Kirchner and Fritz Bleyl while studying in Dresden. Together they formed *Die Brücke* (The Bridge) group. The name was a quotation from a passage by Nietzsche about youthful initiates making a bridge towards a new future. The group's relaxed, communal lifestyle and contemporary morals are reflected in the many studio scenes with young girlfriends and models that Schmidt-Rottluff, Heckel and Kirchner painted in the years after they met. They also travelled together to local lakes and more distant parts of the German coasts to paint landscapes and seascapes.

Schmidt-Rottluff's work of this period is characterised by bold colours placed directly adjacent to one another using vigorous brushwork. Around 1910–11, after his confrontation with ethnic sculptures in the museums of Dresden and Berlin, his compositions became more block-like. He also made sculptures and joined his fellow Expressionists in reviving older German traditions of the woodcut. Schmidt-Rottluff was particularly prolific, producing around 600 woodcuts by the mid-1920s. His art was defamed during the Third Reich and removed from museum collections. However, he continued to work and after the war and was appointed a professor at the Academy of Fine Arts in Berlin. Throughout his career he remained a figurative artist, specialising in the depiction of landscape. **(SR)**

Karl Schmidt-Rottluff
1884–1976

Thomas Schütte is a German artist who creates installations, models, sculptures and photographs, as well as watercolours and drawings of great immediacy and delicacy. These works oscillate in theme between the suggestion of public and utopian ideals, an interest in the graphic language of power, the inscription of meaning within particular spaces, and the description of personal and subjective experience.

Early in his career, Schütte developed the notion of a 'repertoire' – a stock of different types of work or 'fields' of activity to which he regularly returns. These interrelate in what he calls 'a balance of contradictions', allowing interpretations of his work to remain as flexible as possible,

and creating the sense of a simultaneity of interests, materials and forms rather than a linear progression from one type of work to another.

Schütte's works, including public sculptures and installations, have revealed his political interests, referencing the Holocaust, the plight of asylum seekers and refugees, and the rise of neo-Fascism in post-unification Germany. In *United Enemies*, subtitled *A Play in Ten Scenes*, he was influenced by a study trip to Rome that he had undertaken a year earlier, at a significant moment of change and upheaval for Italian politics. The resulting installation centres on tiny modelled male figures, perhaps inflected by classical statuary, bound together and shown under glass domes like those used to display stuffed birds and animals. Prints lining the room provide close-up views of the figures' often distorted and comically caricatured faces. The work suggests how humanity is bound together whether we like it or not, sharing the same fate. The diminutive scale of the figures makes their struggles appear petty, creating a gentle satire on the nature of human politics and communication. **(ED)**

From *United Enemies*
1994
Lithographs on paper
Each work 64 x 95 cm
Purchased 1995

Thomas Schütte
born 1954

Merz
Taking the name from a fragment of text in one of his collages, Kurt Schwitters coined the term *Merz* in 1919 to refer to his assemblages, and subsequently used it to for all his works, including his poetry. An artistic 'movement' that included Schwitters alone, its underlying principle was the allocation of equal worth to all materials. For Schwitters, *Merz* was an aesthetic style that signified freedom from social, cultural and political conventions. **(MB)**

Kurt Schwitters is best known for his collages of discarded materials, which he called *Merz*. While associated with both the Dadaists and Constructivists, he was never part of either movement. His collages, performances and writings bear similarities to the work of the Dadaists, but differ in intent. Whereas Dada was a self-proclaimed anti-art, espousing defiantly negative principles of disruption and rejection, Schwitters's *Merz* were essentially constructive, reassigning value to discarded fragments by positioning them within a constructed composition. There is a systematic rigour to his assemblages, built on structures derived from Cubism. He extended the principles of *Merz* to the interior of his house in Hannover, where he created his first *Merzbau*, a precursor to contemporary installation art.

After being branded a 'degenerate artist' and forced to leave Nazi Germany, Schwitters escaped first to Norway and then, when that country was invaded, to England. *Picture of Spatial Growths – Picture with Two Small Dogs* 1920–39 (p.95) was one of a few works he managed to have brought out of Germany. He reworked the surface of the picture in Norway, adding further layers of papers and objects, including the two small china dogs that give the work its title. Also assembled in Norway, *Opened by Customs* 1937–8 is typical of Schwitters's compositions, a highly ordered arrangement featuring pieces of rubbish and fragments of German and Norwegian newsprint. The title was added to the work by Schwitters's son, taken from two customs labels included in the composition. **(MB)**

Opened by Customs
1937–8
Paper collage, oil and pencil on paper
33.1 x 25.3 cm
Purchased 1958

Kurt Schwitters
1887–1948

Richard Serra's abstract sculptures explore the innate properties of heavy materials, and the way in which our physical awareness is determined by space, place, time and movement. His early work from the late 1960s emphasised physical processes over final form, and included a series of works created by throwing molten lead against the walls of his studio. Serra also made a number of short films at this time.

By 1969, Serra had begun producing his 'prop pieces', sculptures whose parts are balanced solely by forces of weight and gravity. His sculpture *2-2-1: To Dickie and Tina*

1969, 1994 is an example of such a self-supporting configuration. It consists of two pairs of lead sheets and one single sheet, which stay upright only by the force and weight of another rolled lead tube that rests on one corner of each of the sheets. The result is both dramatic and slightly threatening. A later work, *Trip Hammer* 1988, seems even more precarious. One sheet of steel stands upright, 2.6 metres high and 1.3 metres deep, and balances on an edge 5 centimetres wide. Another sheet rests horizontally on this thin edge, its only other means of support provided by its minimal contact with the wall.

Serra has continued working with large-scale assemblies of sheet metal, but since 1970 his work has been increasingly site-specific. The more recent works are often vast in scale and while seen by some as poetic configurations of space, have been criticised by others as too confrontational. In the 1980s, *Tilted Arc*, a 120-feet-long, 12-feet-high curving wall of metal installed in the centre of the Federal Plaza in New York City, caused intense controversy, and was finally removed for scrap. **(SH)**

2-2-1: To Dickie and Tina
1969, 1994
Lead antimony alloy
132 x 349 x 132 cm
Purchased with assistance
from the American Fund
for the Tate Gallery 1997

Richard Serra
born 1939

Untitled A
Untitled B
Untitled C
Untitled D
1975
Photographs on paper
Each 41.8 x 28.4 cm
Presented by Janet Wolfson
de Botton 1996

In the mid-1970s many artists were using photography to record performances, but Cindy Sherman was one of the first to pioneer photography as a fine-art medium in itself. Although she has made herself the prime subject of her pictures, her work can scarcely be described as self-portraiture. Rather than using the medium to explore her true identity, she employs costumes and make-up to project alternative personae derived from her imagination.

Sherman studied to be a painter but was drawn to the idea of using make-up as a form of painting, her own body becoming the canvas. *Untitled A, B, C* and *D* 1975 belong to an extensive series of photographs in which she transforms herself from one character to another. The make-up used is deliberately crude, but despite the theatricality of the images, she nevertheless successfully implies a range of characters, including a young girl, an older woman and a man. Masquerade had earlier been employed by the Surrealists as a means of exploring the nature of desire and sexual identity. Sherman uses it to test the boundaries between race, class, age and gender.

Sherman's interest in artifice is further explored in her *Film Stills*, in which she casts herself as the subject in imaginary film scenes. She described how the female types in these images were derived from the plethora of images absorbed from cultural sources such as film, TV, advertisements and magazines, as well as real acquaintances who served as role models in her youth. Detached from any real scenario, Sherman's evocative *Film Stills* invite the viewer to construct their own narratives around the images. **(HS)**

Cindy Sherman
born 1954

David Smith's sculptures combine both monumentality and spontaneity in remarkable synthesis. He grew up in Indiana, where he formed an admiration for trains and railroads. Aged nineteen he worked as a welder and riveter in a car factory, developing a deep respect for the materials iron and steel. He stated [of steel]: 'What it can do in arriving at form economically, no other material can do. The metal itself possesses little art history. What associations it possesses are those of this century: power, structure, movement, progress, suspension, destruction, and brutality.'

Smith trained as a painter, however, coming to sculpture through collage and relief works. In *Home of the Welder* 1945 he draws flat planes together to form a volumetric whole with references to Egyptian building models and reliquary houses. The influence of Surrealist sculpture, particularly Giacometti's early work, is evident in the depiction of a dream world. Smith creates a symbolic tableau using objects such as the millstone and chain to express the frustration and sense of confinement that he felt in relation to his work at this time and his childless first marriage.

Wagon II 1964 was made just a year before Smith's life was tragically cut short by a car accident. The sculpture demonstrates his ability to bend and draw in steel with apparent effortlessness, combining a sense of repose with an underlying suggestion of powerful latent energy. The wheels are both practical and symbolic, liberating the sculpture from a static position on a plinth and suggesting nature's eternal cycle. **(MP)**

Wagon II
1964
Steel
250.2 x 306.5 x 167 cm
Purchased with assistance from the American Fund for the Tate Gallery, the National Art Collections Fund and the Friends of the Tate Gallery 1999

David Smith
1906–1965

Frank Stella first came to prominence with a series of abstract geometric paintings in the early 1960s. Reacting against the demonstrative style of such Abstract Expressionists as Jackson Pollock and Franz Kline, he followed instead the more conceptual approach of Jasper Johns, whose paintings of the American flag stressed the object-nature of works on canvas. In his earliest work, Stella used compositions of stripes that emphasise the paintings' rectangular structures. In the famous *Black Paintings* 1958–60 narrow bands of black enamel are separated by fine lines of unpainted canvas that echo the horizontal, vertical or diagonal axes of the rectangle. *Six Mile Bottom* belongs to the subsequent series of *Aluminium Paintings* 1960–1 characterised by a similar use of aluminium paint, reinforcing the two-dimensionality and symmetry of the picture surface. In this series, as is visible in *Six Mile Bottom*, Stella cut away the small rectangles of canvas that were excluded by the logic of the striping pattern. He further developed this process in the following series of *Copper Paintings*, cutting away much larger areas of canvas and eliminating the original rectangular form.

Stella's insistence that 'what you see is what you see' was a significant influence on the development of Minimalist sculpture, particularly that of Donald Judd, in its simplicity and quasi-industrial repetition. During the mid-1960s Stella began using colour and polygonal canvases; by the 1970s he was combining organic forms and gestural brushstrokes with the earlier geometric structures in complex wall reliefs that have evolved into wholly three-dimensional structures. **(EM)**

Left:
Hyena Stomp
1962
Oil on canvas
195.6 x 195.6 cm
Purchased 1965

Right:
Six Mile Bottom
1960
Metallic paint on canvas
300 x 182.2 cm
Purchased 1972

Frank Stella
born 1936

Surrealism

In his *Surrealist Manifesto* of 1924, the movement's leader André Breton declared: 'Surrealism rests on the belief … in the omnipotence of the dream, and in the disinterested play of thought.' The Surrealists acknowledged the power of the unconscious, the suppressed and the irrational. As the means towards this intellectual, sexual and political liberation they drew upon and modified the (often contradictory) theories of Freudian psychoanalysis and Marxist politics. This synthesis is evident in the title of their first periodical: *La Révolution surréaliste*.

In these early years the Surrealists actively explored the potential of the irrational. Breton and the other poets, including Paul Eluard and Robert Desnos, found release from conscious control through word games and automatic writing (unedited word association). In the belief that everyone could be an artist, they collaborated on techniques such as the game of visual 'Consequences' known as *Cadavre exquis* (Exquisite Corpse). The painters, including Joan Miró and André Masson, found individual ways of adapting automatic techniques to pictorial form. Their fluid line and open fields of colour evoke the liberated world of the unconscious. Automatism would gain strength periodically within Surrealism, notably in the 1940s work of Matta and Arshile Gorky in America.

Simultaneously, Surrealist art evoked the illusory space of dreams, following the example of Giorgio de Chirico. Ernst adapted this mode in the 1920s, and Yves Tanguy, René Magritte (around whom a Brussels group formed) and Salvador Dalí painted inexplicably disrupted situations. Their explorations also shifted into a wide variety of media. Photography and film were introduced through Man Ray's experiments and the explosive impact of *Un chien andalou* (1929), on which Dalí collaborated with Luis Buñuel, while Alberto Giacometti's sculptures encouraged Dalí to promote provocative Surrealist objects that could infiltrate everyday life.

The movement was regularly subject to bitter internal disputes, which included defections to a rival group around Georges Bataille's periodical *Documents*. However, fragmentation was matched by internationalism in the 1930s as Surrealism broadened its reach through a string of exhibitions linked to sister groups in Brussels, Prague and Tenerife. The *International Surrealist Exhibition*, held in London in 1936 (see p.26), was the first to challenge the way in which art was displayed. With Breton, the artists Roland Penrose and E.L.T. Mesens set up striking juxtapositions of small works against large, realistic against abstract. Such extraordinary exhibitions attracted wide publicity (25,000 visited the London show in a month) and a stream of new recruits. There was a notable number of women artists among them, including – in Britain alone – Eileen Agar, Lee Miller and Leonora Carrington.

Among art movements, Surrealism was unusually long-lived (continuing into the 1960s), and this may be attributed to the potency of reconciling 'the real and the imagined … the communicable and the incommunicable'. When Breton, Matta, and others were exiled to New York during the Second World War, Surrealism made its impact on the Abstract Expressionist artists they encountered there, including Gorky and Jackson Pollock. Surrealism's legacy is still discernible; its assertion of the often transgressive liberation of the mind has profoundly marked subsequent cultural activity. **(MG)**

Top:
Man Ray (1890–1976)
Indestructible Object
1922–3, remade 1933,
editioned replica 1965
Wooden metronome
and photograph
21.5 x 11 x 11.5 cm
Presented by the Friends
of the Tate Gallery 2000

Above:
Luis Buñuel (1900–1983) and
Salvador Dalí (1904–1989)
Un chien andalou
1929
Film still
Courtesy BFI

René Magritte (1898–1967)
The Reckless Sleeper
1928
Oil on canvas
116 x 81 cm
Purchased 1969

The first impression on entering a Tomoko Takahashi installation is often one of utter chaos. Hundreds of objects are strewn across the floor, attached to the walls, even hanging from the ceiling. But on closer inspection a sense of some kind of underlying order begins to emerge. Takahashi spends many months collecting together the objects and recycling them into her work, usually setting up home within the exhibition site for the duration of its installation. Her work may be read as a critique of today's throwaway society, although her primary interest is the symbolic and personal meaning contained within her materials.

Drawing Room was first shown at the Drawing Center in New York in 1998. Takahashi kept all her post over the preceding year, including love letters, bills, faxes and junk mail. She then performed the ritual of reading each item out aloud before obliterating the text with marker pens and affixing the documents to the wall and ceiling, simultaneously exhibiting and obscuring her personal life. In characteristic fashion, patterns begin to emerge – in some parts of the room, pieces of paper are grouped together by colour or size.

When the work was acquired by Tate, Takahashi reconstructed the installation, working with conservators and curators to make detailed plans regarding the positioning of the elements. The 'drawings' are so densely packed together in some places that they appear to be swarming like insects. Some additional elements were added at this time, including the desk and chair, which appear to have been swallowed up by all the paperwork. **(HS)**

Drawing Room
1998
Mixed media
Presented by the Patrons of New Art (Special Purchase Fund) 2002

Tomoko Takahashi
born 1966

Yves Tanguy is known for the subterranean worlds he created, in which strange, biomorphic forms exist in empty landscapes. Having joined the Surrealist movement in 1925, he became fascinated with automatic drawing, creating images spontaneously from his imagination. He regularly participated in the Surrealist game of the 'exquisite corpse', where players would draw one part of a 'body' secretively, fold the sheet over and pass to the next player until a bizarre whole being was completed.

Despite receiving no formal artistic training, Tanguy had a great facility with paint, creating seamlessly smooth surfaces and minutely painted organic forms. He developed his distinctive language during the late 1920s and early 1930s, and while his biomorphic images are said to be derived from the rock formations he had seen in Brittany, they appear to have little in common with the real world. Tanguy progressively honed his compositions, and following a visit to South Africa, his landscapes became expansive voids, which appear to extend into infinity. In *Azure Day* 1937, only two vague, cloud-like accumulations help to differentiate between sky and land. In the foreground, strange skeletal beings are grouped in confrontational formations. Their delicately pastel-coloured shapes and the apparently benign title of the work appear incongruous when viewed against the threatening atmosphere that pervades the composition. **(LA)**

Azure Day
1937
Oil on canvas
63 x 81.2 cm
Accepted by H.M. Government in lieu of tax on the estate of Cynthia Fraser, Chairman of the Friends of the Tate Gallery 1965–71, and allocated to the Tate Gallery 1996

Yves Tanguy
1900–1955

Dorothea Tanning has worked as a painter, sculptor and printmaker, and most recently as a writer and poet. She became involved with Surrealism in the 1940s, after meeting the group of artists in exile in New York from Paris during the Second World War, including Max Ernst, whom she later married. Her paintings from that period draw on personal and literary narratives of childhood fantasies and nightmares.

Tanning loved Gothic novels as a child and many characteristics of the genre are present in *Eine Kleine Nachtmusik* 1943. The title 'A Little Night Music' is borrowed from one of Mozart's most popular and light-hearted chamber works, and Tanning's painting certainly has more than a little of the 'night' about it. A dreary hotel corridor is the setting for a sinister and unnerving scene of unexplained events and unseen forces; a giant sunflower appears to menace or bewitch two young girls, one of whom leans lifelessly in a doorway while the other's hair stands on end, either through fright, static or a wind that affects nothing else in the scene.

Tanning's work evolved in the 1950s, as she experimented with different painting and, later, sculptural approaches. However, her use of motifs such as mirrors and flowers – symbolic material, almost always evoking the female human form – and dreamlike elements remained constant. She currently lives and works in New York. **(RL)**

Eine Kleine Nachtmusik
1943
Oil on canvas
40.7 x 61 cm
Purchased with assistance from the National Art Collections Fund and the American Fund for the Tate Gallery 1997

Dorothea Tanning
born 1910

Illegitimate I
1997
Oil on canvas
210.1 x 131.1 x 2.3 cm
Purchased 1998

Luc Tuymans is one of a handful of artists responsible for the reinvigoration of painting during the 1990s. The arrival of Conceptual art in the 1960s and later lens-based media such as photography and video had suggested that painting was an outdated and irrelevant medium, out of joint with a new age of radical technological and social developments. Part of Tuymans's success is based on his confrontation with the anachronism, inadequacy or 'belatedness' of painting, as he describes it.

Born in Antwerp in 1958, Tuymans briefly interrupted his career as a painter in the 1980s to become a filmmaker. Subsequently he has infused his paintings with filmic techniques such as close-ups, cropping, framing and sequencing. In addition he draws much of his subject matter and imagery from newspapers, films and television. His subject matter ranges widely from major historical events such as the Holocaust or Belgian colonial politics, to paintings that depict psychological states and emotions, to the banalities of wallpaper patterns or Christmas decorations. The undoubted centrality of subject matter in these works is undercut by their characteristic evasiveness, by what is left out or avoided rather than what is explicitly represented.

Illegitimate I 1997 is part of a group of works completed and first exhibited together, which express a sense of sickliness and contamination. The hazily rendered image is perhaps reminiscent of a traditional wallpaper motif, or the outline of female reproductive organs. Tuymans embraces ambiguity, enjoying the possibility of multiple interpretations for his work. He paints on unstretched canvases pinned to the wall, making numerous preparatory drawings and photographs, but insists that the time spent actually painting is always confined to a single day. **(ED)**

Luc Tuymans
born 1958

*Quattro Stagioni
(A Painting in Four Parts)*
1993–4
Purchased with assistance from
the American Fund for the Tate
Gallery and Tate Members 2002

This page, left to right:
Primavera
Acrylic, oil, crayon,
and pencil on canvas
313.2 x 189.5 cm

Estate
Acrylic and pencil on canvas
314.1 x 215.2 cm

Autunno
Acrylic, oil, crayon
and pencil on canvas
313.6 x 215 cm

Inverno
Acrylic, oil, and pencil on canvas
313.5 x 221 cm

Cy Twombly's paintings are distinctive for their inventive use of gesture. The abstracted forms on his canvases are produced through various different methods of applying paint, ranging from gentle brushwork to harsh scrapings, impasto daubs and graphic inscriptions. He developed his style in the wake of Abstract Expressionism and the 'action painting' of artists such as Jackson Pollock.

Twombly moved from his native America to Rome in 1957 and immersed himself in classical culture. The subjects of his paintings are often derived from literary and mythological sources and frequently feature fragments of text from classical poetry.

His works also evoke transience and decay. He often rubs out or overworks sections of his paintings, suggesting the passage of time and alluding to the broader sweep of history. The delicacy of these erased passages acts as a metaphor for the fragility of memory. These erasures are particularly evident in the blackboard paintings that he began making during the late 1960s.

Quattro Stagioni 1993–4 is a series of four large paintings representing the seasons and the cycle of life, death and rebirth. The strong colours and expressive mark-making on the canvases suggest the emotive nature and violent changing of the seasons. The bright reds of spring and the searing yellows of summer contrast with the earthy browns and greens of autumn and the more solemn, muted blues and blacks of winter. The abstracted form of a boat recurs in the paintings, suggesting the passage to the underworld in the Egyptian Book of the Dead. **(RT)**

Cy Twombly
born 1928

Vorticism

Launched in London in 1914 by the artist, writer and polemicist Wyndham Lewis, Vorticism was a British rival to Futurism. The name was given currency by the title of the journal *Blast: Review of the Great English Vortex*, whose publication marked the launch of the movement. Vorticism shared the Futurist enthusiasm for the energy and dynamism of the modern industrial and mechanical world. However, the Vorticists rejected the Futurist attempt to convey the romance of speed, referring contemptuously to 'automobilism' and the 'accelerated impressionism' of Futurist painting. Instead they sought a more profound, architectural and abstract expression of this vision, exemplified in, for example, Lewis's *Workshop* of 1914–15 (p.156).

The first of *Blast*'s only two issues contained among other material two aggressive manifestos by Lewis 'blasting', in highly eccentric language and typography, what he considered to be the effete and backward-looking nature of British art and culture: 'BLAST First (from politeness) ENGLAND … CURSE ITS CLIMATE … DISMAL SYMBOL … of effeminate lout within.' But he then 'blessed' England for its maritime and industrial power, as well as its tradition of satire, and proclaimed the Vorticist aesthetic: 'The New Vortex plunges to the heart of the Present … we produce a New Living Abstraction.' The only group exhibition of the Vorticists was held in London in 1915, and as the First World War gathered pace, Vorticism, like so much else, came to an end, although in 1920 Lewis made a brief attempt to revive it with Group X.

The other Vorticist artists were Lawrence Atkinson, Jessica Dismorr, Cuthbert Hamilton, William Roberts, Helen Saunders, Edward Wadsworth and the sculptors Jacob Epstein and Henri Gaudier-Brzeska. David Bomberg was not formally a member of the group but produced major work in a similar style.

Very few Vorticist paintings have survived, but there is a substantial body of works on paper. Outstanding paintings are Lewis's large *The Crowd* 1914–15, which evokes a revolutionary event in a stark urban and industrial setting, and David Bomberg's two large canvases *The Mud Bath* and *In the Hold*, both of 1913–14. Of his work Bomberg wrote: 'I appeal to a *sense of form* … in some work I completely abandon *Naturalism* and Tradition … My object is the *construction of Pure Form*.' He also wrote, 'I live in a *steel city*'. Among major surviving Vorticist sculptures are works by Gaudier-Brzeska and Epstein, which present a mechanistic, modernist image of man and nature. Gaudier's giant carving, *Hieratic Head of Ezra Pound* 1914, is a Vorticist portrait of the American poet who played an influential role in avant-garde circles in London from 1909–20 and strongly supported Vorticism. Epstein's *Rock Drill* 1913–15 (p.107) combined a real machine with the highly abstracted life-size figure of its operator to create a towering and powerful image of modern industrial man. All that now survives of this work is the figure's torso, cast in bronze. **(SW)**

Henri Gaudier-Brzeska (1891–1915)
Bird Swallowing a Fish
c.1913–14, cast 1964
Bronze
31.8 x 60.3 x 27.9 cm
Purchased 1964

Right:
Front cover and page
from *Blast*, no.1, July 1914
Tate Archive

Below:
Edward Wadsworth (1889–1949)
Abstract Composition
1915
Gouache, pen
and pencil on paper
41.9 x 34.3 cm
Purchased 1956

Celebrity
Warhol's comment that 'in the future, everyone will be famous for fifteen minutes' seems to have been borne out in the late twentieth and early twenty-first centuries, with the popularity of reality TV and greater public access to professional broadcast media. Celebrity remains a modern fascination, and thus a common subject of art. Painters as diverse as Elizabeth Peyton and Wilhelm Sasnal have made portraits of well-known actors, models and musicians, while Sam Taylor-Wood has used her famous friends, including Elton John, David Beckham, Marianne Faithfull and Robert Downey Jr in her artworks.

Warhol not only made portraits of celebrities, but became a celebrity in his own right. With his white-blond wig and deadpan speaking style, he was arguably the first artist of the media age to cultivate his persona as a recognisable 'brand', although a precedent can be found in Salvador Dalí. In the UK, art has periodically made the front pages of newspapers. In the 1970s controversy raged over the artistic merit of Carl Andre's *Equivalent VIII* (p.61), which became known as the 'Tate bricks'. More recently artists including Damien Hirst and Tracey Emin have actively cultivated their own media image as part of their artistic practice. **(RT)**

One of the most celebrated figures of the twentieth century and arguably the most important proponent of American Pop art, Andy Warhol began his career as a commercial artist. As an illustrator for magazines and the advertising industry, he developed a distinctively clean and simple graphic style. His earliest works as a fine artist are drawings and paintings depicting consumer goods and images from the popular press.

In the early 1960s he began making images using silkscreening. This technique allowed for repetition of images on a large scale. The replication serves to depersonalise the images that Warhol chose and ultimately to render them equally banal or profound, regardless of whether they depict consumer objects, famous faces or electric chairs.

Many of his most recognisable pictures were sourced from the media and convey his fascination with celebrity and mortality. His works featuring Marilyn Monroe, Elizabeth Taylor and Elvis Presley depict the stars at the height of their fame. The blurring and fading that result from the intrinsic deterioration of the image in the silkscreening process suggest the inevitability of decay and death. In his images of Jacqueline Kennedy during the hours after the assassination of President John F. Kennedy, Warhol fetishises the First Lady's anguish, highlighting the media's morbid and compulsive fascination with private grief broadcast on a public scale.

In addition to his portraits of celebrated figures of the day, Warhol made several series depicting 'disasters' including car crashes and people jumping from high rise buildings in suicide attempts. These suggest his enduring interest in creating modern memento mori, images that act as reminders of mortality. **(RT)**

Andy Warhol
1928–1987

Left:
Self-Portrait
1986
Acrylic and screenprint on canvas
203.2 x 203.2 cm
Presented by Janet Wolfson
de Botton 1996

Marilyn Diptych
1962
Acrylic on canvas
Each 205.4 x 144.8 cm
Purchased 1980

Video Art
In 1965 Sony introduced the Portapak portable video system and changed art practice at a stroke. Like many new technologies it was originally developed by the military, but artists working outside the mainstream, as well as avant-garde dancers and filmmakers embraced the new medium enthusiastically, avidly exploiting what it offered in terms of instant replay, portability, and solitary, economical filming, which could allow a new intimate relationship between the body and the camera. Video was not easily commodified, it could connect audiences and events immediately and directly in a way that traditional painting and sculpture could not, it was an important tool for documenting performance and happenings, and it could be used as a vehicle for critiquing mass media TV and Hollywood. Early uses by artists such as Bruce Nauman, Nam June Paik and Yoko Ono included live video feeds, and unedited real time footage.

The 1980s saw the development of video sculptures and installations, where the works became integrated into structural and architectural features giving a sense of permanence to a medium that in its infancy had traded on its immateriality, transience and fragility. By the 1990s video had become a key and at times dominant medium in international art exhibitions and as fears over longevity and conservation diminished, was increasingly acquired by major museums and private collectors. Cinema style and multiple projections immerse the viewer in a total visual and aural environment. The medium continues to offer a connection with the real world of TV, Internet, surveillance cameras and video games. **(ED)**

Gillian Wearing first came to prominence in the early 1990s for works featuring real people in real settings. While her photographs and films use the tropes of documentary reportage and reality television, her interest lies in the psychological subtext beneath the appearance of everyday life. She explores how the most intimate facets of our psyches are communicated to others.

For her photographic series *Signs that say what you want them to say and not Signs that say what someone else wants you to say* 1992–3 she photographed passers-by on the London streets holding placards on which they had inscribed messages. The signs range from the didactic to the emotive, revealing the complex inner world of each individual and the extent to which they are prepared to reveal themselves to a complete stranger.

The strategy of encouraging personal disclosure is also evident in Wearing's *Confess All On Video. Don't Worry You Will Be in Disguise. Intrigued? Call Gillian* 1994. The work's title was the wording of an advertisement she placed in the London listings magazine *Time Out*. Several participants responded, confessing personal stories on camera while wearing masks to protect their identities. Wearing's video functions as a contemporary equivalent of the confessional or the analyst's couch. The audience is invited to share the cathartic experience of the participants' 'talking cure' while drawing their own assumptions about the relative truth or fiction of the various narratives.

In *10-16* 1997, adults are shown lip-synching recorded interviews with young people between the ages of ten and sixteen. Putting the adolescents' words into the mouths of adults emphasises the enduring fragility of youthful hopes and fears with humour and poignancy. **(RT)**

10-16
1997
Video
Presented by the Patrons of New Art through the Tate Gallery Foundation 1998

Gillian Wearing
born 1963

Turbine Hall
Rachel Whiteread's installation for Tate Modern's Turbine Hall in 2005–6, *EMBANKMENT*, was the sixth commission in the annual Unilever Series (see p.20). The piece was built on site from approximately 14,000 hollow white polyethylene casts made from ten differently sized cardboard boxes. Taking inspiration from both the warehouse and the arctic landscape, it explored themes of personal and collective memory. The Unilever Series began in 2000 with Louise Bourgeois's *I Do, I Undo, I Redo*, three giant bronze towers which visitors could climb to view the space, followed by Juan Muñoz's intervention in the architecture *Double Bind* (p.43). *Marsyas* (2002–3), Anish Kapoor's spectacular site-specific sculpture, was made from three circular frames stretching red fabric the length of the space (pp.38–9), and was followed by Olafur Eliasson's atmospheric *Weather Project* (2003–4), almost appearing to double the space's height with its mirrored ceiling and indoor 'sun' (p.12). In 2004–5, Bruce Nauman's audio installation *Raw Materials* (p.32) radically did away with any form of material transformation in the space, using only sounds sampled from his work of previous years. **(CW)**

Rachel Whiteread studied painting at Brighton Polytechnic (1982–5) and sculpture at the Slade School of Fine Art (1985–7). Her sculptures are made by casting the interior spaces of familiar objects such as a bath or a table, using plaster, resin or rubber, processes usually associated with the preparation of sculpture rather than the finished work. The intimate, domestic nature of her earliest works such as *Shallow Breath* 1988 – a cast of the space beneath the bed in which the artist was born – or *Ghost* 1990 – a cast of the interior of a living room in a terraced house similar to her childhood home – laid the foundations for the melancholic representation of memory evident in her body of work to date.

Whiteread, who won the Turner Prize in 1993 and represented Britain at the Venice Biennale in 1997, is one of the few artists of her generation to have worked on public sculpture of monumental scale. These major works include *House*, a life-sized concrete cast of the interior of a condemned terraced house in London's East End (1993, destroyed 1994), the cast of an entire library for *Holocaust Memorial* in Vienna (completed 2000) and *Monument*, a resin cast of the empty plinth in Trafalgar Square (2001), for which it was made. For the Unilever Series Turbine Hall commission at Tate Modern in 2005, Whiteread created *EMBANKMENT*. Comprising approximately 14,000 casts made from ten differently sized cardboard boxes stacked and built up in the space, it formed a labyrinthine installation speaking of personal history – but never revealing what the box might have contained – and of both the museum's industrial past and its present, as keeper of collective memory. **(CW)**

Untitled (Air Bed II)
1992
Polyurethane rubber
122 x 197 x 23 cm
Purchased with assistance from the Patrons of New Art through the Tate Gallery Foundation 1993

Rachel Whiteread
born 1963

Photographic Credits

Index

Page numbers in *italic* type refer to illustrations; **bold** numbers refer to main entries.

J

Janco, Marcel 95
Japanese prints 77
Johns, Jasper **141**, 201, 202, 212
  0 through 9 141, *141*
  Flag series 201, 220
Jones, Joan 138
  Lines in the Sand: Helen in Egypt 41
Judd, Donald 14, 22, 37, *37*, 113, 136, 140, **142–3**, 173, 182, 220
  Untitled (1972) 142, *143*
  Untitled (1990) 173, *173*
  Untitled (DJ 85-51) 142, *142*
Judson Dance Theater 182
Jung, Carl Gustav 57, 198

K

Kabbalah 57
Kahlo, Frida 36
Kahnweiler, Daniel-Henri 92
Kandinsky, Wassily 62, 64, **144**, 177, 180, 207
  Cossacks 144
  Green Sound 144
  The Yellow Sound 144
Kapoor, Anish 14, 116, **145**, 173, 205
  Ishi's Light 29, *30*, 57, 145, *145*
  Marsyas 37, *38–9*, 41, 235
Kaprow, Allen 138, 190
Kelly, Ellsworth **146–7**
  Broadway 146, *147*
  White Curve 146, *146*
kinetic sculpture 121, 138
Kirchner, Ernst Ludwig 110, **148**, 214
  Bathers at Moritzburg 148, *148*
kitsch **192**, 202
Klee, Paul 64, 177
Klein, Yves **149**, 188, 205
  1KB 79 149, *149*
  Anthropometries 138, 149
  Fire Paintings 149
Kline, Franz 57, **150**
  Meryon 150, *150*
Koepcke, Addi 114
Kollwitz, Käthe 127
Koolhaas, Rem 47
Koons, Jeff 192, 202
  Three Ball Total Equilibrium Tank... 202, *203*
Kosugi, Takehisa 114
Kosuth, Joseph 89
  Clock (One and Five), English/Latin Version 89, *89*
Kounellis, Jannis 29, 66, 75, 116, **151**
  Untitled (1968) 67
  Untitled (1979) 151, *151*
Krasner, Lee 57, **152**
  Gothic Landscape 152, *152*
Kristeva, Julia 164
Kruger, Barbara 127, 202
Kuitca, Guillermo **153**
  Untitled 153, *153*
Kusama, Yayoi 78

L

Lacan, Jacques 78
Land art 66
Landy, Michael 188
Lane, Brian 114
Larionov, Mikhail 125
Latham, John 89
Lautréamont, Comte de 63, 96, 163
Le Corbusier 154
Léger, Fernand 101, **154–5**
  The Acrobat and his Partner 154, *155*
  Leaves and Shell 154
  Still Life with a Beer Mug 154, *154*
Lewis, Wyndham **156**, 230
  The Crowd 230
  Workshop 156, *156*
LeWitt, Sol 89, 113, 140, **157**, 173
  Five Open Geometric Structures 157, *157*
  Six Geometric Figures (+Two) 157
  Two Open Modular Cubes/ Half-Off 173
Lichtenstein, Roy **158**, 196, 201
  Whaam! 158, *158*, 202
Lipchitz, Jacques 92, **159**
  Sculpture 159, *159*
Lippard, Lucy 66, 89
Liss, Carl
  Travel Fluxkit 114
Live Art Development Agency 41
Live Culture symposium 41
Loktev, Julia 41
Long, Richard 14, 25
Lucas, Sarah 61, 96, 188

M

McCarthy, Paul 164, 192
  Bighead 41
  Blockhead 40, 41
McEwan, Ian
  Saturday 34
Maciunas, George 114, *114*
  FluxUS 114
McQueen, Steve **170**
  Drumroll 170, *170*
Magritte, René 81, 86, 96, **160–1**, 222
  The Annunciation 160, *161*
  The Future of Statues 160
  Man with a Newspaper 160
  The Reckless Sleeper 160, *223*
Mail art 114
Malevich, Kasimir 30, **162**, 173, 205
  Dynamic Suprematism 162, *162*
Mallarmé, Stéphane 81
Malraux, André 112
  Imaginary Museum 22, *23*
Manzoni, Piero 66, 116, 138, **164–5**, 205
  Achrome 164, *165*
  Artist's Breath 164
  Artist's Shit 164, *164*
Marclay, Christian 27, **166**
  Sounds of Christmas 41
  Video Quartet 166, *166*, 202
Marden, Bruce 205
Marinetti, Filippo Tommaso 21, 76, 119, 144
  Cover of *Zang Tumb Tumb* 119
  The Foundation and Manifesto of Futurism 119
Martin, Agnes **167**
  Morning 167, *167*
Martin, J.L. 187

Marx, Karl 27, 222
Masson, André 222
'Material Gestures' display 26, 29–30, *31*
materials **75**
Matisse, Henri 29, 36–7, 92, 113, 152, **168–9**, 210
  The Snail 14, 22, 168, *169*
  Trivaux Pond 168, *168*
Matta, Roberto 222
Matthieu, Georges 64
Mayor, David 114
Meireles, Cildo **171**
  Eureka/Blindhotland 171, *171*
Mendieta, Ana 138
Meryon, Charles 150
Merz 95, **216**
Merz, Mario 66
  Cone 66, *67*
Merz, Marisa 66
Mesens, E.L.T. 222
Metaphysical Painting **86**
Metzger, Gustav 114
Metzinger, Jean 92
Mexican muralists 198
Michaux, Henri 64
Mies van der Rohe, Ludwig 177
Millennium footbridge 17
Miller, Lee 163, 222
Minh-ha, Trinh T. 41
Minimalism 61, 78, 81, 90, 105, 113, 114, 140, 142–3, 157, 167, **172–3**, 182, 186, 201, 202, 205, 220
Seriality 143
Miró, Joan 29, **174–5**, 222
  Message from a Friend 174, *175*
  Painting 174, *174*
  A Star Caresses the Breast of a Negress (Painting Poem) 174
Miyajima, Tatsuo 116, **176**
  Lattice 176, *176*
modernism 68, 202
Moholy-Nagy, László **177**
  K VII 177, *177*
  Vision in Motion 177
Mondrian, Piet 92, 152, **178–9**, 180, 187
  Composition B/(No.II), with Red 178, *178*
  Composition with Yellow, Blue and Red 178
  The Tree A 178, *179*
Moneo, Raphael 47
Monet, Claude 14, 25, 26, 29, 100, 143, **180**
  Impression: Sunrise 180
  Water-Lilies 180, *180*
monochrome paintings **205**
montage 27, 70, 95, 132
Moore, Henry 107, 133, **181**, 187
  Recumbent Figure 181
  Upright Internal/External Form 181, *181*
Morandi, Giorgio 86
Morris, Robert 66, 75, 173, **182**
  Untitled 143, *182*
Motherwell, Robert *56*, 57
Munch, Edvard **183**
  The Sick Child 183, *183*
Muñoz, Juan **184**
  Double Bind 42, *43*, 235
  'Raincoat drawings' 184
  Towards the Corner 28, 184, *184*
Musgrave, Victor 114
Muybridge, Eadweard 68

N

Nabis 77
Namuth, Hans 199
Nash, Paul 187
National Gallery 45
Nauman, Bruce 75, 138, **185**
  Double No 185, 202
  Good Boy Bad Boy 25
  Raw Materials 33, 235
  Untitled (Three Large Animals) 185, *185*
neo-Conceptualism 106, 137
Neo-Concretism 171
Neo-Plasticism 178
New Realism 130
New York School 57
Newman, Barnett 25, *56*, 57, 112, 167, **186**
  Adam 57, 186, *186*
  Eve 57
Nicholson, Ben 133, **187**
  1934 (relief) 187
Nietzsche, Friedrich 76, 86, 110, 214
Nolde, Emile 110
  The Sea B 111
Nouveau Réalisme 64, 81, **188–9**, 201, 212

O

objet trouvé 188
Oiticica, Hélio 171
Oldenburg, Claes **190**, 201
  Counter and Plates with Potatoes and Ham 190, *200*
  Soft Drainpipe – Blue (Cool) Version 190, *190*, 201
  Soft Drainpipe – Red (Hot) Version 190
  The Store 190
Omega workshop 156
Ono, Yoko 114, 138
Orozco, Gabriel 41
Orphism **101**, 125
Ortega, Damian 41
Orwell, George 137
Ottinger, Ulrike 41
Ozenfant, Jean 154

P

Page, Robin 114
Paik, Nam June *114*
Pane, Gina 138
Paolini, Giovanni 66
Paolozzi, Eduardo 131, 201
Parker, Cornelia **191**
  The Distance (A Kiss with added string) 208, *208*
  Thirty Pieces of Silver 191, *191*
Pärt, Arvo 41
Pasmore, Victor 131
Patterson, Ben *114*
Penone, Giuseppe 66
  Tree of 12 Metres 66
Penrose, Roland 222
Performance Art 114, **138**, 188, 190, 198
Pevsner, Antoine 121
photography 72, 218, 222
photo-emulsion paint 70
photographic reproductions 22
Rayographs 163
solarised 163
as source 68, 207
photomontage 95, 132
Piano, Renzo 47
Picabia, Francis 95, 101, 163, **192–3**
  The Fig-Leaf 192, *193*
  The Handsome Pork Butcher 192
  Hot Eyes 192
  Otaiti 192, *192*
  'transparencies' 192
Picasso, Pablo 25, 26, 27, 29, 30, 36–7, 80, 92, 93, 121, 158, 159, 187, **194–5**
  Bottle of Vieux Marc, Glass, Guitar and Newspaper 92
  Bust of a Women 79
  Girl in a Chemise 194
  Seated Nude 93
  Still Life 194
  The Three Dancers 194, *195*
  Weeping Woman 25, 194, *194*
Pissarro, Camille 100
Pistoletto, Michelangelo 66
  Venus of the Rags 66
'Poetry and Dream' display 26, 27, *27*, 29
Polke, Sigmar 37, **196–7**
  Printing Errors 196
  Triptych 196, *196*, *197*
Pollock, Jackson 26, 29, *56*, 57, 63, 112, 143, 150, 152, **198–9**, 222, 229
  Summertime 198–9, *199*
  Yellow Islands 198
Pop art 22, 27, 64, 81, 92, 105, 130, 131, 141, 158, 188, 190, **200–1**, 202
post-Impressionism 26
Postmodernism **202–3**
Pound, Ezra 230
Pousette-Dart, Richard *56*
primitivism **79**
Prince, Richard 202
Process art 75, 182